Thought and Language

J. M. Moravcsik

London and New York

First published 1990
by Routledge
First published in paperback 1992
by Routledge
11 New Fetter Lane, London EC4P 4EE

Simultaneously published in the USA and Canada
by Routledge
a division of Routledge, Chapman and Hall, Inc.
29 West 35th Street, New York, NY 10001

© 1990, 1992 J. M. Moravcsik
Disc conversion by Columns of Reading
Printed in Great Britain
by T. J. Press (Padstow) Ltd, Cornwall

British Library Cataloguing in Publication Data

Moravcsik, J. M. (Julius M.)
Thought and language. – (The problems of philosophy)
I. Title   II. Series
401.9

Library of Congress Cataloging in Publication Data

Moravcsik, J. M.
Thought and language / J.M. Moravcsik.
p.   cm.—(The problems of philosophy: their past and present)
Bibliography: p.
Includes index.
1. Languages – Philosophy   2. Thought and thinking.   3. Ontology.
1. Title   II. Series: Problems of philosophy (Routledge (Firm))
P106.M588   1989
401 – dc19   89–6285 CIP

ISBN 0 415   07105 4

Contents

Preface

This book centres on a certain way of surveying a variety of theories of language, and on outlining a new proposal of meaning within the framework set by the survey. One of the key features of both survey and proposal is the insistence on the need to locate theories of language within a large framework that includes questions about the nature of thought and about general ontological questions as well.

In this age of specialization it is not surprising that most treatments of language, thought, or ontology are of a more restricted nature, focusing on this or that topic within one of these areas. But, as we shall see, the topics are interrelated. Some theories of language assume a Platonist ontology, while others require nominalism to be true. We shall also encounter two ways of viewing the semantic core of natural languages, and this contrast will be shown to be related to construing thought as either essentially pragmatic or essentially non-pragmatic in nature. These kinds of interdependency will be highlighted both in the survey and in the proposal. Clearly, we have learned much from recent detailed work on the nature of language and the nature of thought. This volume was designed with the hypothesis that occasionally we need to look at the forest, and not just at the trees. Within such an enterprise one cannot argue for every detail in the same manner as in works with a more narrow scope. I hope that the synoptic aspects of this volume will compensate for that.

This book deals in an interconnected way with both very general and very specific issues. At one end of this spectrum we find discussions of the contrast between realist and nominalist ontologies, while at the other we encounter analyses of specific lexical items of English. This spectrum is presented in such a way as to show that, while we know quite a lot about language and thought, there is a great deal that we do not know and, possibly, will never know.

My interest in the nature of language has two very different sources. On the one hand, I have been working with classical and modern languages throughout my career, and this work has led me to ask questions about the nature of language, in contrast with questions about specific languages. On the other hand, since my student days at Harvard in the mid-1950s, I have been exposed to the approaches to natural languages developed by Quine and Chomsky. Though these approaches differ greatly, a common element between them is the attempt to link proposals concerning the structure of natural languages to large issues concerning human nature and reality in general. I have been thinking during the past decades of how to put together my views on these issues into a coherent whole. The outline of a lexical theory, which I published in 1981, suggested the focus around which I could organize these reflections. What emerged is a theory about language and thought, with a defence of the underlying ontological commitments.

I am indebted to many people for help and stimulation. I learned much from Professors Quine and Putnam, both of the Harvard faculty. My link to MIT over the years, and especially contact with Professors Chomsky and Bromberger, have also been of great help. I am especially indebted to Noam Chomsky for his kind encouragement and helpful criticisms. I spent many years at the University of Michigan, where both William Alston and Richard Cartwright taught me much about the philosophy of language and metaphysics. Other colleagues and students at Michigan helped also. It would be impossible to acknowledge my debt to all of them individually. Barbara Humphries who is now at Wayne State University has also been a source of stimulation. At Stanford I had many fruitful exchanges with Jon Barwise, Joan Bresnan, John Etchemendy, Dagfinn Follesdal, Dov Gabbay, Georg Kreisel, Dan Osherson, John Perry, Patrick Suppes, Tom Wasow, and several others. There are so many students from whom I learned much over the past twenty years that individual acknowledgements would be impossible. However, my interactions with Scott Soames, which happily continued after he left Stanford, need special mention. There are also researchers at other institutions whose critical suggestions have been of great help. Among these Carl Ginet at Cornell, Asa Kasher at Tel-Aviv University, and Jonathan Stavi at Bar Ilan University especially come to mind. I have been fortunate to have had close contact with the philosophers of language at UCLA over the past two decades. Special thanks should go to David Kaplan and Joseph Almog.

Work on this book has been supported by a number of institutions. The Philosophy Department of Stanford University and the Center for the Study of Language and Information have generously supported my efforts. Much of the work for this volume was done at the Center for Advanced Studies in the Behavioral Sciences on support provided by the National Science Foundation, No. BNS–8011494. The last stages of writing were done mostly at the Institute of Advanced Studies at Tel-Aviv University, supported through the generosity of Raymond and Mortimer Sackler. I am grateful for the hospitality of this institution.

Finally, I wish to express my gratitude to Professor Ted Honderich who kindly invited me to contribute to his series, and whose encouragement helped throughout the course of working on this essay.

PART ONE   PROBLEMS

CHAPTER I

Ontology

Tersely stated, ontology attempts to answer the twin-questions: 'What exists?' and 'What is it for something to exist?' These questions surface also in the form in which 'exists' is replaced by 'is real'. Not surprisingly, some philosophers think that the two formulations are equivalent, while others disagree. These questions are not so far removed from the level of common sense as it might seem at first glance. Dreams, bad conjectures, and superstitions, among other things, often make us ask about some putative entity: 'Is this real?' At times we end up with a contrast between what is real and what only seems to be, and at other times we juxtapose what exists but is only a surface phenomenon with a fundamental underlying element of reality. We raise these questions and form these contrasts in contexts of specific investigations or in particular psychological states. Ontology borrows the contrast of appearance and reality from common sense and projects it across the cosmos.

One can trivialize the ontological question by answering it with long lists of specific times and kinds. The philosopher, on the other hand, wants as answers not endless lists of specifics, but broad categories of reality. The basic ontological categories, though any one of these can be found at times denounced as not genuine and at other times passionately defended, remain surprisingly constant through the history of western philosophy. These include: the abstract and the spatial, the recurrent and the non-recurrent, the atemporal and the temporal, the actual and the possible or necessary. We shall concentrate on only a few of these debates, examining those that are most relevant to the theories of thought and language that will be presented in the subsequent chapters.

3

The cosmic projection of the appearance versus reality distinction leads philosophers not only to debates about what exists and what does not, but also about what are more fundamental and what are less fundamental elements of reality. The former are supposed to explain the latter. Thus some ontological theories are not mere inventories but consist of proposed explanatory patterns. Modern ontologies like the realism of Moore and Russell, dealt with at pp. 138-40, are more like inventories, while the early classical ontologies of Plato and Aristotle concentrate on ontological explanatory structures. Plato's Forms are not only real, but also have a fundamental ontological role. Their existence and nature explain and make possible the existence of everything else. Aristotle's substances have the same status in that ontology. But even in the more inventory-like ontologies, positing two or three fundamental categories of reality within which one is to capture the diversity of what there is, amounts to an attempt at clarification, making the many one, and thus bringing order into the chaotic.

We shall introduce the notion of ontological priority to capture the distinction between the more and less fundamental. Entity A is ontologically prior to entity B if and only if the existence of B depends on the existence of A, but not the other way around. This notion brings out the sense in which Plato took Forms to be prior to all else while Aristotle assigned the same honorific place to his substances. The philosophical dependency proposals are conceptual. Hence there may be situations in which one conceptual dependency relation makes A prior to B, while another one reverses the order. Another problem with this notion is that not all conceptual relations count as ontologically relevant dependency relations. There is, however, no general way of characterizing the conceptual dependency relations that all philosophers regard as ontologically relevant. Different schools have different views on this issue.

Though the two questions: 'What exists?' and 'What is it for something to exist?' are conceptually distinct, philosophers tended to link the issues together. If a philosopher is convinced that only material things exist, it is easy to lapse into a position according to which to exist is to be material. Or, to take an historical example, to think that to exist is to be perceived. It is clearly desirable, however, to keep the questions distinct, and to formulate an account of what it is to exist that is neutral with regard to the various ontological theses. The advantage of doing ontology in this way is that one has a neutral conceptual background against which rational examination of competing ontological theses can take place. If, for example, materialists and anti-materialists mean different things by their uses of 'exists', then their ontologies would be difficult to compare, and could even turn out not to be in conflict with each other. Such an interpretation would, however, distort the historical facts. Such distortion would also be involved if we said that materialists and anti-materialists argue about what it is to exist. Few if any such arguments can be found in the historically influential presentations of the materialist position.

To some the task of explicating what it is to exist seems too formidable. They advise us to try our hand at the seemingly more modest enterprise of providing criteria for what it is for a theory to be ontologically committed to the existence of certain kinds of entity. Additional criteria can then be added to evaluate theories in terms of more or less adequate ontological commitments. This is the programme embraced some time ago by Quine. In his earlier writings he attempted to give an explication of ontological commitment that was supposed to be neutral between rival ontological theories and would not commit us to entities that everyone would not accept as real. Quine's criterion, however, only applies to theories that can be translated into his 'canonical language' which is, roughly, first-order predicate calculus with certain interpretations (Quine, 1953a). Unfortunately, even this seemingly more modest enterprise ran into trouble. Quine's proposal was tied to certain technical notions such as that of a variable and the notion of quantification, which make sense only within certain formalisms. Not surprisingly, the difficulties turned out to be technical as well. Detailing these would take us too far from the main purpose of this work. Some of the problems centred on the issue of whether the proposed criterion was as ontologically neutral and uncommitted to abstract entities as Quine thought it to be (Chomsky and Scheffler, 1958). Other difficulties emerged when one considered the proposed criterion in the light of formal results in logic about translatability. It turned out to be the case that in the light of these results and Quine's criterion, the best ontology would be one in which only

5

numbers were acknowledged as real – a conclusion that pleases the Pythagoreans, if there are any left, but hardly Quine. In his subsequent writings, Quine introduced various further technical notions to avoid this conclusion; the jury is still out on that one (Quine, 1969).

Let us return to the project of formulating a neutral criterion of what it is to exist. We shall carry out the project in an informal intuitive way, not tying the results to formalisms. This is, after all, the way in which most of the important ontologies have been presented in western thought. In fact, most of the ontological positions were invented before the formalism of symbolic logic within which Quine's proposal is couched came into existence. The intuition guiding the proposal is that what exists must have a qualitative nature, and likewise, what has a qualitative nature must exist. Thus what exists must be the subject of true propositions other than simply existential ones. Furthermore, what does not exist cannot be the subject of true qualitative propositions. If we had the collection of all true singular propositions, then we would also have a handle on all that exists. The proposal is, therefore, that a necessary and sufficient condition for what it is to exist is to be the subject of some true propositions. Giving this characterization of existence in terms of a necessary and sufficient condition does not commit us to further views about the full meaning of 'exists'. It is easy to see that this analysis is indeed neutral between materialism and its foes, or an ontology of abstract entities and its critics.

Unfortunately, the proposal faces several difficulties only some of which can be met by adding qualifications. First, there are many views about what it is to be a subject. There are grammatical, semantic, and logical criteria, and these do not coincide. What is the grammatical subject of a singular sentence may not be its subject on the basis of semantic analysis (for details see Russell, 1905). Again, a theory of logical reconstruction might yield a still different notion of subject, or eliminate the notion altogether. One might try to cut the Gordian knot by saying that the subject of a proposition in our sense will be whatever the proposition is about. Unfortunately, about-ness is not a sufficiently clear semantic notion to bear such a conceptual burden. Philosophers do not always agree what a sentence, or the proposition it expresses, is about. Consider, for example, 'John

6

smokes Marlboros'. This could be construed as being about John, or about Marlboros, or about smoking. More sophisticated explorations of this concept have not yielded satisfactory results either (Goodman, 1972, chapter VI). Thus the proposal needs to be supplemented by the lame disclaimer 'pending a satisfactory analysis of the notion of subject'.

Further difficulties emerge in connection with negative existential propositions. Our proposal requires a reinterpretation of such propositions in such a way that the non-existent entity does not emerge as the subject. Such interpretations are available but are not beyond controversy. Finally, the proposal is not meant to exclude formal ontologies within which domains of non-existent objects are admitted in order to have the tools for formulating adequate analyses of propositions of all kinds with abstract and non-abstract objects, qualitative, existential, and non-existential content, etc., for such theories too admit the difference between what exists in reality and what does not (e.g., Parsons, 1980; Zalta, 1983).

Let us see now how one would compare different ontological theories in terms of our criterion. Realism claims that abstract recurrent entities, sometimes called universals, exist, while nominalism claims that no recurrent entities exist. According to our criterion, for nominalism to be successful it will have to reconstruct all of the truths that seem to be about recurrent entities to be actually about combinations of non-recurrent entities. Likewise, a materialist who denies that there are purely mental entities will have to show how all truths that seem to be about mental entities can be shown to be really about material entities. Even if at any given time we do not know how to carry out these programmes of reinterpretation, one could argue against an ontological thesis by showing that the favoured category or categories suffer from obscurity or even incoherence. Of course, obscurity has to be understood here in a logical sense. Common-sense intuitions, especially of the crude variety, are no guides to what is or is not a legitimate part of reality. (I am indebted to Neil Delaney for the felicitous phrase: 'the podaic projectibility criterion', which says: 'if you can kick it, it exists, if you can't, it ain't.') As we shall see, there are general criteria of adequacy for ontological categories that transcend historical and cultural limitations, unlike notions like what is 'odd' or a 'strange entity'.

7

Ontological proposals and their assessments must be kept separate from epistemological issues. For example, we proposed to examine claims about what are subjects of true propositions, but we did not specify that the propositions in question must be known or even knowable. We might have reasons to believe in the reality of a certain entity even if it can be shown that the nature of this entity cannot be known by us. For example, we might be able to prove that it is reasonable to admit the existence of certain very large numbers, or of God, or of faraway galaxies. In particular, epistemological claims such as those of empiricism, according to which all of our informative non-tautologous knowledge of reality is based on information received through the senses, must be laid aside when assessing ontological claims. Empiricism proposes some constraints on the realm of human knowledge. One cannot deduce from that alone limitations on the realm of what exists. To be sure, in a complete philosophy one would like to see harmony between one's ontology and epistemology. But to rule out from the start any ontology that seems to cause trouble for one's epistemology is like fitting the glass slipper to the lady's foot by chopping off her toes.

In this chapter we shall review ontological debates about universals and non-recurrent entities called particulars. One might hold that only universals exist, or that only particulars exist, or that both types exist. Within the latter view there are those who do and those who do not want to argue also for the ontological priority of one of these categories. We shall also review ontological debates about the reality of modalities such as necessity and possibility. The actualist denies the reality of these modalities, though he could admit them as mind-dependent conceptual entities playing key roles in the way – human conditions being what they are – humans organize experience. We shall then turn to the examination of two kinds of particular: material objects and events. We shall consider views according to which events do not exist, or are at least ontologically posterior to material objects. There are many other ontological debates. Some are about facts, others about time, space, and still other aspects of reality. We shall concentrate on the issues enumerated because these provide the right background for the questions about thought and language that we shall raise. Can we have an adequate analysis of thought without events? Can we have an adequate analysis of language and its syntactic and phonological constituents without positing the ontological reality of universals? Can we account for verb- and aspect-semantics without assuming that in many sentences of subject–predicate form verbs introduce events? The debate between materialists and dualists is also relevant to our concerns, but we shall leave the discussion of that matter to the second part.

Before launching into an outline of the debate between realism and nominalism, another problem involving another sense of 'realism' needs to be mentioned, only to be laid aside. This problem, discussed primarily by Kant, concerns the alleged gap between reality as such and reality as known through human experience. We are asked to consider the possibility that all of the categories mentioned – particular, universal, space, time, etc. – are constituents of the phenomenal world of human experience only, and that we might not have any *a priori* reasons to ascribe these also to a mind-independent reality. The 'realists' in this debate think that the basic categories of experience correspond to those of the real world, while the phenomenalists are sceptical about this. Since all of the issues that we shall consider would emerge regardless of which side one chooses, we shall not devote much space to this important topic. But at least the bare outlines of a moderate realism are worth mentioning. According to this view, we might not have *a priori* reasons to show that realism in this context is right, but that there may be good empirical reasons to suppose that realism is likely to be true. One could cite the success of the human mind in coming to understand reality, and suggest that one of the contributing causes might be our ability to approximate with our categories those of reality. There are several other arguments to the effect that even if one cannot prove the realist to be correct, one need not embrace phenomenalism. Realism is not an all-or-nothing proposition. A moderate version of it can turn out to be more reasonable than the available alternatives.

Realism and Nominalism

The paradigmatic examples of particulars traditionally have been

9

entities with both spatial and temporal or at least only temporal location. Thus material objects in the broad sense, such as living things, mountains, buildings, stars, and islands are particulars, and so are events such as the Battle of Waterloo, the birth of Jesus, and Vladimir Horowitz's last concert. Mental events such as Cleopatra's thinking of Anthony at a particular time are also particulars, and according to some philosophers these have only temporal locations. The paradigmatic cases of universals are attributes such as being a human, being a triangle, or being made of wood. Many but not all philosophers regard numbers also as universals. This dichotomy is not claimed to be exhaustive of reality. Sets, types such as the 1982 Volkswagen, or letter-types, and various other candidates for reality might not fit into either slot (see Cartwright, R., 1962).

Philosophers do not rest content with these intuitive and common-sensical examples. They point out that there are particulars not contemplated by common sense. For example, the object whose parts are all of the red surfaces in the world is a particular, and so are things made up of all the greens, blues, browns, etc. It is fairly easy to extend our intuitions to these large-scale particulars that are designated by what the linguists call 'mass terms', i.e. terms that do not pluralize but behave otherwise as general terms (for discussion see Goodman, 1951; Moravcsik, 1973.) There are also universals outside of common sense. Many of these are not introduced by a single word of some Indo-European language. An example would be the universal of being either a mathematician or six feet tall, or both a barber and a bridge-player, etc.

These are huge collections of items, and not all of these correspond to common-sense intuitions. Hence the urgency for definitions. This task, however, turns out not to be easy. Traditionally, the key difference between universals and particulars has been claimed to be the fact that universals are recurrent while particulars are not (e.g., Stout, 1923; Moore, 1923). The attribute of being intelligent, for example, recurs repeatedly in instances such as Newton, Semmelweis, and Einstein, but a particular made up of all of the water on earth can have only parts not instances and does not recur. It is interesting to note that nothing in this characterization says that particulars must be in space and time. Thus additional burden is placed on the notions of recurrence and being a part.

Recent attempts at clarifying the notions of a universal and a particular involved working out the ontological theories in formal presentations. Nominalists attempt to clarify the notion of a particular, and then try to show that all truths can be presented without assuming the existence of universals (Lesniewsky, 1931; Goodman and Quine, 1947; Goodman, 1951). These enterprises need to meet the following conditions for metaphysics. First, the formal accounts must link up to the pre-theoretic intuitions of what particulars are. Second, the systems have to meet formal criteria of consistency and clarity. Thirdly, the undertakings have to deal with the key examples of human knowledge, such as mathematics. Among the various formal presentations of both realism and nominalism, we shall select Nelson Goodman's *Structure of Appearance* because of its avowed attempt to meet these criteria, and because nominalism has a greater need to be seen in this way, while there have been many good, less formal, defences of realism.

In Goodman's system there is a basic primitive notion, 'overlap', and in terms of this one can explain the identity and individuation conditions of particulars. Two alleged particulars are identical if and only if there is a complete overlap between them, and they are distinct if the overlap is not complete. This can be understood intuitively if we think of the particulars – or individuals, as Goodman calls them – as sums of parts. Two particulars are not identical if one has at least some parts that the other lacks. This 'mereological' conception (*meros* in Greek means 'part') has been used by several philosophers to discuss the nature of particulars (see for example Moravcsik, 1973).

Given this bare sketch, it is time to turn to the consideration of the motivations for nominalism. First, as in any theoretical field, so in philosophy too there is a desire for simplicity, economy, and reduction of the elements posited in a theory to a minimum. Two questions arise with regard to this motive. First, is nominalism really a more economic theory than realism? Secondly, are parsimony and economy legitimate motivations in ontology? As we shall see, it is far from clear that nominalism is really a more economic theory than realism. To be sure, nominalism does without one of the fundamental categories of realism, namely universals. But this has to be balanced with consideration of the theoretical structures that nominalism has to carry in its reductionistic programmes of what are for realists relatively simple structures explaining the predication of properties of particulars or simple sentences of arithmetic. The nominalist analysis for many of these patterns turns out to be more complex than the realist proposals. Secondly, is it really sound to assume in ontology that 'God loves parsimony'? It is one thing to say that in our theories of science, humanistic fields, etc., we should not posit entities unnecessarily, but it is quite different to claim that the universe contains only those entities that are essential for its functioning. Nature and the abstract realms may very well be 'wasteful', ontologically speaking.

This motivation inspired various reductionistic programmes, centring mostly on the stronghold of the realist: mathematics. These programmes, conducted by some of the best minds in the philosophy of mathematics, have failed, and no new ones of comparable stature have emerged in recent times. (The most important such efforts were those by David Hilbert, and the combined efforts of Quine and Goodman. See Kreisel, 1958; Goodman and Quine, 1947.).

Another motivation has been the conviction that the nature of universals is unclear, or even possibly incoherent. Arguments embodying this motivating intuition need to be spelled out very carefully. Not any kind of unclarity is ontologically relevant. Throughout history there have been many kinds of entity whose nature was at a particular time unclear but whose existence was not in doubt. The history of our theories about the heavenly bodies provides a fine example for this. At different times people had very different theories about what these entities were, but had no rational ground for doubting that they existed. Thus the charge of obscurity or unintelligibility has to be made ontologically relevant. One of the most prominent recent representatives of this kind of attack on universals is Quine. And indeed, Quine is very much aware of the need to show the alleged unintelligibility to be ontologically relevant. He claims that universals are unintelligible from the point of view of establishing for them criteria of identity and individuation. If Quine is right, then this is certainly a powerful ontological criticism. For how can we rationally accept the existence of an entity or a kind of entity if there are no conditions for their retaining identity and their being individuated in some non-arbitrary way? Of course, in a very abstract sense Quine and everyone else know when two universals are identical. They are identical if and only if they have all of their properties in common. But Quine's point is not only that we do not know when this is the case, but also that there does not seem to be any fact of the matter that would determine when this state obtains. Quine is, furthermore, concerned with the individuation of universals. For example, if the meanings of lexical items of languages are universals, what facts determine when two meanings are identical? Note that this question is ontologically deeper than the epistemological complaint that we do not know when two meanings are identical. To give another example, if, e.g., chemistry is said to be studying correlations between chemical properties, what facts determine whether we are talking about one or two such properties in any given context?

Even if philosophers like Quine could prove this charge, by itself it would not support nominalism. For the claim that universals are in ontologically relevant ways obscure does not support the claim that particulars should be the centre of one's ontology. For that we need the additional premiss that the nature of particulars is in ontologically relevant ways clearer than the nature of universals. And indeed, the intuition that this is so has been a third historically important motivation behind nominalism. This motivation survives even if nominalistic programmes, especially their reductionistic schemes, can be shown to have failed. Quine is not a nominalist, but holds the view that one should limit one's ontological commitments to non-particulars of any sort to a minimum. This view is backed by Quine's position according to which the nature of particulars is clearer than the nature of universals and other non-particulars. It is clear that perceptually verifiable empirical facts do very little to help with the individuation of universals, and claims about synonymy and property-identity in the various sciences rest ultimately on certain kinds of well-trained intuitions. This may or may not be sufficient. However, we must take a good hard look at the nature of particulars. The fact that we have empirical knowledge of many of these is the kind of epistemological consideration which – as we stated on p. 8 – should not have bearing on this matter.

Is the nature of particulars clear in ontologically relevant ways?

Utilizing parts of a paper by Hao Wang (Wang, 1953) we shall sketch some of the intellectual worries about this notion which is on the common-sense level so obvious. Wang's primary purpose is to criticize Goodman's calculus of individuals from a formal point of view. Nevertheless, several of his points have metaphysical significance. As noted above, what Goodman calls individuals we call particulars. As Wang sees it, Goodman offers three explanations for his notion of an individual. First, by giving an everyday example, he wants to capture our pre-theoretic intuitions concerning this notion. The example he gives is the state of Utah. For the non-nominalist the set of the counties of the state of Utah, and the state itself, are two distinct entities even though located in the same spatial region. The nominalist does not countenance sets. For him there is the state, and the sum of all of the counties of the state, and these are the same individual. Is this example helpful? That depends on how well one understands the notion of sum in such a context, and whether Goodman can really show that everything one wants to say about one of the putative entities can be reduced to the truths one can express about the other. Secondly, Goodman uses the notion of content to link his notion of an individual to our common-sense notion of a particular. But as Wang shows, even if one restricts the notion of content to physical things, it is not clear enough to give us a firm grasp of what particulars are. For example, a carton containing some stuff has the same content as a similar container but with the outermost layer of the carton removed. Still, for Goodman, or for any other nominalist, these would be two distinct individuals. Thus the attempted explications do not seem clear. This is especially worrisome because the lack of clarity affects conditions of identity and individuation.

Matters become worse when we realize that the formal calculus – Goodman's second way of explaining the fundamental notion of nominalism – does not have any clear links to our pre-theoretic notion of particulars. As we saw, the key primitive of the calculus is 'overlap'. This in turn is supposedly linked to the notions of 'part'. Two individuals partly overlap if and only if they have some parts in common. So, particulars turn out to be entities that have parts but not instances, or 'members', in the set-theoretic sense. Is our ordinary notion of part strong enough to carry such a conceptual burden? For example, symphonies and poems have parts, but not in the same way in which such paradigmatic particulars as loaves or islands have parts. One would like a characterization of what it is that parts of poems and parts of loaves have in common.

Thus we come to the third characterization of Goodman's individuals. An individual is anything that satisfies Goodman's calculus. This calculus is a version of what we called mereology. Wang's discussion of the calculus centres on certain formal problems, and the contrast he uses is between mereology and set-theory, not a theory of properties. Nevertheless, some of his key points can be utilized in our metaphysical discussion. For Wang wants to know whether the nominalist admits an infinite or a finite number of particulars into his ontology. When the universe is restricted to a finite number of individuals, then the distinction between set-theory and the calculus of individuals collapses. If, however, we admit an infinite number of individuals into our ontology, then the intuitions supporting the notion of a particular weaken considerably.

We can see this informally in two ways. First, whatever intuitions we have about the physical parts of a physical body tend to vanish when we consider an object that is infinitely divisible. Why is the notion of a table with infinite number of parts any clearer than a property such as being wise with an indefinite number of instances? Alternatively, if universally quantified sentences of the form 'All A's are B's' can be reduced to be about a finite conjunction of particulars, then nominalism makes intuitively good sense. But if standard truths of this form have to be interpreted as having an infinite number of entities as their subject, then the difference between this reading and the one about universals is small enough not to support strong ontological preferences. As Wang points out, however, it is highly dubious that we could render the truths of mathematics, geometry, and the other sciences and humanistic disciplines to be about finite collections.

These considerations show that while the nominalist has some legitimate complaints about universals, the realist can counter with a number of similar worries about particulars.

The realist accepts both universals and particulars. Let us start with a bad argument for realism, only to use it as a contrast to the more legitimate arguments. The bad argument starts with the observation that English is a 'realist' language in the sense that it provides the resources to talk about and in terms of universals. The argument then goes from this premiss to the claim that English has realist ontological commitments, and then to the claim that this shows realism to be true or to be likely to be true about reality. This argument has many flaws. The crucial mistake here is to talk of the ontology of a natural language like English. From the fact that a language makes it possible for us to refer to a kind of entity, it does not follow either that the language as such has this ontological commitment or that the competent users of the language should carry this burden.

The better arguments for realism are based on claims that some of our key branches of knowledge such as mathematics, geometry, linguistics, etc., cannot be explicated adequately unless we assume that these disciplines have domains of universals as their object. (For a fine exposition of this view for mathematics, see Bernays, 1964.) Other arguments consider the empirical sciences generally, the counterfactual force of their laws and principles, and hence the plausibility of interpreting these too as being about correlations of properties. If correct, would not the truth of a law of science be independent of the accidental fact that the universe contains the collection of actual particulars that it happens to contain?

Later we shall offer a solution to these problems. At this stage we should sum up what we have covered by distinguishing the four possible positions:

1. Only universals are real.
2. Only particulars are real.
3. Both universals and particulars are real.
4. Universals are concepts, i.e., mental entities.

The fourth position is sometimes called conceptualism. We have not treated it in this survey because its strengths and weaknesses will be seen in our review of theories of thought. We have not treated the first position in any detail either, since if it were true, then neither the author nor the readers of this volume – nor the volume itself – would be particulars, and thus the discussion of the thesis would have to be carried out by creatures of a higher order, e.g., universals, if these can communicate.

In comparing different ontological conceptions the notions of identity and individuation figured prominently. It is time to turn to a discussion of their metaphysical role and significance.

Identity, Individuation, Persistence

We can approach the notion of identity informally by relying on our common-sense notion of qualitative sameness. We commonly speak of two things sharing some features or parts and thus being partly the same. Extending this notion, one can say that when two things are completely the same, then they are identical. This intuition is meant to be captured by the principle that two things are identical if and only if they have all of their properties in common. This principle admits of more than one interpretation, depending on whether one includes under 'property' also spatio-temporal ones, and whether one assumes relative or absolute time. Thus some metaphysicians defend the claim that two things could share all of their properties in any intelligible sense of that term, and still be distinct (see Black, 1952; Hacking, 1975). Since this issue does not figure in our discussion of theories of thought and language, we shall lay it aside.

If identity is primarily a concept of logic, and the metaphysical issues surrounding it are exhausted by the discussion of the identity of indiscernibles and related matters of haecceity, i.e. special property of being identical, then why should this concept be of continued interest to us, and how does it relate to ontological scepticism? As we saw, Quine's demand for the clarity of ontological posits is paraphrased by some in terms of 'criteria of identity'. Hence we need to examine this notion. The phrase 'criteria of identity' is infelicitous, for it covers – or covers up – three things. First, it can be an epistemological notion. As such it would lay out conditions under which we can know elements of a given kind to be identical or distinct. We shall not deal with this notion, since, as was pointed out, what we can know or not know has no direct bearings on whether entities of a given type do or do not have a distinct and coherent nature of their own. Secondly, this notion can specify the most general conditions under which two things are identical. But, as we saw, this is a matter of Leibniz's law.

According to a third interpretation 'criteria of identity' is really meant to point out principles of individuation and persistence, taking 'principles' in a realist, and mind-independent sense. This is the tack we shall take in this chapter. Let us consider the application of individuation to the class of positive integers. To say that the kind 'positive integer' is linked to a principle of individuation is to say that there is a principle in accordance to which there is a true answer to a question like: 'How many positive integers are there between 5 and 9?' We can contrast this situation with asking the nonsensical question: 'How many nonsenses were there in the prime minister's speech?' The kind 'nonsense' does not carry with it a principle of individuation. It yields, however, a quantitative interpretation, even though it introduces abstract items. For example, to the question: 'How much nonsense was there in the prime minister's speech?' a true answer might be: 'Twice as much as in the president's speech'. We started with these examples to show that individuation cuts across the abstract–concrete dichotomy. A principle of individuation is, then, a principle determining plurality for members of a given kind of ontological category. Persistence conditions are a species of individuation principles, specifying unity and plurality across time. Applying the correct persistence principle should determine the truth or falsity of statements like: 'This is the same woman whom I met at MIT twenty years ago'.

Let us consider now examples from the spatio-temporal realm. The kind 'cow' carries with it a principle of individuation. Thus there is a true answer to a question like: 'How many cows are there in this meadow?' Or in the case of triangles: 'How many triangles are there on this blackboard?' There may be epistemological or perceptual difficulties in answering on some occasions questions of this sort, but that does not affect the status of the kind. The metaphysical point is that if an alleged kind is linked to a principle of individuation, and even apart from epistemological problems there is no principle that would provide factual basis for answering questions of the sort illustrated above, then the proposed ontological category is suspect.

The same considerations apply to matters of persistence. The kind 'human' is linked to a persistence principle, and it is in virtue of this that a statement like 'the young student at MIT twenty years ago is now the professor of linguistics at a

18

distinguished institution' is true. The demand for individuation affects also kinds like water, iron, red, that do not carry individuation principles. To be sure, we cannot ask: 'how many waters?' except in unusual contexts in which we refer to kinds of water. But water is a liquid, and the generic kind 'liquid' does carry a principle of individuation. In the same way, red is a colour, and gold is a metal. The generic kinds must carry individuation principles in order for the species to have sufficient ontological clarity.

Let us suppose that an ontologist introduces his favourite ontological category, the gloms. Gloms are supposed to play a key role in the structure of reality. But upon investigation it turns out that even for an omniscient being there would be problems with individuating gloms and determining their conditions of persistence. This would be a good reason for suspecting the existence of gloms, and not wanting an ontology in which they play key roles. Furthermore, the reasoning involved here is very different from the kind that leads us to suspect witches, ghosts, and leprechauns. (This way of conceptualizing matters of identity and individuation is not above controversy. For partly different views, see Geach, 1962; Wiggins, 1967; Perry, 1970; Griffin, 1977).

Having shown the need for individuation and persistence conditions, we shall now examine the metaphysical status of the principles embodying these conditions. It seems initially plausible to suppose that the propositions describing truly these principles are necessary. After all, these principles define a crucial part of the existence and nature of classes of entities. Though it may be contingent that humans exist, and that some are fat while others are not, some are short while others are tall, etc., it does not seem to be contingent that the two people in this room, for example, are two humans and not one or three. If the two entities singled out exist and are humans, then they are necessarily two humans. Let us consider another example. The person wanting to claim that persistence and individuation principles are contingent would have to say, for example, 'This event happens to be a rainstorm, and it just happens to be one rather than ten rainstorms'. To show the oddity of this stance, let us push the matter further and ask, could one say something like the following: 'This entity happens to be an event, but it could have been . . .'? Is it contingent that it is an event and that it is one event? What would the 'this' refer to in the envisaging of such alleged possibilities?

Of course, it could happen that we change our conceptual framework in a drastic way, and stop positing categories like material object, event, or even universal and particular, but this would not leave us with new categories and the same old entities. Our new conceptual framework with its new individuation principles would carve out new kinds and new classes of entity. There is no bare, propertyless 'I know not what' that could support as a substratum the different conceptual frameworks.

In this discussion it seems natural to assume that each entity has the kind or property under which it falls and which determines the individuation conditions for it, essentially. Thus, for example, an event is necessarily an event, and a human being is necessarily a human being. This view is called essentialism. Metaphysicians differ on the question of whether one can work out an intelligible scheme in which entities are individuated by principles of individuation without invoking some form of essentialism. There are many versions of essentialism. Those denying the doctrines of essentialism are either opposed to realism with regard to universals or denying the reality of the modalities. The interesting and complex issues separating different versions of essentialism do not affect what we shall consider under the headings of thought and language. Hence we shall omit discussions of these. (For some interesting examples of essentialism see, Kripke, 1972; Almog, 1986).

The question of whether individuation principles are necessary is distinct from the issue of the extent to which individuation and persistence principles are contaminated by pragmatic human interest. As so often in philosophy, the extreme positions are less plausible and viable than the middle ground. Brief reflection on terms for artefacts and certain human activities should convince us that some individuation principles are indeed affected by human interest. Were it not for our interest in games, nobody would individuate events in such a way as to have what we call a game of cricket or baseball come out as one event. The same goes for machinery such as that needed for excavation or moving earth. But it is a long way from these obvious common-sense observations to the sweeping conclusion that all of the individuation principles reflect human interest and need. As we turn to biological classifications, we need to distinguish the claim that some of the lower level classifications reflect pragmatic interest (sub-species of pigs, etc.) from the claim that this is also true of the higher parts of classificatory pyramids, involving genera such as animal, reptile, etc. (For an interesting discussion see Dupre, 1981.)

But even if one could show that all classificatory schemes carrying individuation principles are contaminated by pragmatic considerations, what would this show? It certainly would not suffice to defeat the 'realist' who insists that there are genuine individuation conditions for elements of nature even if we can only approximate these as we increase our understanding of nature. If one denies this, what would prevent us from lapsing into Eleatic monism; i.e. that view that reality is an indivisible unit, with any carving up into a plurality purely illusory?

To conclude this section, the matters surveyed should lead us to the following three questions:

1. Are there general principles of individuation ranging over, e.g., all particulars, or at least all material objects and all events, respectively, or is individuation a matter of differing principles from kind to kind?
2. How do individuation principles for particulars differ from those for universals?
3. What kind of pragmatic contamination of our carving up of the world into kinds would cast serious doubt on the realist stance towards individuation principles?

Later we shall consider a proposal to answer these queries.

The Modalities

Humans are planning and explanation-seeking creatures. We need for both of these fundamental activities projections of the actual world into possibilities, and the limits of these projections in terms of necessity. Planning involves considering what could be done. The possibilities tell us what can be done, and necessity shows what cannot. Similar considerations apply to explanation.

21

An explanation is more than a mere description of what is the case. If what is proposed has any genuine explanatory power, then it should tell us not only what happens, but also what could and could not happen. If an explanation is successful, it shows why something had to happen, and why something else could not have happened. We can leave here the various meanings of 'can', 'could', 'must', etc. open. All that is needed at this point is the simple observation that explanations deal with more than just what happens to be the case.

These reflections show that the human cognitive life is dynamic, i.e. it deals with modal notions such as the potential, the possible, the necessary. If we had a book of all of the singular truths about the world, this would still leave us intellectually dissatisfied. We would want to know: 'but why?' Some people might say that all we can obtain as answers to such a further question is the presentation of regularities, i.e. general statement of the basic form: 'All A's are B's.' But for most people these statements should be law-like and carry counterfactual force. And this brings us once more to the modalities. (For an attempt to minimize the modal influence on counterfactuals, see Goodman, 1955.) The extreme sceptic will say that he does not understand counterfactuals. This must be surely a theoretical objection, and if serious, should focus on the ontological status of some elements of counterfactuals. On a basic cognitive level we all understand and implicitly use in our thinking counterfactuals. Nobody has difficulties assenting to such obviously sage counterfactuals as: 'If cows had wings, we would carry big umbrellas.'

Showing that possibility and necessity are vital parts of human thought is not the same as showing that these are genuine ontological constituents of a mind-independent reality. Maybe the modalities are needed only as aids to human understanding, but once we consider the world apart from the human frailties associated with our imperfect modes of understanding, the modalities are not needed for an adequate ontology. Thus from a metaphysical point of view, we can take three positions with regard to the modalities.

1. *Realism.* According to this view the modalities are as genuine ontological components of a reality with or without minds, as particulars or universals of the sort we surveyed.

22

2. *Conceptualism.* According to this view the modalities are mind-dependent or mental constructs, needed for human understanding only, but not for the orderly functioning of reality.

3. *Scepticism.* According to this view, the modalities are not conceptually legitimate notions. They can be shown to be defective in some way that is agreed by neutral criteria to be ontologically relevant.

We shall deal with conceptualism later. In this section we shall consider realism and scepticism, and shall start with arguments favouring realism.

The first such argument revolves around the interpretation of principles of individuation. As we saw, these divide reality into an intelligible plurality both in the abstract and the spatio-temporal domain. They do not merely show how in fact some entity is constructed so as to be distinct from others and persist through time, but how it must be. That is to say, the conditions of persistence, for example, show what changes are possible for the entity and what changes are impossible, in the sense that these will destroy the entity in question. For humans, becoming pale or thin are possible changes, becoming a corpse destroys the entity. Thus if we need individuation principles in order for reality to be an intelligible plurality, and if these require the modalities, then the modalities should be parts of a legitimate ontology. The sceptic has to show either that all of individuation is merely a matter of pragmatic considerations, or that one can give non-modal interpretations of the individuation principles.

The second argument centres on what we shall call constitutive relations. Let us consider a ring and the gold of which it is made. Are these the same or different material entities? There are things true of the ring that are not true of the gold. For example, someone made the ring and designed its structure; but these things are not true of the gold. There are also things true of the gold, such as its being a precious metal and its having been mined in Transylvania, that are not true of the ring. Thus by our criterion of reality given earlier we should conclude that these are separate entities that happen to coincide in their spatio-temporal location. One would insist on the nature of spatial coincidence even in the unusual case in which the ring came into existence at

23

the same time as the gold. Even then it is true that the ring was designed by a craftsman while the gold was not. Furthermore, the persistence conditions for the ring only partly overlap with those for the gold. Certain replacements of parts would count as destroying that piece of gold, but not that ring. If this is an adequate account of the matter, then we need to distinguish between identity and mere spatio-temporal coincidence. But for this we need the modalities.

The third consideration rests on the interpretation of the laws of science. We saw already that the laws of science are taken normally as having some explanatory force. This requires that they have counterfactual force. The modalities offer an adequate and natural way of spelling out counterfactual force. They also allow us to say that the laws of science hold not only for those things that happen to be in the world, but would hold also if the population would have been different – within certain limits. The sceptic would have to show that we can account for the explanatory force of the laws of nature and for the accidental nature of the world's population being exactly what it is, without bringing the modalities into the analysis.

The fourth consideration is that we seem to have intuitions of necessity, apart from any practical pragmatic interests (see Kripke, 1972). We have intuitions that birds could not be events, that walking could not be a mammal, etc. A theory of the modalities systematizes these intuitions. There are other theories that systematize our logical, linguistic, moral, etc. intuitions. The sceptic would have to show why the modal intuitions are more suspect than the other kinds.

In recent times, however, an influential sceptical argument has been presented by Quine which, if sound, would cast doubt on the legitimacy of the modalities, regardless of how the sceptic answers the four points made above (see Quine, 1953c).

Quine points out that a legitimate logical operator should obey the standard laws of logic. The modalities of necessity and possibility are expressed in formal logic as sentential operators. Inferences involving legitimate sentential operators should preserve validity under the substitution of identical for identicals. Thus, for example, the following inference is valid:

It is not the case that Napoleon is an English king.

Napoleon is identical with the husband of Josephine.
It is not the case that the husband of Josephine is an English king.

We seem to run into trouble, however, when we attempt to construct inferences with analogous structure involving the modalities. Let us consider the following:

Necessarily, 9 is an odd number.
9 is the number of the planets.
Necessarily the number of the planets is an odd number.

We start with true premisses, in the second line we substitute identicals for identicals, and nevertheless we end up with a false conclusion. Quine concludes that arguments of this sort show the modalities to be fundamentally suspect. Indeed, if there were nothing left to be said on this matter, Quine's conclusion would seem unavoidable. We should consider, however, other ways of paraphrasing what on a clear intuitive level is the same argument. Let us try, for example, the following:

The number 9 is necessarily an odd number
The number 9 happens to be the number of the planets
The number that happens to be the number of the planets
is necessarily an odd number.

This version of the argument also contains a substitution of identicals with identicals and has true premisses and ends up with a true conclusion. It seems, then, that more adequate informal formulations preserve validity, and show the logical modalities to be operating legitimately within logical frameworks.

The sceptic will not rest content with this reply. He will demand further clarifications. He wants to know what we mean by phrases like 'is necessarily an odd number', or 'happens to be the number of the planets'. The force of this move depends on what is meant by 'clarification'. The phrases in question are well understood, and are as legitimate parts of standard English as the phrases occurring in the previous argument. An informal clarification points out that the suspected phrases introduce the attribution of properties to individuals as necessary or contingent.

They also separate genuine identity from mere coincidence. These distinctions can be explained by going back to our initial point in this section about planning and explaining as parts of human cognition. Examples of planning and explanations will illustrate the distinctions just drawn. Explicitly or implicitly we ask ourselves often whether an entity has a property on account of its nature, or only accidentally. An entity has a property necessarily if it has it under all conceivable circumstances, for example, if it is dictated by persistence conditions.

Thus the debate should turn on the legitimacy of appeals to conceivability and to persistence conditions. But these are issues on a separate plane; logic alone does not decide these matters. There is also a further issue, namely how to fit the arguments as paraphrased adequately above, into a good formal analysis of logic (e.g. an attempt by Follesdal, 1965.) But we must be careful not to put the cart before the horse. It is not legitimate to throw away a metaphysical proposal if it can be defended on the normally accepted grounds, only because we might have difficulties fitting it into an available formal framework. Formal logic is supposed to analyse the data of science, metaphysics, and common sense. Occasionally, formal work can force us to reconsider some of the 'data', but this should be done only in face of overwhelming evidence. In the case of the modalities the existence of such a state does not seem to have been established.

Events and Material Objects

There are sounds, motions, walks, thoughts, whispers, rain, thunder, growth, birth, destructions of various types, and many other temporal entities that we shall label events. They contrast with humans and other animals, mountains, stones, oceans, artefacts, continents, and other such entities that we shall label material objects, knowing that this use stretches the ordinary meaning of this phrase. There may also be other kinds of particulars. But for our purpose of explaining what is needed for an adequate theory of thought and language this dichotomy is the most crucial to be drawn among particulars.

Events or temporal happenings, including what are called ordinarily states, will be considered without any prejudice for or against any subclass. Some events like thinking are mental, while others like digesting are physical. Some events like osmosis are natural while others like signing an agreement are institutional. Some events like pushing or pulling require agents while others like rain, thunder, or sound do not. This variety need not be taken as evidence for the ontological promiscuity of our category. We find an analogous heterogeneity among what we label here material objects. Some of these, like a sceptre, are institutional, while others like a tree are not. Some like biological specimens involve growth and development while others like heaps of sand do not. We ascribe causal agency to some, e.g. animals, while to others, like a board, we do not.

Events are located primarily in time. Their spatial locations, as we shall see, remain inexact. Material objects in our wide sense are either concrete, or have concrete parts, or are aspects of something concrete. They have definite spatial location.

The distinction between material objects and events, whose roots go far back into history, seems to have two main sources. One of these is the pattern of actor – or agent – and action, in terms of which we interpret so much of our experiences. We extend it often to conceptions of natural forces. This is why occasionally such concepts are interpreted in anthropomorphic terms. The other source is the decomposition of nature into changes and subjects for changes. One can imagine a book of truths that chronicles the history of nature, and think of this as containing accounts of all of the material objects and the changes that these undergo. One could then think of events in our broad sense as both the states in which the subjects participate and the changes that mark the transitions from one state to another.

The historical hypothesis that these are the sources for the dichotomy would also help to explain why there have been philosophers who want to say either that events do not 'really' exist, or at least that they are less fundamental than material objects. For though in modern times we think of causal laws as relating classes of events, we ascribe causal power, potency, and agency to material objects. (For more on this see Cartwright, N., 1983.) This, together with our penchant for a uniform ontological interpretation of simple truths of subject–predicate form concerning particulars in nature, suggests the metaphysical scheme according to which there are material objects with various kinds

27

of properties, and that within this scheme everything true can be expressed without the need to posit additional categories of particulars. On this view, 'Socrates is wise' and 'Socrates is walking in the Agora' have the same basic structure, i.e., particular and property.

One might be puzzled how anyone could deny the reality of events, but the philosopher so inclined would say that the mere fact that we seem to refer to these entities is weak evidence for their reality. As Quine once put it, we talk about doing something for the sake of charity, but we need not posit the reality of sakes. Furthermore, they would say that our assertions and knowledge about events will be captured within their ontology of material objects and properties. Thus they agree that the situation is not analogous to eliminating talk of witches or ghosts.

A milder version of the anti-event thesis says that there are events but they are ontologically posterior to material objects. To say that material objects are ontologically prior to events is to say that events depend in some ontologically relevant way on material objects, but these objects have no such dependency linking them to events.

For purposes of surveying the situation we can distinguish the following ontological views.

1. There are only material objects. Purported truths about events can be reduced to truths about material objects and their properties.
2. There are events and we need not posit material objects, for truths purportedly about these entities can be reduced to truths about events and properties.
3. The two categories of event and material object are equally fundamental.
4. Material objects are ontologically prior to events.
5. Events are ontologically prior to material objects.
6. There is an ontologically relevant two-way dependency between material objects and events.

As we shall see, there is also yet another position according to which the dichotomy should not be regarded as fundamental.

In our history the first important contrast between philosophers concerning the ontology of events is between Plato and Aristotle. In Plato's *Timaeus* we find the following fundamental elements: Forms, instantiations, motions, and a space–time–matter mix, described as a 'receptacle'. Within this framework the category of material objects does not have a fundamental role. Yet Plato thinks that within this scheme we can express all of the important laws of nature. In contrast, for Aristotle an account of nature is basically an account of material substances and their interactions. Aristotle's material substances are best described in modern terms as sources of energy and potentiality. In this framework the closest thing to an event is an interaction between substances. These are not regarded by Aristotle as having the same ontological status as substances. Neither framework is more parsimonious than the other. The following consideration, however, might sway one towards the Aristotelian conception. Events are ontologically 'dense', i.e., they are continuous as much as time is. Material objects, on the other hand, can be thought of on the common-sense level as being scattered in space and time. What is on the surface more tractable by perception seems to earn in the eyes of some philosophers privileged ontological status.

Whitehead was a metaphysician who took events to be the basic kind of particular, and one can find the outlines of such a view also in Ramsey's writings (Ramsey, 1931). In recent times some philosophers attempted semantic analyses to support the opposite view, namely that events do not have an ontologically legitimate status. (As an example, see Horgan, 1978.) There are no recent examples of the view according to which events are ontologically prior to material objects. On the other hand, Strawson represents the point of view according to which material objects are ontologically prior to events (Strawson, 1959). Different sets of facts are cited by Whitehead and Strawson in their favouring of different priorities. The favouring of events rests on the assumption that modern physics has or will show the most fundamental and minute elements of reality not to be material object-like. On the other hand, Strawson's arguments are supported by a way of construing common-sense organizations of experience. This rough contrast is suggestive. It indicates that metaphysicians at times might be talking at cross-purposes, for they try to account for different 'data'.

In the second half we shall develop a proposal according to which both material objects and events are equally fundamental types of particulars, and there is a two-way dependency between these categories in terms of individuation and persistence. But before we move to a more detailed consideration of some of the issues separating the different positions we need to consider a position according to which the dichotomy is not ontologically fundamental.

Quine develops a canonical language within which all of the truths of the sciences can be encoded. He proposes that within this interpreted language we treat time as just another dimension, like the spatial ones. In this treatment he recasts physical objects as spatio-temporal continua underlying both the notion of a material object and that of event. His notion of a 'physical object' includes both what we call events and what we call material objects. This latter distinction according to Quine does not affect the fundamental ontological categories. (This view is developed in earlier writings of Quine, but for a terse statement and defence of the view, see Quine, 1960.) Quine admits that we need the notion of material objects in order to explain some salient facts about human language-learning in general, and reference in particular. We also need this notion to explain a key usage of general terms; namely having some divide their reference. This semantic notion is the analogue of what we called earlier certain properties being linked to principles of individuation. Quine thinks, however, that the use of the notion of material object to account for certain cognitive processes does not qualify it as demarcating a fundamental ontological category.

One can agree with Quine about the facts cited, and still defend the ontological legitimacy of the two categories. For one has to spell out individuation and persistence conditions for Quine's spatio-temporal continua, or 'process-things' as Strawson calls them in his criticism of Quine. Suppose, however, that process-things turn out to be implicitly like mass terms. That is to say, they do not come with non-arbitrary principles of individuation. Taking these as fundamental will not solve the problem of individuation. Thus we see the need to admit events and material objects as basic ontological categories, barring the truth of some reductionist thesis, for it is in reference to these that we spell out non-arbitrary conditions of reference and individuation. As we saw, classes of permissible and non-permissible changes characterize persistence. But these changes are events, or according to some reductionistic theses some equivalent of complexes of material objects and properties.

This would be, then, briefly, a defence of the ontological relevance of the two categories. The defence grants Quine that the task of ontology is not just to capture ordinary usage of natural languages or conditions of language learning. We can still regard the categories of material object and event as ontologically genuine if it turns out that these categories are needed to spell out conditions of individuation and persistence for particulars.

We shall turn now to Strawson's account that interprets material objects as basic particulars, and events as entities that depend in the relevant way on material objects. In order to understand Strawson's dependency claims, we must understand a notion that plays a key role in these claims, namely the notion of an identifying reference. Strawson wants to argue that we can identify in this sense material objects without identifying events but not the other way around. This, according to Strawson, establishes ontological priority (Strawson, 1959, p. 17).

In considering this claim, let us first see if one can draw from matters of identification ontological conclusions. Such an inference requires that successful identifying reference should have existential import. That is to say, the referent, or identified entity, must exist. Strawson's examples of identifying particulars involve relating these to our spatio-temporal framework. For, as he points out, a purely qualitative singular reference to a particular, no matter how complicated, leaves open the possibility that the particular in question has an 'identical twin' somewhere. Strawson thinks that the key to locating things in our spatio-temporal framework are three-dimensional objects, i.e. material bodies.

He explains identification first in a person-to-person communicational context. Speaker *S* identifies particulars to hearer *H*. Success is attained when they lock into the same entity. One can have more or less relaxed requirements about the specificity of the audience. It can be an individual, a group, future humans, etc. No matter how strict or relaxed the conditions of the intended audience, identificational success requires only the following:

1. both the speaker who does the identifying and the intended audience, present or remote, should be able to turn their attention to the intended region of their respective phenomenal spaces;
2. the audience should focus on what both speaker and audience take to be existing in the relevant region of space and time.

In short, successful person-to-person identification in this sense does not require that the referent should exist; it seems to me that it requires only that speaker and hearer should take it to be existing. Thus, for example, in a community that has communal hallucinations, members may successfully identify to each other all kinds of objects in definite spatio-temporal regions. One cannot conclude from this that the putative entities exist. In order for successful identification to have existential import, one must add that the individuals involved in the identifying have veridical identifying capacities. This assumption cannot come out from Strawson's notion of identifying reference alone. (For an expanded version of this point, as well as for more material on the sections to follow, see Moravcsik, 1965.)

Let us assume for sake of argument that this matter can be resolved in a satisfactory way. Is Strawson's claim of ontological priority tenable under those conditions? Strawson has two notions, those of identification and re-identification. These correspond roughly to our notions of individuation and persistence. Let us look at what Strawson wants to say about identification and re-identification.

Strawson claims that we can form individuating references to material objects without referring to events, but not the other way around. One of his examples is that of animals and births (Strawson, 1959, p. 51). He admits that from 'this is an animal' we can conclude 'there is some birth which is the birth of this animal', since there are no animals without births. He also agrees that 'this is a birth' entails 'there is some animal the birth of which this is'. But he thinks that to say 'this is an animal' entails merely 'this was born' without reference to a specific event, while referring identifyingly to a birth will not be possible without referring also to the animal of which this is the birth. One might restate Strawson's point sympathetically (not relying on the peculiarities of the English language that gives us 'born' and 'human', but not 'animalish') in the following way. I can give an identifying reference of an animal without also identifying its particular birth. But one cannot refer identifyingly to a birth without specifying the particular animal whose birth it is. One could go on, complicating the discussion, but let us grant Strawson the point. Is it not true that as long as he admits that from 'this is a birth' if follows 'there is an animal of which this is the birth' and from 'this is an animal' it follows 'there is a birth which is the birth of this animal' no existential and hence ontological priority follows from the identificational asymmetry? For the fact that in the one case I need to refer only to some event while in the other case to a specific material object does not establish ontological priority.

Let us now turn to another point concerning persistence or re-identification. Strawson claims that the re-identification of events like a battle or a thaw will require reference to the bodies that are participants in these events. Thus, for example, a successful re-identification of a battle will involve being able to re-identify roughly the same group of original participants or a partly different group causally related in appropriate ways to the original participants. This seems to hold true for many kinds of event introduced by verbs of Indo-European languages.

Strawson's crucial move is, however, to claim that there is no such dependency of material objects on events. He writes: 'If, on the other hand, we consider the identity through time of material bodies themselves, we shall indeed find that a fundamental requirement is that which we have already noted, viz. continuity of existence in space; and determining whether this requirement is fulfilled may turn on identifying places; but this, in its turn rests upon the identification of bodies' (Strawson, 1959, pp. 55–6).

Let us first note that continuity in space will not do as a sufficient persistence condition for many kinds of material bodies. For example, human bodies persist in time, and although they are continuous, the condition of such existence does not include a requirement of sameness of parts through space. On the other hand, for a material entity like a collection of body cells it does. Thus both continue through time but in different ways. There is

33

also the case of a live human and his corpse. This illustrates the fact that mere continuity in space is not enough. In this case we do have continuity in space but two distinct material objects. The crucial issue seems to be how many parts must survive and in what arrangements. To this question there seems to be no general answer for all material bodies. The matter is settled kind by kind. Different kinds of material bodies have different persistence conditions. Furthermore, while some material bodies are continuous, others like mountain ranges or some lakes are not. Again, we need to view the issue kind by kind.

So far we have made out a case for persistence conditions varying among material bodies from kind to kind. This does not yet show their dependency on events. That step follows when we reflect on the fact that exchanging some parts for others, or just losing parts, or increasing the number of parts, are changes and hence events. Thus the persistence conditions for various kinds of material bodies involve events and event-types. We see here, then, the exact analogy of the dependence that Strawson claims to have shown to hold between events and material bodies. Thus these arguments, while unearthing many interesting facts about reference and identification, fail to show the ontological priority of material objects over events.

Let us illustrate the parallel situations with regards to persistence. What are persistence conditions for a concert? There must be some continuity, though intermission is allowed. There must be some continuity of participating humans, though even here there is some latitude. Presumably there is also sameness of the building, and to some extent also of instruments. The pieces played must fall into some prearranged order. We see, then, that some reference to material bodies is being made.

Now let us consider the persistence of a lake. The lake may lose quite a lot of water in the summer, and then show a marked increase in water level when the rains come again. The lake can also 'move' to some extent, that is to say, it need not keep the exact contours that it has at the start of its existence. But all of the items we referred to, increase, decrease of water levels, change in the coloration of the water, etc., are changes and hence events. The only way to get rid of the dependency is to claim that statements about changes and thus events can be eliminated by some semantic trick. But then the same can be said about the persistence conditions of events. Maybe we can describe these by talking only of events and complex properties thus eliminating the need to refer to material objects.

In this discussion we have left so far the notions of an event, its individuation and persistence on an intuitive level. It is time to turn to a number of accounts of what events are and how they fit into our theories of reality. A number of such accounts have been given recently. There are two contexts in which the ontology of events must be faced. One of these is action theory, and the other is the study of the causal laws of science. Action analysis is relevant, since on the surface it seems obvious that actions constitute a subset of the class of events. The laws of science seem relevant since we articulate causal laws as relations between sets of events.

We are faced with the following options. It could be that all events are particulars, or that all are universals, or that there are both kinds of event. Particular events would be the Battle of Waterloo, the death of Julius Caesar, or the inauguration of President Carter. It is easier to fix our attention on particular non-recurrent events when the descriptions of these also contain proper names of some of the participants. But even in these cases ordinary language may leave matters undecided. What about references to Mayor Hines' breakfast or Betty Grable's triumph? These phrases could be taken to pick out one event respectively, or series of recurring events. The mayor presumably has breakfast every day, and a successful actress like Betty Grable could have had a series of triumphs. A sentence starting with 'Arthur Schnabel's great performance of the "Hammerklavier" ' can continue with 'evoked the greatest applause ever in Carnegie Hall', or with 'elicited shouts of "bravo" each autumn in Philadelphia'. And, of course, there is always the availability of paraphrase. We can talk of Jones and a particular event of walking in the Cambridge Commons, and also of Jones having the property of having walked in the Cambridge Commons at such-and-such a time. Even locutions like 'a certain' or 'a particular' are ambiguous. A certain smile can be shared by more than one woman, and a particular walk by more than one walker.

One may want to limit events to only one of the categories of universal and particular, but strong arguments are needed to support such an ontological stand, given the liberality of our language. As Davidson pointed out, in such ontological matters claims of parsimony are not sufficient. He says about parsimony: 'What's so good about it? Clarity is desirable, but parsimony may or may not make for clarity' (Davidson, 1970, p.27). Davidson's own metaphor suggests that he thinks of the introduction of universals to explain locutions like 'I did it again' as 'using a cannon to shoot a mouse' (ibid.). We shall lay aside metaphors and concentrate on Davidson's reasons for thinking that events are real, they are particulars, and on his conception of their nature.

One consideration supporting the existence of particular events is that they contribute to making certain propositions true. A sentence comparing two explosions in terms of loudness seems to be true in virtue of two particular events having certain relational properties. Again, we assign responsibility to human agents in virtue of certain relations that they have to specific particular events.

These considerations would not weigh heavily with those like Chisholm who think that only event universals exist (Chisholm, 1970), for such philosophers would translate statements like the above example into other more complex ones in which certain properties relating agents, event-properties, and times are ascribed to individuals.

The view that events are basically universals gains strength from the realization that most of our ways of specifying events, such as 'walking across the Quad', 'writing a letter to Aunt Jenny', etc., introduce repeatable events and hence universals. Davidson, however, points out that one can account for recurrence without positing universals. For one can regard what we call recurrent events such as smoking a pipe as an event with many spatio-temporally discontinuous parts, each of which is in the ordinary sense an event of my smoking a pipe (Davidson, 1970, p.28). Of course, each of the parts, i.e. my smoking the pipe on several occasions, need not be exactly the same. In building the bigger entities out of their parts a certain latitude is permissible. Indeed, one can add, the same holds for specifying instances of a universal. We do not assume that all instances of a universal like being a human or being a triangle must exhibit exact qualitative sameness. Still, this argument shows only that we can account for the common-sense notion of event recurrence without positing universals. It does not show the necessity of acknowledging particular events.

Other considerations, however, point strongly in that direction. Davidson points out that in many cases two event descriptions containing co-extensive singular terms introducing a participant in that event are typically regarded as singling out the same event (Davidson, 1970, p.29). Thus, to use our own examples, the event of kissing Molly is the same event as the event of kissing the parson's daughter, assuming that Molly is the parson's daughter. This is so, even though kissing Molly and kissing the parson's daughter are two distinct universals. The most natural way to account for the facts in such contexts is to say that given that 'John kissed Molly last night' is equivalent to 'John kissed the parson's daughter last night' we mean to refer with these sentences to one particular event with two participants, namely Molly and John. Any attempt to reduce this to circumlocutions avoiding reference to a particular event seems less perspicuous than the interpretation just given.

Additional evidence is furnished by Davidson with reference to the semantics of adverbial modification, and our ability to count events and place them in a temporal order. The former kind of evidence could be dismissed by the metaphysical purist on the ground that it reflects merely a semantic peculiarity of natural language and thus perhaps a certain way in which humans organize experience. This does not furnish premises for ontological conclusions. But this could not be said about the second kind of evidence. We cannot help but order temporal slices in succession and place ourselves into this flow of events. Planning and explaining what happens to us are fundamental to rationality. These activities seem to involve reference to particular events. Thus very little is gained by trying to analyse away the successive stages of our own lives into a framework in which we are only parts of complex property specifications. If, however, we admit particular events into our ontology we need to deal with their conditions of individuation and persistence.

According to one proposal events are identical if and only if they have the same causes and the same effects (Davidson, 1969). The intuition behind this proposal is, presumably, that the realm of events consists of causal chains. Items with the same position in these chains are identical. Thus, for example, the event of the veterinarian keeping the cat from having certain diseases and the event of the veterinarian giving the cat certain injections are the same event, and they can be shown to have the same causes and the same effects.

There are problems with this view. Let us consider two ways of specifying what seems intuitively the same event, namely my lunch yesterday, and my most unpleasant hour yesterday. The causes for my lunch yesterday were: making reservations, entering a certain establishment, ordering from the menu, etc. The effects are: leaving the restaurant with enough food in my stomach, driving away from the restaurant, etc. Let us look, however, at the causal ancestry of my most unpleasant hour yesterday. This would typically include: noisy room, arrogant waiter, fight with the waiter over conditions, bad company, etc. These seem reasonable candidates for having caused my most unpleasant hour, but not for having caused my lunch yesterday.

Someone might say that the 'real' description of the event is in terms of its being a lunch, and that the other description points only to an aspect of the event. But one could turn this around. Why not regard the description in terms of unpleasantness as the 'basic' description and its being a lunch as the feature? It seems that one might need a form of essentialism, according to which being a lunch is an essential constituent of the event. But Davidson does not want essentialism. Perhaps someone might say that the description that is closer to physical descriptions should be the basic one. But in our case both descriptions are equally close to – or far from? – the physical level. Still others would say that the description that is within a framework of causal regularities should prevail. But in our case both descriptions and the candidates for causes that we picked out are within frameworks of causal generalizations. Noisy rooms, bad company, and incompetent waiters typically cause miserable hours, and making reservations, driving to a place, entering the restaurant, etc. typically cause lunches. It seems, then, that the proposal under consideration is doing the job in some cases but not in others. In Part II we shall see how this can be incorporated into a theory.

Apart from the issue of convincing cases, there are two more problems with this view. One of these is the charge of conceptual, though not formal, circularity. It seems that we have to understand the notion of an event in order to understand the notion of causal chains (Brand, 1977, p. 332 points out that the account is not formally circular). Some might find the notion of conceptual circularity strange. But all it means is that there are concepts that cannot be made intelligible without invoking a certain other notion, whose intelligibility, in turn, leads us back to the previous concepts. We can certainly understand the notion of causality without understanding the notion of an event. But we need the more specific notion of a causal chain. Apart from such 'local' phenomena as genealogy, or finding the producer of an artefact, we do not have a handle on the notion of causal chains, except when viewing this under the general notion of events succeeding each other and being causally related.

If the above objection does not seem convincing, the next one ought to cause discomfort even to the person who is a true metaphysician at heart. For the account seems to assume that all events have causes and effects. What about uncaused events, and the ones that do not have effects? (This issue is raised, though not exactly in this form, in Brand, 1977; and Moravcsik, 1965.) Kant thought that the principle that every event has a cause is an *a priori* synthetic truth. The evidence for this is, to put it mildly, not very strong. There were many periods in our history in which people did not think that there were no random events. For example, early Greek cosmologies did not assume in general any such principle, and it is absent from Plato's cosmology. It is a matter of controversy if Aristotle ever accepted it, and some Hellenistic philosophers clearly denied it. It would be interesting to determine to what extent this principle was prevalent in the western world before Newton and Descartes. Furthermore, one could not deduce this principle as a basic principle of human rationality from the fact that infants from the earliest age look for what we call causal links among some of their experiences. (For evidence, see Michotte, 1963.)

On the basis of these considerations we should not close our minds to other alternatives. One of these is the proposal by Brand according to which events are identical if and only if they occupy necessarily the same spatio-temporal location (Brand, 1877, pp. 332-3). The proposal is introduced by the demonstration with reference to such cases as swimming in a pool and catching a cold at the same time, that mere contingent spatio-temporal coincidence will not do. As we shall see, this account does not capture all of the relevant cases. But apart from that, even if it was observationally adequate, it would offer an account that does not distinguish events from material objects. For as we saw, in those cases too – as in the case of the gold and the ring that it constitutes – there may be spatio-temporal coincidence. Thus if we accept this analysis, we shall have to find some other way of telling material objects apart from events. Let us return, however, to examples. A human body and a series of collections of body cells occupy the same spatio-temporal region. Perhaps a few cells could be different, but if many of the cells were replaced, there would be a different body. Thus in a metaphysical rather than logical sense, the two are necessarily in the same spatio-temporal region. Nevertheless, the persistence of body cells is not the same as there being a persisting human body. Let us look for analogues in the case of events. There are bodily changes such as growth, illness, recovery, ageing, etc. We can single out necessarily co-extensive changes in the various collections of body cells. Thus we have necessary spatio-temporal co-existence, but still two distinct series of events.

The last example suggests that we should consider event individuation to be simply a matter of property instantiation. According to this view, if in the same spatio-temporal region two distinct properties are instantiated, then we have two events, regardless of whether the co-extensiveness is accidental or necessary. This view, however, requires that we posit not only events as particulars but also event universals.

Given the language of everyday or scientific language, we seem to need event universals as much as the posit of any other entity. For research is often oriented to finding out whether a certain kind of event or event universal has or lacks instances. Thus event universals guide empirical research and particular events emerge in connection with experimentation and the discovery of answers.

This could be viewed, however, as just a matter of the human perspective, involving incomplete knowledge and understanding. The fact that in our thought-processes involving research into new domains event universals have priority does not show that these universals are ontologically fundamental. A better argument can be formulated, however, by reference to the individuation and persistence conditions discussed above. These govern permissible and not permissible changes for different kinds of entities. These items are change-types, or change universals, and thus event universals. Thus if someone accepts the thesis that there are persistence and individuation conditions of the sort sketched, he should accept also event universals. In other words, individuation conditions are property complexes that are parts of the natures of various natural kinds.

Let us return to event individuation and consider proposals making use of universals. According to Kim (1970b), events are combinations of objects, properties, and certain times. Thus Socrates' walking at a certain time is an event, and Socrates' walking is an event universal. Identity for events is sameness of object, time, and property exemplified. Thus Socrates behaving unselfishly before his death and Socrates behaving altruistically before his death are the same event, on the assumption that the property of behaving unselfishly and the property of behaving altruistically are the same property.

We can make a change in this proposal in order to bring it into line with a suggestion made above, namely that the positing of basic metaphysical distinctions should not depend on contingent assumptions about the rough nature of the working of the world. Thus we should regard such expressions as 'it is raining', 'it has been hot', 'it flashes on the horizon', or 'there was a great crash', as introducing events, regardless of whether current (or future?) physics analyses these into occurrences involving material objects. In our ontology we should leave room for objectless events.

The reformulation of Kim's account amounts to dropping the requirement that all events must have material objects as participants. One of the challenges faced by this proposal is showing how events differ from material objects. Linguistic usage cannot be the final arbiter. What if, instead of talking about tables and houses, we use locutions like 'it tables here' or 'it houses here'? Apart from aesthetic considerations, the usage could be adopted without much inconvenience. Such usage would encourage us to view material objects also as property instantiation at certain times. Still, intuitively it seems clear that we do not want to posit a different material object for every property instantiation in a certain region at a certain time. And it seems less counter-intuitive to say that about events. Thus it seems that one could distinguish Kim's conception of events from our conceptions of material objects.

Two problems seem to remain. One concerns the persistence conditions. A process like osmosis has its own persistence conditions governing what is or is not still the same process after the passing of a certain amount of time. In the case of events, as in the case of material objects, mere continuity is neither a necessary nor a sufficient condition of persistence. An event like a walk admits of some kinds of interruption but not others. If I walk to the bus stop from my house and stop for a newspaper at the kiosk, this still counts as one walk. If, however, I interrupted the walk to the bus stop by calling at a friend's house for a philosophical chat that lasts half a day, then what I participated in counts as two walks. Each kind of event has its own conditions of what kinds of interruption do or do not interfere with persistence. Nothing in the individuation conditions given so far accounts for this phenomenon. There are also cases in which we have two continuous processes such as kinds of growth and degeneration, and these still count as two rather than one event.

Another problem arises when we consider whether we should have uniformly intensional conditions on event individuation, i.e. property identity. In some cases such individuation is plausible. When Jones is thinking of humans and featherless bipeds, it seems plausible to say that we are dealing with two events. For it seems that thinking of humans and thinking of featherless bipeds involves entertaining two thoughts; hence we should regard the phenomena here as two events. On the other hand, we saw earlier examples in which mere co-extensiveness in time and space, and sameness of participants seem sufficient for individuation. Kissing Molly, for example, and kissing the parson's daughter are, under the right circumstances, the same event, but longing for Molly and longing for the parson's daughter seem to be different events, even if they occur at the same time. An overambitious young man might yearn for what he takes to be two distinct women, even if – possibly to his relief – they turn out to be the same person. When we turn in the second half to constructive proposals, we shall see ways of accounting for this amorphous situation.

In considering examples of purported events, we made free use

of mental events and resisted the suggestion that our philosophizing not consider objectless events. Someone might wonder
whether there might not be good reasons to have a theory of
events with an inherent predisposition towards materialism or
physicalism. If one could be sure that the distinction between the
mental and the material can be made out on *a priori* grounds,
then such a move might be justified. We shall see, however, in
our examination of the nature of thought that these assumptions
are not well grounded. If the distinction between the mental and
the material is open-ended, and the issue between materialism
and dualism – and other alternatives – an empirical one, then the
predisposition suggested is not warranted.

We shall turn to yet another way of distinguishing events
from other kinds of particulars. The proposed distinguishing
mark is that events in our sense can have aspects attached to
them, while this is not true of material objects. The syntax of a
language like English provides evidence for this. Aspects attach
themselves to verbs introducing events, and do not attach
themselves to nouns introducing material objects. Thus, for
example, we have phrases like 'she is walking', or 'she has
written a book', but nothing analogous in the case of nouns like
'mountain', 'building', etc. Not surprisingly in tense logic, i.e. the
branch of logic dealing with past, present, future, and aspects like
progressive and perfect, we define the tenses by reference to the
flow of time, the occurrence of events, and the positions of the
speaker and intended audience with reference to that flow.
(Rohrer, 1978 provides a good recent survey.) Interpretation of
this work shows a difference between material objects and
events, and also shows the need to posit particular events located
at various points and intervals in time.

Let us concentrate on two basic aspectual features: the
progressive and the perfect. In terms of these we can express the
various ways and manners in which events and processes are
spread over time. (For a recent attempt at a more formal
characterization, see Gabbay and Moravcsik, 1980.) We can
characterize the progressive in the following rough intuitive way.
The progressive introduces a certain structure into the event
introduced by the verb to which it is attached. For example, we
can attach the progressive to 'walk' and obtain, e.g., 'he was
walking'. The expression 'walk' denotes periods of intervals in

43

which walking takes place. These intervals need not contain at every instant actual occurrences of walking. But the progressive directs us to such sub-periods; i.e., the ones in which actual walking takes place, and relates these to certain other events. For example, 'he was walking home when he heard the fire engine'. The perfect, on the other hand, takes a given process and specifies for it a certain point of completion. For example, 'she has built a house'. This phrase introduces a period of house building, and the perfect indicates completion; and hence that the activity is no longer continuing. There are various formal ways to show why completability is attached to some events and processes, but not to others, and hence how attaching the perfect to a verb helps us to delineate sequences of events that can be seen as having structures of beginning, continuing activity, and completion.

Someone might try to express all of this in a system within which we posit only objects and properties, but it is questionable whether this could be done, and whether the ensuing formalism would have any philosophical explanatory force.

The objector could reply that viewing time as a flow of events with happenings and completions may be just part of the human conceptual framework. If 'completion is in the eye of the – linguistic – beholder', then we cannot draw any consequences from these data for ontology, even if it turns out that these two aspects are parts of every natural language. Humans are active, and they have aims, projects they want to complete, etc. But need we look at the universe in this way *sub specie aeternitatis*? The issue shades into general discussion of the need to see the world under teleological or functional aspects, in connection with, e.g., biology. (This objection was voiced by Professor Quine in conversation.)

It seems, then, that we need a theory of events that can distinguish events from material objects without relying on the aspectual treatability of events. At the same time it should be a theory that provides a framework for the semantics of tense and aspect. We shall see in chapter 4 how this can be carried out.

In summary, we reviewed the issue of whether we need a theory of events that can distinguish these entities from material objects, whether we need to posit events, and if so, whether we need both event universals and particular events. We also considered various attempts to provide individuation conditions for events, including principles of persistence. We considered as our examples events from various categories such as the mental and the physical, the object-less and the object-dependent.

We omitted discussions of many other important ontological issues concerning the division of the realm of particulars into subspecies. But we shall see that the notions developed and the issues raised affect in important ways what philosophers want to say about the nature of thought and analyses of language.

The fact that we can make sense of events in this general way, prior to restricting our attention to sub-classes, is of importance for what follows. For it shows that one cannot start a theory of thought or language by saying that purely metaphysical considerations have already ruled out events in general, or mental events, or for that matter materialism. Furthermore, if all of the categories surveyed have ontological credentials, then they can be used as the framework for a 'rich' theory of thought and language, making use of universals, particulars, modalities, and events of various kinds. We shall be able to link what we said about individuation and persistence to theories of semantics. Our survey showed why some philosophers try to reduce ontology to a slimmer base. But we also adduced considerations supporting doubt that increase in conceptual clarity or explanatory power can be found in the proposed reductionisms.

CHAPTER II

Thought

What is thought and thinking? This question is at least as old as western philosophy. It will occupy us throughout this part of the book. It is not the same question as asking about the meaning of 'think' and 'thought' in modern English. In different languages in different historical periods different words are used to cover the variety of phenomena associated in pre-theoretical common-sense thinking with thought. This concept encompasses many different processes. We shall give it the label 'cognition' and leave it undefined since the many different states and processes under the label do not admit of a sharp delineation. Here are some examples indicating the subject of our inquiry. Thinking of something, having a concept of something, understanding, explaining, thinking, and believing. Corresponding to these verbal notions we have nouns like thought, concept, intelligibility, belief, judgement. In addition to these positive notions cognition includes also doubt and questioning. There are two ways of indicating a common element among the items cited. One of these is to claim that for these activities and states and for the expression of their results language is necessary. This claim needs qualifications. One of these is that the need for language is related to these activities and states attaining a certain level of complexity. This level is empirically determined, and today opinions vary as to where to draw the line. But it is worth noting that as phrased here the claim does not rule out animal cognition of various kinds. The other way of finding the common denominator is to claim that expressing what goes on in these states and activities is one of the key tasks of natural languages. According to this view, language may or may not be needed for every cognitive process. It does not rule out pre-verbal or non-

46

verbal thinking. It does say, however, that language typically expresses or embodies the outcome of various cognitive processes.

Some of the words used in listing examples of cognition have a process-product ambiguity. For example, 'thought' or 'belief' can refer either to what we think or believe, such as '2+2=4', or to the mental processes and states of thought and having a belief. Our task will be to shed light on both process and product.

Cognition as we delineated it is the subject of both common sense and scientific reflection. Our task will include examining how cognition can be treated on both of these levels, and to see how the levels can be related to each other.

Regardless of which of these two ways we take, cognition as we use this notion here is that part of mental processes and states that centres on the interaction of thought and language. It should be stressed that this is only a small part of the subject called Philosophy of Mind. That vast subject includes, among other things, the mind–body problem, free will, determinism, feelings and emotions, causal links between the felt cognitive experiences and physiological states, the relation of minds to machines, and many other topics. This essay does not deal with these. It deals with the mental from the point of view of sketching various proposals of how to integrate a view of cognition with views of language. Those aspects of cognition are treated that are important for understanding how language can express or embody thoughts. The proposals to be presented are compatible with many views concerning the other larger issues in the philosophy of mind.

A salient fact about cognition is that we typically cannot identify specific episodes of thinking, believing, etc. without a characterization of what is being thought or believed in that episode. In contrast, we can identify states of persons being in pain, without always knowing the sources – be these causes or objects – of pain states. Cognition, then, has 'objects' in a special sense. These objects – or contents, as some prefer – can be described as a first approximation to be complexes of abstract objects, such as concepts, theories, or propositions, or possibly sentences. In this chapter we shall consider various conceptions of the relation between thought and its objects. As we shall see, some deny that thought needs to have objects in a special sense, and think that thinking has only 'content', while others think that object and content in this context are equivalent.

The stress on the objectual nature of cognition confronts us with an option in strategy. One might try to treat cognition as just another biological process, like digestion. Thus the main emphasis within such an account would be on causal laws, with some attention to the functional specifications of various states and mental or physiological structures. Alternatively, we can take the objectual nature of cognition as fundamental and focus on the question: 'How is it possible for the mind to deal with such objects?' Within this enterprise, the question of whether it is possible to give a theory of cognition that would predict exactly who will think or believe what and when, is left open as an empirical issue concerning which at present we have no decisive evidence.

Let us consider a recent statement of what a philosophical analysis of what we called cognition is. In his book Robert Stalnaker writes:

> My topic is the abstract structure of inquiry – the enterprise of forming, testing, and revising beliefs. My goal was to provide a philosophical foundation and motivation for an apparatus for describing that structure – an apparatus that might help to clarify the relationships among some problematic concepts in the theory of knowledge and the philosophy of mind, concepts such as belief and conditional belief, presupposition and presumption, probability, counterfactual dependence, causation, and explanation.
>
> (Stalnaker, 1984, p. ix).

This elegant statement captures what many philosophers of cognition today would regard as the core of what needs investigation and analysis. And clearly, it would be very difficult to deny that forming, testing, and changing beliefs are among our key mental processes, and that some of the others on our initial list must assume that these processes take place. Nevertheless, we should note at the outset that this is not the only way of conceiving of the focus of investigation.

At the heart of Stalnaker's conception are humans as belief-forming creatures. The elements of these beliefs are presumably concepts, and these represent sorting things into groups according to similarities, the perception of which may or may not be influenced by human interests. The terms making up sentences expressing what we believe are labels for sets determined by similarities. According to this view humans are primarily labelling and information processing creatures. Of course, Stalnaker would add that we do many other things as well, such as theorizing and explaining. Within his approach, however, one would build the more complex structures out of the more basic elements of beliefs and their content. Theories and explanations, on this view, are sets of sentences and what they express, related in certain ways.

Though all of this sounds very sensible, it is worth exploring alternatives. I shall sketch one here, though it is more difficult to present this with the conceptual tools favoured by recent analytic philosophy than Stalnaker's programme. At this stage I shall merely present an outline of this alternative, leaving its elaboration and defence to the second half of the book.

According to this conception, humans are basically explanation-seeking and puzzlement-removing creatures. Our puzzlements are only partly linked to matters of practical concern. Our concepts are formed by first finding something in our experience problematic, and then being able to remove the puzzlement by fitting the phenomena into explanations; these may be the forging of certain patterns, finding analogies, formulating definitions revealing basic constituency, or finding the elements in an entity that enables it to function as it does. Concepts collect either phenomena that seem problematic or include explanatory schema that answer questions of the sort: what is it, on account of what can it function, how can it generate these effects?

For example, some humans find it puzzling that when people make certain noises at each other, they can make sense of it. Something, be it a warning, expression of emotion, or information, is being transmitted. Out of such puzzlement arise our concepts of speaking, listening, understanding, and we forge the concept of language to explain what makes these activities and states possible. The concept must have ingredients that play key roles in more detailed explanations of these linguistic activities and their cognitive correlates.

As an other example, let us consider the interesting fact that among women in a social unit there will be one with special biological and emotional ties to a given child in that community.

Wonderment at this leads to the formation of the concept of a mother. The ingredients of this concept must play a key role in explanations of various maternal activities.

These illustrations show that within this alternative approach, the basic units are not beliefs but explanations of a restricted sort. Concepts, beliefs, acceptance of information in general, are abstractions from the cognitively more basic unit of explanation giving. To be sure, explanations of the sort under consideration must contain units that can be assessed as true or false, but the fundamental assessment of explanations is not in terms of veracity, but in terms of their being insightful, deep, illuminating, adequate, etc.

The basic units of Stalnaker's object of analysis are entities that are true of false, and whose nature has been investigated by recent analytic philosophy. The basic units of my alternative cannot be assessed merely as true or false, nor is it clear that the objects of what are on this account basic cognitive states can be expressed fully in propositional form. Furthermore, notions like finding something problematic, finding an explanation insightful, and understanding a theory are among the most difficult targets of cognitive psychology, and have not been clarified to any great extent in analytic philosophy. Thus it might raise philosophic eyebrows for me even to include these in a philosophical sketch of cognition, and be positively flirting with fate to attempt to make these fundamental. Nevertheless, such a proposal will be articulated later and made the foundation of a theory of lexical meaning.

Among the problems to be surveyed here we find questions about the ontological status of cognition, the status of recent influential theories of cognition in psychology, and approaches to the characterization of the key properties of thought and cognition in general.

Ontology and Semantics

The traditions of Cartesian and post-Cartesian philosophy construe the problem of the ontological status of cognition and its elements in terms of the contrast between mind and body. We noted earlier that cognition covers only a small part of the 'mental', but since this term is used so widely in recent literature, we shall adopt this nomenclature, with the qualification stated here, to be understood. The contrast of mind and body suggests that there are only two alternatives: materialism or dualism. In this brief survey, however, we shall see that there are many more options, and thus the key notions of any ontology of cognition should be subjected to the same philosophic scrutiny.

The more general ontological issues surveyed in chapter 1 also come into play in these discussions. For many of the mental phenomena are interpreted by common sense as felt experiences. Thus it would sound odd for someone to say that my being puzzled about a philosophic problem right now or my thinking of Christopher at this moment should be analysed as properties. Our intuitions are more comfortable with an ontology that admits events as well as material objects, and posits with respect to both categories both universals and particulars. The realism–nominalism debate is also relevant to our discussions of cognition. For if realism is viable, then we can characterize the objects of thought as complexes of universals. If nominalism is right, then these objects must be reducible to complexes of particulars. Furthermore, as we shall see, certain conceptions of cognition require that nominalism be adequate. For a fully naturalistic or materialist conception of cognition would require that the relation between thought and its objects be just another causal link, and causal links hold between collections of particulars.

We should separate the ontological status of cognition and its elements from semantic issues, such as whether one can translate all sentences containing mental terms into another language that contains only materialistic terms in the relevant places of the translation. Such programmes are called reductionist theses. The following shows that the semantic issue of reductionism is not the same as assigning ontological status to thinking. Someone could maintain a materialist ontology without being committed to the success of the relevant semantic reductions. For example, it could be held that ultimately all mental entities are material entities, but that something concerning humans interpreting their own mental processes forces them to talk within a language that contains, ineliminably, mental terms. Or someone might show that a materialist translation of all mental terms can succeed, but at the same time deny that this shows mental entities to be less fundamental ontologically than material ones. For in normal circumstances translation is a symmetrical affair. From the fact that two languages are inter-translatable it does not follow that the ontological commitments of one are more fundamental than the commitments of the other. Thus the materialist who wants to base his ontological preferences on semantic arguments must show more than translatability, and the dualist who wants to justify positing irreducibly mental entities must do more than just show the failure of a materialist reductionistic semantic programme.

We shall start with a consideration of materialism with regards to cognition. This is the view adopted by most philosophers of language and practitioners of 'cognitive science' in the past few decades. Materialism in this context claims that all pre-theoretically mental or cognitive phenomena as well as the phenomena and concepts required by a scientific account of cognition can be explained within a framework that posits on the level of particulars only material entities. Thus a materialist account of cognition should show how to dispense with both immaterial mental entities and with universals as objects of cognition. A weak version of this view holds that although there are non-material particulars, these are ontologically dependent on material entities, in the sense of ontological dependence explained in chapter 1. Since most recent writings on cognition hold the stronger view, we shall restrict this brief survey to this position. (For some representative writings, see Smart, 1963; Armstrong, 1968; and Churchland, 1979.)

We need to ask of materialism, as well as of its rivals, the following questions:

- Are its basic notions conceptually clearer than those of its rivals?
- If the basic notions keep changing, does the tradition have enough continuity to render these notions intelligible?
- Is the hypothesis that cognition can be explained within the favoured ontology empirically viable?

The concept of matter has not remained fixed through history. Aristotelian matter is very different from Newtonian matter, and both differ drastically from the 'matter' of contemporary physics. If we insisted that matter is just what people in the time of Descartes and Newton thought it to be, then we would have to say that modern physics is not materialist, for it does not posit extension as the most fundamental element in the physical world. Thus a defence of materialism would have to fall back on the claim that the tradition is continuous enough to allow us to talk about a unitary property of being composed of matter. Philosophers have held different opinions on this issue. A choice on this question influences one's view on how to answer the first of the three questions posed above. For if the notion of matter is not sufficiently clear from the tradition, then how can we compare it to the concept of the mental and immaterial? Indeed, if neither notion is drawn sharply, perhaps the whole contrast is less fundamental than tradition would lead us to believe.

On the matter of empirical viability we find again a wide variety of opinions. As we shall see, this is affected also by the disagreement on what the facts are that a theory of cognition is supposed to be able to explain. The basic difficulties have remained the same over decades. One is the relating of felt experiences to the physiological mechanisms, and the other is to explain how the brain can symbolize the objects of cognition on the assumption that nominalism fails. Furthermore, one must not assume that the more we know about the physiological mechanisms of cognition on the one hand, and the structure of the abstract objects of thought on the other, the more convergence we shall see. It could be that the more we know about these two concepts, the less any close correlation will seem plausible.

We shall now ask what motivation one might have for adopting a materialist theory of cognition. One possible motive is the claim that material entities are better understood than immaterial mental ones. Another, stronger one would be the conviction that mental entities belong to the category of ghosts and witches. A third motive could be the conviction that only a materialist account could find a proper place among the sciences.

None of these claims that might provide motive for materialism is self-evident; in fact, all of them are badly in need of support. It is difficult to argue for the first two in a non-question-begging way. Unless one were prejudiced in the first place in favour of materialism, what reason would one have that the regular systematically characterizable flow of events we call mental experience belong into the same class as the scattered and emotionally influenced experiences and mental states that led to the positing of ghosts and witches? And again, unless one started out with a materialist notion of what it is to understand something, why would one think that mental entities are not well understood?

The third possible motive admits of more unbiased discussion. It rests presumably on the conviction that all of the other sciences can be reduced at least in their ontologies eventually to physics, and thus – by induction? – the same should hold of a science of cognition. Underlying this view is a commitment to the 'unity of the sciences', according to which all scientific explanations have basically the same form, and all sciences can be eventually shown to be parts of a unified network of explanations. Though this view was popular in the heyday of positivism, it has very few if any defenders among contemporary philosophers of science. In any case, as a motive for an ontology, the claim is not strong. It suggests that we have to wait until the debate about the 'unity of the sciences' is settled (if ever) before we can justify the materialist ontological commitment, a commitment with far-reaching consequences.

The lack of clarity of the notion of matter, and the difficulty of finding clear-cut motivation for materialism suggest that, perhaps, it is more fruitful to consider a version of materialism called 'physicalism'. According to this view, the basic elements of the universe are those posited by physicists, and thus cognition too has to be explained eventually in terms of those entities. Thus Gilbert Harman writes:

> the plausible and widely held view that in some sense there are no facts over and above the purely physical facts. Scientists believe that the totality of physical facts completely determines all other facts and that, in particular, all mental processes are completely determined by whatever physical processes there are.
>
> (Harman, 1973, p. 36).

Whether all scientists really hold this view is a sociological question into which, fortunately, we need not enter. But we do need to ask the question 'what is a physical fact or property?', and since the subject of physics changes over the centuries, we should fall back on defining the physical in terms of the tradition of the discipline of physics. Thus 'physical' means 'whatever physics at any given time takes to be fundamental'. We shall have opportunity later in this book to ask why one should ascribe such an honorific – and possibly unwanted – status to the ontological commitments of the physics department.

There is a trivial version of physicalism (Harman, 1973; Chomsky, in conversation). For given the human conceptual inertia, it is reasonable to suppose that whenever physics enlarges the domain of what it takes the ultimate constituents to be, we shall simply stretch the meaning of 'physical' rather than admit a new category for this discipline. There are, however, also non-trivial versions of physicalism. For example, a physicalist might say that our experiences of thinking, having concepts, etc. that do not involve any awareness of material processes are not to be trusted in ontological matters. Or one might insist that no explanation of cognition can be complete until it is reduced to physiology. These non-trivial versions of materialism require a great deal of justification.

Apart from the positive and as of now still programmatic aspects of materialism and physicalism, these views also have a negative critical role to play in reflection on cognition. For they are presented as alternatives to dualism, i.e. the view that there are two basically different kinds of particulars: the mental and the physical. Cognitive processes are supposed to involve interactions between these two kinds. The physicalist challenges the intelligibility of the alleged interactions, and challenges the conceptual feasibility of talking about non-material non-extended entities whose structure determines interactions with physical things. The dualist might resort to positing only mental events and not mental substances, but if his theory is to rival that of the materialist in explanatory power, it will have to do more than just relate classes of events.

Let us now ask of the special category of the dualist, namely the mental, if it is conceptually as clear as the favoured kind of its rival. For Descartes the two kinds were contrast-dependent, and one was as clear as the other. There was the extended and the non-extended, the spatial and the non-spatial. The contrasting pairs seem conceptual twins. But it is one thing to say that certain pairs of concepts are contrast-dependent, and another to show that both elements of these pairs are equally viable candidates for that which determines a domain of entities for empirical study. One difficulty with the mental is that, apart from evidence based on self-reflection, it is primarily a negative category, i.e. the immaterial, non-extended, etc.

The view that in terms of experience mental phenomena are qualitatively different from physical ones does not yet lead to the positing of mental entities as what explains cognition, but only entities that call for explanation. For example, are mental representations non-material 'mental' entities? If so, their status cannot be justified by mere appeal to the felt qualities of direct cognitive experience, since everyone concerned agrees that most mental representations cannot be experienced directly.

Still another view of the mental construes its key mark to be intentionality (e.g. Searle, 1983). According to this view, mental events such as seeking, looking, asking, intending, calling attention to, etc., are distinguished by the fact that human intentions are necessary for their occurrence, and that their 'objects' are interpreted as a result of these intentions. The intentional is then viewed as uneliminable, either semantically or ontologically. We shall have opportunity later to see to what extent ascribing intentions to an agent is really necessary in order to ascribe to it cognitive activity.

We should note that an 'objectual theory' of cognition is different from both materialism and dualism. For it says that cognition is to be defined and characterized in terms of relations to the abstract domains that constitute the objects of cognition. It leaves questions such as whether these relations involve material, immaterial, neutral, etc. entities open as an empirical issue, not to be settled by philosophical fiat. It also claims that we can find out a great deal about human cognition without waiting for the question about the material and the mental – and other candidates – to be settled.

This sketch suggests that none of the conceptions is free from philosophical difficulties. At the same time, all of them provide frameworks for empirical accounts to be formulated. Thus it may be that a choice between them will depend to a large extent on future empirical research following the different conceptions here outlined.

So far we have enumerated conceptions differing in their ontology. There is yet another, non-ontological version of dualism. (This can be culled in different versions from scattered remarks in the writings of Chisholm and Chomsky.) According to this view the mental is not ontologically distinct from the physical, but differs from it in structural organization. That is to say, the occurrences of the different kinds of cognition do not follow either mechanistic or probabilistic causal laws, but are determined by principles, perhaps only partly known or knowable, unique to cognition.

There are also possibilities apart from materialism and dualism. There is nothing sacred about the number two. One can be simply a pluralist, and posit a number of different basic constituents for different aspects of the universe. Perhaps there are different constituents for the physical, the biological, and the mental. Once we give up the 'unity of science' thesis, various forms of pluralism become available. There is no reason to regard any of these pluralistic schemes as any more or less 'scientific' – whatever that phrase is supposed to mean – than a unitarian view like materialism.

Apart from the monistic scheme versus pluralism contrast, there are also less well-known versions of monism. One of these is neutral monism, championed in this century in some of Russell's writings. According to this view there is only one kind of basic building block for reality, and its nature cannot be described as either material or mental. Being physical and being mental are two aspects of this neutral ontological substratum and we can see things under one or the other of these key aspects. Philosophers in the best Socratic tradition should champion the conceptual underdog. Thus the lack of popularity of this view should not count against, but, if anything, for the project of further exploring it.

Finally, with regards to each of these positions we should keep asking whether there is any conceptual or philosophical ground for preferences, or is the choice really an empirical one. In chapter 1 of this book we saw conceptual arguments for and against realism and nominalism. But the positions presented in this part so far seem of a different nature. The Cartesian question of whether we should distinguish extended from unextended entities sounds like an empirical question. It is like asking whether we need to bring a theoretical construct into a certain empirical explanation. The burden of proof seems to lie on the side of those who claim that any one of these views can be shown to be preferable on purely *a priori* grounds. To say that the identity or lack of identity of some mental and some physical entities is an empirical question does not force us to commit ourselves to any particular view about the logical status of statements of identity. Even if one were a monist of some sort, one could hold the view that all identity statements are necessary, but that we discover these on empirical grounds. (On these issues, see Kripke, 1972.)

Some Psychological Theories of Cognition

We shall look in this section at two psychological theories that have attempted in our times to look at cognitive phenomena in some detail. The two views to be considered first were inspired by materialist preferences. They attempt to formulate theories of cognition that admit not all cognitive processing to be a matter of the functioning of internal material structures and yet account for all of the relevant phenomena without violating the canons of materialism. We shall start with a consideration of behaviourism. Behaviourism is, however, not a single, tightly organized theory. It is, rather, a collection of theories held at different times by different people, with certain overlapping themes. We shall restate these themes as claims. The following is a reasonable summary.

1. The vocabulary of that part of psychology which describes cognition should consist only of behavioural terms.
2. The intelligent mental operations of humans are definable in terms of actual and potential behaviour.
3. That part of the vocabulary of psychology which introduces the observables in connection with cognition should consist of behavioural terms.
4. The fundamental facts that psychology needs to explain can be described on the level of behaviour.
5. Psychological explanations of thinking should be in terms of behaviour.

6. Psychological explanations at their best link environment to behaviour, and show how the former can change the latter.

In order to appreciate the force of these claims, let us consider what it takes to deny any one of them. One might deny 1 by insisting that the vocabulary can include terms referring to introspectible non-behavioural entities like feelings and sensations. The denial of 2 can take the form of claiming that what we call intelligent operations, such as calculating, proving, or explaining, cannot be explained solely within a behaviourist vocabulary. One can deny 3 by insisting that we can also observe some of our inner states, such as remembering or believing, and that the terms describing these states are not behavioural. A denial of 4 could grant that much of the evidence used in psychology is behavioural, but that the fundamental facts to be explained arise on a deeper level. For example, a fundamental fact of cognition is that people under certain circumstances can master a language; but this fact itself is not directly observable: it is something that we infer from observable experience. Thus the denial would separate what is evidence for or against psychological hypotheses from the level at which the fundamental facts to be explained are. In defence of such a stance, one can draw analogies with other sciences. In physics, chemistry, or biology some of the important facts to be explained – e.g., electricity, gravity – are not on the level of the observable. This does not mean that we do not use observables as evidence for or against hypotheses attempting to explain these facts. The denial of 5 could proceed by claiming that even if one were to grant that all the evidence we have is a matter of behaviour, the explanations themselves, in particular the explanatory factors, should be sought on a deeper theoretical level. Physics might be, once more, a good example. For in this discipline the observable is explained repeatedly in terms of the unobservable. Finally, 6 brings up the question of how much of human cognitive activities can be explained in terms of environmental influences and how much of it depends on innate mechanisms. Historically speaking, this issue is often decided by people in terms of what they take to be the more optimistic outlook. At a time when people think that what is innate is basically fixed, but that we can do a lot to manipulate the environment, 6 sounds like an optimistic message and thus gathers followers. At other times we think that we can change the internal, genetic factors; at this point the denial of 6 too carries an optimistic message.

The fact that we have shown what it takes to deny any one of these theses speaks in favour of behaviourism, to the extent of showing it to be a powerful non-vacuous set of theses, or at least challenges. Reflecting on these sketches of possible denials should convince us that several of the theses are to be settled by empirical research and not by philosophical argument. For example, the question of how much environmental influence and how much of an innate mechanism is responsible for children learning mathematics seems like a straightforward empirical issue, rather than a matter of philosophical manifestos. Still, some of the claims involve methodological choice. For they deal with what should count as evidence, what should count as facts to be explained, and what should count as adequate explanation of cognition. If one thinks that evidence, fundamental facts to be explained, and the conceptual status of the explanatory mechanisms represent different conceptual and ontological and epistemic levels, then some of the behaviourist theses will be rejected. On these issues of the relations between evidence (must it be observable in all cases?) and fact (are not some of these inferred from observation?) we should make use of what philosophers of science say about other disciplines.

Not all of the theses entail each other. The various proposed strictures on evidence, fact, and explanation are independent of each other. If one accepted 1, then all of the constraints on evidence, fact, and explanation would follow; on the other hand, one could maintain any one of 3, 4, or 5 without embracing also 1. Thesis 6 brings up an issue that is independent of general matters of methodology.

While in the cursory survey we stressed the differences between behaviourist claims, one should note also the conceptual affinity between the different ingredients of what one could call loosely a creed. For all of the theses emphasize the importance of behaviour as the central subject of inquiry for psychology. Behaviourism as an approach is said to have started with J.B. Watson, and had B.F. Skinner as its most eloquent recent champion. (See Watson, 1919, 1925; the latter is seen by some as a more dogmatic statement. See also Skinner, 1957.)

Though this approach had such a long and successful history, there is a problem with its very core. For we must raise the question: what is behaviour? Does it include all of the observable motions of the human body and its parts? Does the notion include only what could be described as physical behaviour? In everyday discourse we would be allowed to say that we observed the grieving widow. Is this a behavioural description? Watson allowed notions like fear, rage, and love. Would a psychologist today describe these as behavioural notions? Can we rely on a common-sense conception of behaviour, or is this notion theory-laden? Some will include under behaviour purposive activities such as searching, building, or reading, while others rule these out on the ground that purely behavioural descriptions must leave out any reference to the purposive or intentional. There are problems also with the notion of observability, for this concept and its range of application changes through history as our technology for observation undergoes changes. For example is observation made through the microscope included? Or, alternatively, can we include descriptions of actions as part of behaviour? What are the units of behaviour? Does an act of kicking a ball count as one unit of behaviour, or are we to break it up into a series of movements of different muscles?

Someone might think that these are pedantic carpings at thriving theory. But we should keep in mind that behaviourism in most of its versions is to a large extent also a negative doctrine. It is against introspectionism, against a teleological vocabulary, against what we shall call 'psychologism', and against the positing of a rich, innate, mental structure. Furthermore, many of these oppositions have philosophical or methodological, rather than empirical motivations. Thus one can justifiably demand more rigour with respect to the basic concepts of the theory, because one wants to know exactly what is excluded and why, and why is what is kept thought to be so much clearer than what is excluded. As an illustration let us take up a notion much discussed by a philosopher sympathetic to behaviourism, namely Quine (1960, pp. 1–111). This is the notion of reference. Is this a behavioural notion? From a rigidly physicalist point of view, what is observable is simply that whenever a certain object comes within the sight of a speaker, then, assuming certain conditions of appropriateness for communication, practicality, etc., that speaker emits a certain set of sounds. But this is true of many cases which we would not want to describe as reference. For example, in typical cases a deer will stand watch over the rest of the herd in the Sierras, and will utter a certain sound whenever an eagle comes in sight. This is a warning signal. Are all warning signals cases of reference? Can we distinguish behaviourally warning signals from cases of reference? Do not the latter involve attention to certain features of the environment which we assume to require conceptual discrimination not on the behavioural level, and assumptions about the state of mind, needs, and intentions of the audience, again not behaviourally specifiable? These questions must be answerable if behaviourism is to play an important critical role in the philosophy of cognition.

There are also other objections to behaviourism, apart from this philosophical questioning of its very core. In this brief survey we shall mention only two. One is raised by Block (1981). He presents an argument showing that we cannot define intelligent activity in terms of actual and potential behaviour. He presents an example of intelligent systems exhibiting the same actual and potential behaviour, but with different internal processing structures. Thus he defends 'psychologism' which is the view that mere description of actual and potential behaviour is not enough for the characterization of intelligence, and that we need to posit also internal representations of concepts and rules in terms of which internal processing takes place prior to or simultaneously with the external activities.

The other criticism is due to Noam Chomsky (1959). He claims that there are fundamental facts about human mastery of languages for which behaviourism cannot account. One of these is a kind of creativity, i.e. the continuous recognition and understanding of novel utterances – utterances that differ in content from any encountered previously. Note that Chomsky here is not pointing to non-behavioural evidence; rather, he is attacking that part of behaviourism which wants to bypass explaining behaviour in terms of internal representation and processing. Chomsky's claim is neutral with respect to ontological debates about materialism and dualism. He simply points to empirical evidence, suggesting the need for positing an internal representation of rules of language, and of generating structures for input sentences according to these rules, regardless of whether the whole process can or cannot be explained on a materialist basis. The other criticism arises out of considering the circumstances under which humans ordinarily learn their first language. The context for such learning is typically one of 'stimulus poverty', i.e. not having enough diversity in stimuli to be able to infer the rules of the language to which the learner is exposed, by known rules of induction. This criticism affects the part of behaviourism we captured in terms of thesis vi. Thus it attacks a part of behaviourism distinct from the parts attacked by Block's argument, and Chomsky's first objection.

Having looked at various behaviourist theses and objections raised against these, let us consider what motivation one might have for adopting this school of thought. One such motive seems to be a yearning for 'objectivity and verifiability'. (I am indebted for this suggestion to Professor Abe Ansel.) In focusing on behaviour, this school concentrates on what they take to be objective as opposed to the subjective, introspective data of individuals. In insisting on behaviour as also the explanatory component, they want to stay as close to the directly verifiable as possible. In assessing this motivation we should keep at least two things in mind. First, even if behaviour is the best kind of evidence that we can have, ultimately we rely in psychology, as in the other sciences, on individual experimenters and their introspective data in reading meters, and other instruments of experimentation. Thus we cannot really separate a science completely from the first person individual report. Second, in order to support the behaviourist's insistence on staying as close to the observation level as possible, one would have to show that, in general, the more a science advances, the more it can close the gap between the observable and the empirical level at which its most basic laws are stated. The histories of such fields as physics or biology do not seem to bear out this hypothesis.

Another motivation is to want to rely on something publicly observable like behaviour and shy away from data such as introspection that are accessible primarily only to the individual subject. But once more, we need to look at this issue without any prejudices. Is it true that with regards to introspective data we cannot achieve intersubjective agreement? For example, in studies of imagery intersubjective convergence seems widespread (e.g., Kosslyn, 1980).

Still other motivations centre on the nature of theoretical posits in psychology. One motive within this class is the conviction that non-behavioural terms in psychology provide bad theoretical constructs. But there seems to be no general argument supporting this stand. One would have to consider each case separately. For example, is it true that the notion of an intelligent device following rules is any less clear than the notion of habituation? Or that purposive intentional notions are fundamentally obscure? Or that positing non-material internal representations cannot be in principle of any explanatory value?

There is a general problem that anyone inclined towards behaviourism has to face. This is the apparent failure of efforts to translate terms denoting cognitive activities into a strictly behavioural vocabulary. We have seen that not even 'refer' has such a translation. What about 'reading', 'writing', 'learning', and 'calculating'? Yet supplying behaviouristic definitions for these terms is required of anyone who is a behaviourist and does not claim that cognition can be explained without the employment of any of these terms.

Finally, a motive is also the desire to stay within the confines of the 'unity of science' view. Ineliminably non-material terms, or abstract structures that do not enter into causal correlations with the physical world, would have to be shunned by such a view. But this raises once more the general issue of the plausibility of thinking any one science to be underlying all of the others, and of thinking that all scientific explanations fall into the same pattern. Furthermore, in all such discussion one must be careful that the term 'scientific' does not degenerate into mere purple prose. By what measure can we say that this or that kind of theoretical construct proposed within any science is 'less scientific' than those of others? The only thing that can reasonably guide us is the history of the sciences. One would have to see what, if any, general characterization fits those theoretical constructs that proved to be successful in the past.

At this point one might wonder why our survey does not devote some space to what is called the 'stimulus–response' (S–R) model of explanation. This model for psychological explanation assumes that our main concern is prediction, and that the prediction of behaviour is best achieved by correlating publicly observable stimuli that the organism is exposed to with behavioural responses. This view assumes a very close link, if not identification, between prediction and explanation. One could argue that predictability does not entail intelligibility and vice versa. But in any case, the S–R model is just one version of behaviourism. One could be a behaviourist and reject this particular version. The difficulties, however, on which we focused, as well as the motivations, relate to behaviourism in general. Any problem that affects the genus will affect, conceptually, the species too.

In concluding this examination of behaviourism, let us summarize the options that this view forces us to consider. We need to decide what we expect of explanations in psychology, and how closely these will be linked to prediction. We need to decide what methodological claims to follow with respect of evidence to be used, and with respect to what we should consider as the fundamental facts to be accounted for. We need to take a stand on the desirable status of explanatory notions in cognitive psychology and their relations to observability. In terms of these options we have to examine notions like behaviour, internal representation, and the 'objects' of cognition.

If one is a materialist and finds behaviourism unacceptable, one can opt for a programme that tries to explain cognition solely in terms of the notions of neurophysiology, leaving out not only mental constructs, but also reference to the objects or symbolic contents of cognitive processes. The most recent such attempt is called 'connectionism'. Within this framework attempts are made to reduce cognitive processing to actions within neural networks, without bringing in any of the notions that we called the objects of thought (Rummelhart and McClelland (eds), 1986; for critiques see Fodor and Pylyshyn, 1988; and Pinker and Prince, 1988). At the very least, such work is interesting in so far as it uncovers correlations between such processes and what we call cognitive states and activities. Whether one could conceptually identify the results of such a programme, even if successful, with what we call cognition depends on a number of philosophical issues some of which will be dealt with in our proposals.

Behaviourism wants to shun positing internal mechanisms as much as possible. Connectionism claims it knows something about these mechanisms. But there is another type of theory that allows us whatever our favourite ontology is, and both give explanatory patterns for cognition and bypass the issue of what the exact nature of internal mechanisms is. This approach has been called functionalism. Most functionalists adopt a materialist ontology, even though the reduction of cognitive terms to materialist ones fails. Yet this does not impose on us a more elaborate ontology. The functionalist, if he is right, can have his materialist cake and eat his non-reductionist semantics too, for he construes the meaning of terms of cognition in what we shall call functionalist ways. This enables the functionalist not to assign to these terms applications with categorical ontological commitments. Functionalism is in principle a theory about the meanings of mental terms, and about the nature of psychological explanations. In order to understand what adherents of this view mean by a functionalist account, we must be careful not to confuse this with more traditional teleological notions such as we find in some parts of biology and in the semantics of some terms of natural languages. For example, terms for artefacts have functional meanings in the traditional sense. That is to say, in the meanings of words like 'chair', 'table', 'house', the dominant component has to do with purpose or use. If one went to a furniture museum and looked at chairs from all cultures in all historical periods, there is very little that one could find as a perceptually distinguishable common denominator. The same applies to houses from different cultures and historical periods. Still, we understand why we should gather these objects with different sizes, shapes, materials, etc. under a common term, for we consider what these are used for and the purposes for which they are designed rather than their particular material compositions. Chairs are objects produced and used primarily for the purpose of having something to sit on, tables to put things on, and houses to provide shelter. To be sure, these are not by themselves necessary and sufficient conditions, but they are the main ingredients, with the rest to be filled in, as we shall see in chapter 6, by context-dependent distinguishing factors that separate chairs from thrones, tree-stumps, pews, etc., and tables from boards, shelves, etc. Some biologists think that similar notions are parts of biological explanations. A digestive system is defined in terms of needed food-transformation processes that result in the organism being fed. Structures and implementation can vary from species to species. We see the same phenomena in connection with verbs. For example, 'build' has a dominant functional in the sense of teleological component in its meaning structure. To build something is to construct a new entity out of previously given material, with the materials and modes of construction left open to be decided case by case.

One could consider the role of teleological notions in the study of cognition. This need not bring one to theological issues. One could use teleology to relate the various features of cognition to evolutionary theories. But modern functionalism as a theory about cognitive psychology is independent of issues of teleology. It takes its notion of function from the literature of mathematics and the computer sciences. (The first and most influential paper is Putnam, 1966.)

We are to conceive of a mechanism or device – abstract or concrete – that is going through a series of successive stages. A function is that which determines and computes the sequence of stages that the device is in. A functional state takes you from non-functionally defined stage to stage. Within a materialist ontology one can think of these stages as material, and in particular physiological, stages. Functional states are not characterized in terms of what actually takes place, or in terms of cognitive structures or processes, be these material or mental. They simply represent whatever it is that takes one from a kind of stage S' to another kind of stage S''. Such specifications resemble some of the software of computers. These specify the functions that link stages in a process. Different 'hardware' results in different kinds of realization of the same program. Thus a functionalist account of thought is independent of specific views about 'hardware', i.e. about specific hypotheses about implementation. Functional definitions will construe mental concepts as specifying what takes us typically from certain cognitive states to certain causal interactions with the environment. Let us consider some examples of this kind of explication. Gilbert Harman thinks that the best way to approach such definitions is to start with simple cases and to make them gradually more complicated. He writes: 'In elementary cases, a belief state that represents a particular thing normally results from the perception of that thing and leads to behavior involving that thing. What the thing is represented *as* depends on this behaviour' (Harman, 1973, p.62). This remark has to be taken for contexts in which the object of belief is perceptually present. Thus given that a human has a certain need, e.g. hunger, and that he sees an appropriate object, i.e. one that can serve as food, belief will be the state that leads him from the inactive stage to the acquiring and eating of the object. Or, to take another example from the literature, 'pain' can be analysed as designating a state caused typically by tissue damage, and having the tendency to cause efforts to get rid of whatever causes the damage, as well as other behaviour (Block, 1980, p.172). This account of pain is consistent with different kinds of realizations, be these physical or purely psychological. Of course, these attempts at definitions will be successful only if they deal also with the less simple cases. Normally, many of the objects of our beliefs at any time are not perceptually present, and involve no behavioural response on our part. Thus the functionally defined notions need to be employed within conceptions that leave room for long chains of functionally defined states, and for potential or delayed behaviour.

In order to be fair to functionalism we should keep the limits of its aim in mind. Functionalism does not say that its analyses of terms of cognition reflect ordinary usage, nor that its explanations of cognitive processes mirror everyday explanations. But the main aim is frankly revolutionary. The mental is redefined not to sharpen everyday usage, but to fit into a scientific theory of cognition. If, occasionally, its claims clash with common sense, then, as long as the science of cognition emanating from this view is successful, common sense will have to yield. This view is backed by the claim that we have witnessed such clashes and the ensuing reform of common sense in the past in connection with the rise of several other sciences.

We have seen so far a rough outline of functionalist definitions. Functionalism is also a proposal about the nature of explanations of cognitive phenomena. These explanations are conceived of as running along two lines. On the one hand, there is the ongoing work within a materialist scheme to find physiological correlates to what we label cognitive phenomena. On the other hand, there are explanations of what we do, desire, plan, etc. in terms of functionally defined cognitive states.

As one can easily see, this view has several advantages. First, it avoids the controversies that surround reductionistic translation programmes of various sorts, since it can agree with the critics of behaviourism that words like 'intend', 'believe', 'think', etc., cannot be defined in purely behavioural terms. It can also remain neutral with regards to reductionistic schemes such as connectionism. It can – though it need not – reject the allegedly dubious theoretical constructs of dualism. At the same time, its analysis of cognition is not trivial. It provides a place for what semantic analysis wants to say about thought and belief, without creating points of conflict with materialist programmes. To use the computer analogy again, the philosophers describe the software the implementation of which needs to be investigated by the empirical sciences. Thus we have a division of labour. We want to know what the functional accounts are of those phenomena that are then investigated in scientific contexts. After all, one might want to say the same thing – especially if one places oneself at an earlier stage of the history of science – about biology. This construes the role of the philosopher as important. For without the specifications of the functional states, how would one know the implementation of what we are to investigate? Finally, this approach gives us a way of talking about belief, reasoning, etc., and what these are supposed to accomplish, without saddling us with what seems to some the burdens of old-fashioned teleology. For in saying that belief is whatever takes us, for example, from the perception of edible object to the action of eating, we do not take a stand on whether each human organ or faculty fulfils some use or purpose in some larger scheme of things.

In spite of all of these advantages there are also some difficulties with this view (for detailed exposition see, e.g., Block, 1978; Bealer, 1984.) First, the functional characterization of cognitive states and activities may leave us with much indeterminacy. That is to say, there may be two different systems, thinking in very different ways, still satisfying the same functional characterization. The weight of this criticism depends on how much indeterminacy one would allow with respect to the characterization of cognition, and how strong one's intuitions are on the strictures applying to whatever we might be willing to call actual thought processes. If we had no access to the internal mechanisms of the human digestive process, how much of a notion would we have of this operation apart from functional specifications?

A second problem faces the functionalist when he moves from giving functional accounts of basic notions like belief and thought, to the more complex ones, such as syntactic language processing, offering explanations, having intuitions of validity, etc. Can one expect that these concepts too will lend themselves to functionalist analysis, or are these 'object'-dependent to such an extent, and free from the constraints of practicality to such an extent, that the functional specifications no longer provide enough detailed structure for the accounts to serve as even partial substitutes of our current notions?

The third problem emerges as we reflect on the relations between the functionalist accounts and the phenomenal experiences of cognition that we all share. In everyday use, thinking, believing, and understanding are not merely explanatory or theoretical notions. We use these expressions also to report certain experiences, and we tie these – though not always reliably – to introspective reports. How does the functionalist account for the fact that certain allegedly physical systems, with functional properties, are capable of having these phenomenal experiences? In a recent paper defending functionalism Robert Van Gulick (1988) writes: 'We simply have at present no theories, functional or otherwise, to explain how a physical system can have a phenomenal life.' He goes on to suggest that this is not a very serious flaw in functionalism. After all, how many theories can explain all observed facts? Functionalism has at this point simply a gap; this has to be balanced by the recognition that it can account for much else.

In reply, however, it should be pointed out that this 'gap' was exactly the point at which Descartes' *Meditations* start. It is undeniable that we humans have these experiences and much in our lives depends on it. We base our understanding as well as our practical planning on it. The 'mentalism' of Descartes was constructed to a large extent to account for this fundamental condition of human existence. Thus in assessing the success of the post-Cartesian schools it is hardly fair to dualism to describe this 'gap' in functionalism as just another fact that it happens not to have been able to explain. What for the functionalist is just another little gap that any scientist has from time to time, is for the dualist the fundamental and central fact on which all theories of cognition are supposed to centre. Thus one certainly could not say that given the traditional outlook on what is important and what is peripheral, functionalism is an adequate replacement for dualism. As we shall see in the next section, the functionalist and theories of similar orientation might not agree with the tradition on what is central.

The last point leads us naturally to placing functionalism in a wider context. As we can see from the examples provided by Harman and Block, the proposed account links cognitive states, though often indirectly, to human actions such as relieving pain or satisfying needs. One might call this an action-oriented or pragmatic conception of human inquiry and cognitive life. But that cognition has this fundamental nature is a huge assumption. There are other, equally viable alternatives. As was mentioned briefly earlier, one can think of humans as basically curious, inquisitive creatures, seeing from time to time various aspects of experience problematic and calling for explanations. According to this conception thought is not fundamentally action-oriented, but has as its primary function the articulation of reality into a series of explanatory patterns. This articulation enables us to act and to change in some ways the environment and ourselves, but the relation between thought and action might be quite indirect.

Functionalism seems to require a pragmatic conception of thought. But a pragmatic conception of thought has as its background the assumption that cognition is a part of 'nature' in the sense in which we assume the empirical sciences to be studying nature. Thus the defence of functionalism leads to the pragmatic conception of thinking, and this, in turn, leads to a naturalistic philosophy of mind. Once more, we are faced with possible alternatives. Naturalism in the philosophy of mind is not the only option. Unfortunately there is little literature in recent philosophy of cognition about these larger questions. Fortunately, one philosopher, Robert Stalnaker, made these commitments explicit. An examination of what he says will help us to consider these issues.

A Naturalistic Philosophy of Mind

A naturalistic philosophy of mind contrasts with at least two other types of theories of cognition. It is viewed as contrasting with dualism. This is, to be sure, a prejudiced way of looking at the conceptual landscape, for a dualist could hold the view that thoughts as immaterial entities are parts of the natural order. But in any case, as Stalnaker sees it, naturalism does not include dualism, and in this he represents what most functionalists would say. Naturalism contrasts also with the theory we labelled 'objectual'. This theory, as we saw, defines thought and other parts of cognition as a basic indefinable relation between certain states and processes whose exact nature is not specified, and the peculiar abstract entities that serve as 'objects' to thought. Still, even in the second contrast lingering doubts remain. We do not have a general *a priori* proof that the mind's grasping of universals could never be a part of what some day will be acknowledged as a genuine 'scientific' account of cognition. For our immediate purposes it is best to lay these doubts aside, and consider what Stalnaker says about naturalism.

Stalnaker modestly calls his conception a 'prejudice' rather than a theory. Nevertheless, his characterization can serve as the starting point for philosophical discussion. He writes: 'Human beings, I assume, are part of the natural order. They are physical objects whose mental capacities and dispositions – specifically their representational capacities – need to be explained in terms of natural relations between natural objects and systems of natural objects' (Stalnaker, 1984, p. x).

We can see the thrust of the preamble by noting ways in which it is used to rule out proposals analysing cognition that are incompatible with Stalnaker's own views. For example, at one point he considers an account of propositional attitudes, i.e. those cognitive relations that establish links between minds and propositions. The account in question involves ascribing to humans a special intellectual capacity to peer at abstract objects. This account is rejected by Stalnaker because it is not naturalistic (Stalnaker, 1984, p.8). At another place, a 'linguistic view' of the objects of propositional attitudes is discussed. The view in question is that such objects have a language-like structure. Stalnaker is willing to consider seriously only those versions of this view that are compatible with naturalism.

These examples show that naturalism is a formidable weapon in Stalnaker's writings. Hence we need to look very carefully at its conceptual foundations. What is naturalism? What are natural objects and natural relations? It seems that Stalnaker has in mind those objects that are in space and time and are causally related. Natural relations would be causal relations and whatever other relations natural science needs to posit in its accounts of the causally related spatio-temporal world. Stalnaker realizes that through measurement and other quantitative specifications, the world of 'natural' objects is also related by science to abstract entities like numbers. His guideline for the study of cognition seems to be that relating humans to propositions or other abstract entities is permissible as long as this is done with the same kind of empirical content as the relating of natural entities to numbers is done by the other sciences (Stalnaker, 1984, pp. 12–14).

This last point shows that it would be an oversimplification to identify Stalnaker's naturalism with what one might call 'causalism', i.e. the view that only causally relateable entities should be regarded as real. Such a narrow view would not only face difficulties in accounting for measurement, but also for geometry, a distinctly non-causal science. The question emerges: can one draw a clear line between the way in which quantitative determinations link material things to numbers and the allegedly non-naturalistic features of the posited human capacity of peering at abstract objects? Perhaps the latter is as yet only a sketch of a notion, but not necessarily more remote from the interaction between the abstract and concrete that we see today in all of the more developed sciences.

Stalnaker's notion of naturalism is clear enough for us to conclude that though behaviourism would be regarded by Stalnaker as a naturalistic theory, he is not committed to it, and that the 'unity of science' theme does not play a major role in motivating naturalism.

Naturalism is as clear or vague as the related concept of nature. Does contemporary science present us with a clear enough picture so that we know reasonably clearly what is included and what is excluded? Opinions on how to answer this question will vary.

We need to consider possible motivations for naturalism. Though the thesis of the 'unity of science', as we summarized it above, does not underlie naturalism, there seems to be at least some 'unity of nature' thesis lurking in the background. In considering this admittedly vague notion, we should be careful not to confine ourselves to extreme positions. One extreme is to think that all of the sciences must use similar theoretical constructs and similar 'natural' ways of relating members of the domains they study. The other extreme is to think that all sciences are equally 'naturalistic', except for cognitive science, which, on this account, sticks out like a sore thumb. But there are many other alternatives. For example, one might think that the empirical sciences fall into several categories. Some are like sub-atomic physics, with indeterminism. Others are like our sciences concerned with 'medium-sized goods', and are deterministic; still others, including the science of cognition, have structures and law-like explanations of their own. The study of cognition is not the only field that suggests that nature comes equipped with a number of categories.

Within the proposal on thought we shall attempt, in Part Two, to add up the conceptual scoresheet on naturalism. We shall now return to the point at which we were considering functionalism, and started out looking at these larger issues. We needed to consider naturalism because it is the background for the 'pragmatic' view on thought, and this is implied by functionalism. Once more we turn for an explicit characterization to Stalnaker. In characterizing what he calls the pragmatic 'picture', he writes:

> Rational creatures are essentially agents. Representational mental states should be understood primarily in terms of the role that they play in the characterization and explanation of action. What is essential to rational action is that the agent be confronted, or conceive of himself as confronted, with a range of alternative possible outcomes of some alternative possible actions.
>
> (Stalnaker 1984, pp. 4, 6, n. 17).

The difference between Stalnaker and those opting for other 'pictures' cannot be about the fact that humans are agents, for this is obvious. Rather, one can draw a number of different conclusions from this fact. As we shall see in the concluding chapter, one can conclude that the agential aspect of our existence should be reflected in lexical semantics. One can also conclude, as we did in chapter 1, that as agents humans are planning creatures, and this involves making use of the modalities. But Stalnaker wants to draw stronger conclusions than these. He thinks that the facts about human agency should lead us to analyse all aspects of cognition as centring on the states and processes that result eventually in action. One consequence of this view is that beliefs, expectations, etc. need not be more finely individuated than the possible outcomes and actions demand. This contrasts sharply with conceptions according to which the main function of thought is to articulate reality and needs to be individuated as finely as the most refined theory of reality demands, regardless of its relations, direct or indirect, to the practical.

Let us consider now some similarities and differences between the pragmatic picture and behaviourism. The pragmatic conception too interprets cognition as leading to behaviour, but it allows itself to describe the relevant behaviour within the terminology of action theory. This could not be done by the behaviourist who shuns all purposive and intentional notions.

Naturalism, with or without the pragmatic thesis, goes well with nominalism. For if nominalism is correct, then all of the objects of thought can be reduced to collections of particulars. The naturalist could then begin to work out a theory of cognition in which the relation between the knowing or understanding mind and its objects becomes a kind of causal interaction. Thus the fact that nominalistic programmes have not succeeded in this century is not irrelevant to the assessment of naturalism. (For recent attempts at programmes helping the nominalist cause, see Field, 1980.) On the other hand, if realist characterizations of the objects of thought prevail, this makes the job of the naturalist that much harder.

Naturalism has consequences also for semantics. As Stalnaker saw, 'If representation is essentially a causal relation, then no predicate, no mental state, can represent in virtue of the intrinsic psychological properties of the person who is using the predicate, or who is in the mental state' (Stalnaker, 1984, p. 21). These remarks occur in the context in which Stalnaker discusses whether Putnam's showing that certain predicates are not 'purely general', i.e. cannot have their meaning specified in purely qualitative terms, should be extended to cover all of the predicates of natural languages. He sees – correctly, I think – that naturalism requires the extension. In the concluding chapter we shall ask whether such an extension is justified.

These reflections show that the 'naturalist' prejudice is indeed a central assumption in a theory like Stalnaker's. It places burdens on one's choice of options in semantics and ontology, it rules out certain types of explanatory hypotheses, and directs attention to others. Furthermore, it is not an obvious truth, or a truth of logic, but rather a substantial claim about humans and the world which they inhabit. In order to help our understanding of naturalism, let us sketch at least how an alternative to it would look.

One version of a non-naturalist theory would start by showing both that the objects of thought need be analysed in a non-nominalist, realist framework, and that the semantics of a natural language must contain some terms whose meaning is purely qualitative. It would proceed by regarding the relation between the mind and its objects as a basic undefinable notion, but would stress that this does not prevent us from raising and answering many illuminating empirical questions about cognition. For one could give a partial characterization of the human mind in terms of some of the salient features of its objects, and general facts about our being able to represent and use these. These characterizations would have the following form. 'Given that we can know, understand, use in explanations, abstract complexes of such-and-such nature and complexity, under normal conditions, X, Y, Z, the following must be true of the human mind.' This programme, which we shall investigate later in the book, would not clash with empirical investigations of the physiology, chemistry, etc. of human cognition. It simply says two things. First, that our conceptions of thought, belief, understanding, etc. do not depend on the outcome of such investigations. Second, that we can know many important truths about human cognition even if the effort to relate physiology to the achievements of the human mind meet only with partial success. If we could come up with a really insightful characterization, from the point of view of cognitive processing, of such human achievements as the composition of Beethoven and Mozart, would we not learn a great deal by exploring the question: what does humans inventing and then enjoying and understanding works with this structure show about the human mind?

Apart from sketching new alternatives to naturalism, we should remember also some of the more traditional options that naturalism seems to crowd out of the picture, but which have not been refuted conclusively. One of these is introspectionist psychology. As we said before, its results may shed light on some aspects of cognition that the naturalistic models fail to handle. If one does not want to take a dogmatic stance on larger issues like naturalism, one has the option – truly pragmatic in the traditional sense of this word – of taking behavioural or physiological evidence where this seems fruitful, and introspective evidence in contexts in which this seems the best move to make. It is arbitrary to assume that all aspects of cognition can be studied equally successfully by restricting ourselves to just one kind of evidence.

Phenomenology, the claim according to which intentional phenomena are *sui generis*, and cannot be made part of a general study whose objects include also the non-intentional, is yet another alternative to naturalism. Later we shall consider the question of how many of the concepts we need for explaining our using and understanding language, are intentional in the strong sense required by phenomenology. (For an illuminating account, see Follesdal, 1988.)

These brief sketches have, I hope, placed naturalism into a wider perspective within which one can see it as one of several options. None of the options emerges as being without any conceptual difficulties.

We have sketched above the conception more directly related to functionalism, namely the 'pragmatic picture'. Let us now consider what non-pragmatic conceptions of cognitions are like. We must separate the claim that cognition is action-oriented from the thesis that acts and processes of cognition must satisfy human needs. Not even the second thesis is self-evident. Cognition can be spontaneous, and need not have any adaptation value, or value in satisfying 'basic human needs', whatever these are. But even if we accept the second thesis, this does not commit us to the first. There are many human needs that are not linked to action-orientation. For example, one could speculate that cognition satisfies such needs as those of curiosity, interest, and the need to relieve the frustration caused by seeing something as problematic. Gaining intelligibility need not be accompanied by a desire to act and to change the environment and ourselves. Passive intelligibility can lead to a feeling of 'having found our place in a larger scheme of things', while active notions of intelligibility lead to wanting to change the world. Needless to say, these are two extremes; perhaps most humans have a tacit conception of intelligence that encompasses both the active and the passive aspects in different ways. Even a cursory glance at the development of the sciences across history and cultures makes one doubt that the action-oriented conception of cognition is culture invariant. The science of astronomy can develop as an aid to navigation, or as a part of religious interests, or as a matter of mere awe and wonder. In ancient China theoretical sciences developed without the stress on the empirical and practical that we witnessed eventually in the western world. Thus these large-scale hypotheses about the nature of cognition should be treated with considerable caution. This is true in general of guesses about the 'functional needs' that allegedly gave rise to various practices. People often say, for example, that writing developed in order to facilitate communication and the dissemination of information. In fact, I am told by students of ancient Chinese culture, writing in China developed as a way for the treasurer to keep records of what is in the treasury, and to convey this to the emperor in a way that would be accessible to practically no one else. Thus in some contexts the point of having writing is to enable people to conceal rather than to disseminate information.

We see, then, that the denial of the pragmatic conception leaves us with at least two alternatives. One is to maintain that cognition satisfies human needs but that some of these do not involve its being action-oriented. The other is to say that cognition functions primarily as articulating reality. The resulting conceptions are linked to action and efforts to change reality in different ways and to different extents in different cultures.

Returning to functionalism, we see now that it has the following problems. First, it rests on larger assumptions about naturalisms and the pragmatic picture that need defence. Second, it will have problems with analysing thought and its content if nominalistic reductions continue to be unsuccessful. Finally, it cannot be regarded as an alternative to dualism if it continues to treat as merely a gap in scientific success the very fact, namely that humans have phenomenal experiences of cognition, that was the foundation for dualistic explanations. The last point shows that we need to step back from the examination of currently fashionable theories, and ask what the nature and basic properties of thought are. Without agreement on these issues, we are unlikely to agree on the feasibility of any one of the current psychological theories as applied to cognition.

The Properties of Cognition

We need to consider the following questions about thought and other ingredients of cognition. In order to keep this survey within reasonable bounds, we shall concentrate on thought in this section. Our questions are:

1. What are the fundamental roles of thought? Representing reality, embodying knowledge, being expressed in language, enabling us to gain wisdom and understanding, or guiding action? How are these roles related?
2. How does thought accomplish these tasks?
3. What properties can we assign to thought in view of these accomplishments?
4. How do we know the objects, nature, and salient properties of thought?

In the last section we dealt with some of the items under 1. However, the answer to this question is not exhausted by theories about what the main role of thought is, for it is clear that thought must be involved in all of the activities mentioned above. Furthermore, one can have different conceptions about how these items are related. For example, if one has a very practical and subjectivist conception of knowledge, then one need not think that representing objective reality must be a condition for embodying knowledge. The further distinction between knowledge on the one hand, and wisdom and understanding on the other, brings up the question of whether the latter have only propositional or sentence-like objects. As we shall see, there are good arguments to show that understanding a proof, theorem, theory, etc., as well as the ensuing wisdom, require also non-propositional objects. But if this is the case, then we have evidence supporting the claim that not all of thought is expressible in language, even at the mature adult level. Finally, as we saw, the role of guiding action is much less of a problem for the functionalist or some other pragmatic conception of thought than for the non-pragmatist. Guiding action requires that thought can be linked to specific spatio-temporal parts of reality. In semantics this is the problem of indexicals like 'current', 'past', etc., or demonstratives like 'this' or 'that'. A satisfactory semantics for these expressions can be the basis for theories of thought that explain how thought is not just representing links between universals but establishes a link, somehow, between humans and specific objects or events. This is a difficult problem. Among the key questions we find whether the link thus established is a causal or a non-causal one. Thought leading to action is not always concerned with the sensibly present. Many of our plans for future action involve objects with which we do not have and never had acquaintance. Thus this issue about cognition cannot be resolved until we look at theories of semantics dealing with the indexical aspects of language.

Most answers to our second question bring up in one form or another the matter of representation. We shall bypass the general philosophic problem of what representation is. For this foundational question goes beyond the confines of studying cognition. It is a problem for aesthetics, semantics, and epistemology as well. In this survey we shall restrict ourselves to considering various views about how thought represents, leaving the basic notion on the intuitive level. Let us consider, then, the hypothesis that thought is primarily representational, i.e. it involves an inner, sentence-like representation of various constituents of its objects as well as the objects themselves. One need not argue for this in one full sweep. As a first step we should consider such objects of thought as are made up partly of constitutive rules, e.g., languages, logic, or mathematics. Games like chess also fall into this category. Thoughts with such objects must embody knowledge and understanding of these objects, and are accompanied by intuitions of what it is to violate the constitutive rules of the objects. Thus it is reasonable to assume that we must have a cognitive representation of a system of rules that derives the right elements of these domains, and thus we need representational thought (Moravcsik, 1969, pp. 411–15). Additional arguments are needed to extend this claim to thoughts with other objects. One such argument would assume that since descriptions of reality at a certain level of complexity are contained by sentences with elaborate syntactic and semantic structures, this articulation must be retained also by thought.

Still another argument would suppose that thought is a form of 'inner talk'. If so, then the individuation of the objects of thought would have to be very fine indeed, while if the pragmatic picture is sound, the individuation can be more coarse (Stalnaker, 1984 p.6).

There are problems with interpreting thought too closely following the model of sentences. One of these emerges when considering thought and language about temporal episodes. For example, on one day I think 'it is raining today'. Then on the next day I recall this thought and express what I remember as 'it was raining yesterday'. On the next day, still another sentence is needed to express what I thought. This leaves us with various options. Are my thoughts on these different occasions tokens of different types of thought? Or is it the same thought, linked to a proposition about the weather on a certain day, but expressed by different sentences? What should be our conception of the relations between thoughts, propositions, and states of affairs with regards to examples of this kind?

There is also the issue of how far we can push the analogy in general. Do we need to posit a non-linguistic, self-interpreting inner language of thought in order to make the representational model complete? (For discussion, see Fodor, 1975; Margolis, 1984, p. 78.)

Among those exploring the representational model today it is assumed that all representation corresponds to units that can be true or false. The reason for this assumption is not empirical but lies in the convenience of representing such units in terms of modern symbolic logic. It is reasonable to suppose, however, that understanding in typical contexts has an object that cannot be exhaustively defined by a set of sentences. Understanding a proof, a new insight, etc. involves not only understanding each of the constituents, but having a grasp of the whole proof, theory, insight, etc. that is more than a mere sum of parts. In view of such grasp we characterize proofs as deep or superficial, insights as deep, important, etc. The difficulty with this proposal is that while it corresponds to our phenomenal experience, it makes it difficult to characterize the objects thus posited in terms of modern logic. (For a full argument defending this position, see Moravcsik, 1979.)

There are philosophers who will object to any representational hypothesis since it relies on the viability of the notion of rule-learning and rule-following. Appeal to conscious rule-following will move only those who do not reject phenomenal experience as data for theories of cognition. Still, one might try an additional step. In many cases of conscious rule-learning and rule-following we achieve only partial results. We frequently fail to live up to the behaviour pattern that we project for ourselves. (This could be labelled the secular and cognitive version of the theological doctrine of original sin.) Thus those denying the legitimacy of the notion of rule-following will also have to deal with the data suggesting that what we aim at in performance and what we accomplish are often not the same; hence self-corrections, feelings of dissatisfaction, etc.

By and large, answers to the second main question involve positing some representational thought. As of now there is no clear alternative unless one attempted to revive a form of behaviourism.

This brings us to the third question. If thought has the roles ascribed to it, and is in some sense representational and can have objects with constitutive rules, what properties can we ascribe to it? We shall consider four proposed properties:

1. Non-trivial level of complexity,
2. Spontaneity,
3. Thought being conscious and non-conscious, and
4. Some thought consisting of intuitions of rule violation.

Rule systems of various sorts can be measured in terms of complexity. Thus if thought is representational, we could establish indirectly levels of complexity that thoughts about such ordinary objects as arithmetic, grammar, logic, or semantic rules for a language provide. We raised earlier the issue of how difficult it is to separate sharply simple signalling systems or other communication systems used by various animals or machines from human language and thought. On the representational hypothesis, one might be able to establish a difference in terms of the complexity of the objects of human cognition and the demand that this places on the cognitive system.

Secondly, one might wish to argue for the spontaneity of thought, i.e. the thesis that there are no causal conditions, apart from other thoughts, that jointly could necessitate the emergence of this or that thought in a person's mind at any particular moment. We met this conjecture already in our review of behaviourism. Those proposing it are not saying that instead of determinism we should adopt an indeterministic model for explaining thoughts, but that thought has its own unique modes of emergence that cannot be assimilated to the emergence of other kinds of entity.

The third proposed property is accepted much more widely than the first two, for phenomenal as well as behavioural evidence suggests that some thoughts are unconscious while others occur on the conscious level. This raises the questions of whether there is any interesting way of separating these two classes, and whether the non-conscious ones are always in principle recoverable for consciousness. (On this topic see also Margolis, 1984, p.69.)

One might call a 'shallow' theory of thought the view that construes most of thought as either conscious or at least recoverable and presentable on the conscious level. As Harman pointed out, such a view might apply to reasons for which we believe something. Often these are not on the conscious level, but up to a point one might be able to recover these (Harman, 1973, p. 69). A 'deep' theory of thought would assume that most of our thoughts are on the non-conscious level, and are in principle not recoverable. When we consider the complex thought processes that go into interpreting sentences, or balancing a cheque account, it is easy to see why thought-processes involved here should not be open to introspection. For the speed required to complete these operations within a pragmatically feasible time makes it imperative that these processes should be non-conscious. As of now, however, we do not have a good principled account showing why some thoughts are conscious, some kinds non-conscious, and among the latter why some are in principle not recoverable. Some of the candidates for the last class are our mental representations of the constitutive rules of the objects such as arithmetic, etc., that we use, mentioned before.

The positing of subconscious representation of rules helps to account for an interesting case of knowledge (Chomsky, 1980). We know in many cases whether a certain string of words is or is not a grammatical part of a language. But in many cases we know this not from experience or explicit learning. Such knowledge in these cases represents intuitions of grammaticality. Thus here we have a type of knowledge without the use of standard empirical evidence. The most plausible hypothesis to account for this knowledge is to suppose that it is based on a structural scheme generated by us on the basis of subconsciously applying rules represented in our minds. Thus a person has knowledge of this sort only if he has the right mental representations. Since these are not on the conscious level, this raises difficulties about how do I know that I know.

There is a temptation for most humans to lean towards the 'shallow' theory of thought. We tend to think that what we know on the basis of introspection is more likely to be under our control than what is non-conscious and non-recoverable. The human desire towards direct self-knowledge and self-control pushes us towards the 'shallow' theory. But we have seen that there is strong evidence on the other side, not to mention the presence of such important adherents as Socrates, Plato, and Freud, who disagree on many important points, but agree that not all knowledge and understanding takes place on the conscious level.

Convergence of data, both introspective and other, supports the thesis that humans have intuitions about logical validity, grammaticality, semantic facts, etc. These intuitions can be interpreted in two ways. According to one view, the very answers we give about, e.g., grammaticality constitute the intuitions. Thus on that view we 'wear our intuitions on our sleeves' and these are introspectible entities. According to the alternative view intuitions of the various kinds are unobservable. Our introspections, answers, other verbal behaviour, etc., furnish evidence on the basis of which we infer what our intuitions are. No kind of evidence is sacred; we avail ourselves of any kind of evidence that bears indirect witness about human intuitions. The first view implies that we are infallible as far as our intuitions are concerned; the second view does not. The first view commits us to introspective psychology; the second view shows how we can accommodate the presence of intuitions within cognitive psychology without becoming introspectionists.

We come to our final question which is about the epistemology of a theory of cognition. One view is that we try to study thoughts as they occur, and use any evidence available, such as those of introspection, behaviour, or physiology. The other view does not deny the utility of all of this kind of evidence, but points out that our actual thoughts, especially as encoded in language in specific contexts, is the result of far too many variables to be presentable as a reasonable object of study. Let us consider the thought that goes into someone ordering in a pub a pitcher of beer. What is actually thought and said is a function of the social context, the conventions of the society, the knowledge of the nature of the addressee, the available language that will be understood, etc. We would need to understand all of these factors in order to give an adequate account of what is being said and thought. Thus it is reasonable for the study of cognition to borrow a page from the books of the other successful sciences, and conceive of the study of cognition as the study of objects abstracted from the real everyday context, and described under idealizations. This is a standard procedure in physics, chemistry, and other such disciplines and is quite neutral with regard to ontological theses or the kinds of methodological debates we see between, e.g., functionalists and dualists.

Of course to say that we want to study thought, language, etc. under idealizations, and then add other variables to describe eventually what in fact takes place, is – or rather should be – a harmless claim. But there may be substantial disagreements on what are good or bad idealizations, and within such debates we cannot settle matters by invoking purely logical principles. We have already seen that there are disagreements on what the fundamental role of thought is. These disagreements will obviously influence people's views on what are the right and wrong abstractions and idealizations.

Perhaps we can illustrate what is involved better if we restrict ourselves to comments about those parts of cognition that constitute certain intellectual abilities or competences. These include the mastery of logic, of languages, and of mathematics. It may include many other kinds of less well understood abilities such as those required for our moral lives and our aesthetic enjoyments. We can characterize such a competence or ability in terms of the following questions:

1. What is expected of a possessor of the competence in question? What does he need to accomplish?
2. What are the general conditions under which humans possess and exercise the competence?
3. What are the characteristic processes?
4. Given that we obtain adequate answers to the first three questions, what do these answers, treated as premisses now, tell us about human nature?

(For elaboration, see Moravcsik, 1969, pp. 407-9.) In cases in which the objects of cognition involve constitutive rules, we can expect insightful characterizations. That humans can master simple arithmetic in normal circumstances, that they can master a natural language, or enjoy a painting or a song, tell us, when specified in more detail, a great deal about human nature.

Noam Chomsky (1965) contrasted competence with performance. But underlying this simple verbal dichotomy we find a number of related distinctions. First, there is the distinction, familiar from common sense and science, between a disposition and its many diverse manifestations. Second, there is a difference between ideal and actual performances. An ideal performance matches that which is prescribed by the constitutive rules of what has been mastered and is being used. Actual performances exhibit not only flaws and the limitations of, e.g., human memory, but are also the function of many other, possibly quite irrelevant, factors such as psychological pressure during an exam. Third, a competence can be characterized under idealizations and abstracted from all other factors that influence actual performance. We can thus characterize grammatical, logical, mathematical, etc., competences, and add only later characterizations of several other competences or in some cases mere psychological or environmental factors that influence actual performance or occurrence. Thus the ideal thought-producer, the ideal reasoner, the ideal economic agent, the ideal rational choice-making agent, or information-processor are all on the same conceptual plane. We need, however, to examine each case and see if the idealizations are appropriate and will, in fact, with the addition of other factors, lead to reasonable hypotheses about what we actually do.

There have also been attempts to argue that many of the idealizations of philosophers and linguists are not helpful to understand human cognitive processes, and that we should make more modest assumptions of what humans can achieve. Some of these conjectures are based on analogies between what computers can do and what we thus assume humans would do. Adjudicating between the rival claims is an empirical question. (For examples of this recent move, see Harman, 1986; Cherniak, 1986.)

Whether we talk about competences or other aspects of cognition, the representational approach suggests that the rules in terms of which we define some of the objects of thought are, in some sense, in the head of the subject. We see from our discussion that this raises a lot of questions. Are we talking about the head of an 'ideal subject', or a real subject under idealized circumstances, or what a real subject actually uses in problem solving, or what he can fall back on, or. . .? This issue is discussed in the literature in the somewhat misleading terminology, as I shall suggest, of 'psychological reality'. (For some discussion, see Moravcsik, 1981a; Soames, 1984a.)

Clearly, talking about mental processing and talking about, e.g., linguistic structures, are not the same thing. There are questions about syntactic or semantic structures that cannot be resolved by peering into someone's brain, and questions about psychology that cannot be resolved by looking at a textbook on logic or mathematics. But this does not mean that there may not be overlapping matters.

An extreme claim of 'psychological reality' would be, for example, to claim that a certain semantic description of components, rules of composition, etc. is actually what an agent uses in everyday conversations. An extremely weak claim would be that the output of a language user can be characterized by the rules of semantics. But there are many other options that lie between these extremes. Thus it would be better to talk about 'psychological relevance', which admits of matters of degree, rather than 'psychological reality', which relies too much on the misleading metaphor of what is or is not in 'the subject's head'. In physics we do not discuss questions about the 'physical reality' of laws and principles that apply to objects under idealizations; why should we do so in the case of cognition?

The rules in question are abstract entities. They cannot be in anyone's head, only their representations. Once we see this, then the question of relevance can be resolved into a series of more detailed issues, some of which we mentioned on p. 85, e.g., what do we use, what could we use, what describes well what we would use under ideal circumstances, or what an ideal agent would use, etc. The fact that we have intuitions of rule-violation does not lead to a thesis that there is a unique description of what exactly we apply 'in our heads'. It leads only to the hypothesis that there is subconscious rule application going on, but the usual strictures about indeterminacy suggest that there is more than one equally good way of characterizing of what the source of these intuitions is.

The issue of psychological relevance affects how we construe the task of enterprises claiming to investigate, e.g., linguistic structure. For the aim may be simply to generate rules that will account for the difference between the acceptable parts of discourse that belong to languages from the nonsensical sequences, or the aim may be to characterize something allegedly unique about all natural human languages. The latter has more psychological relevance than the former; above all, these are enterprises with different aims (see Kasher, 1975).

A Science of Thought?

What would a scientific account of cognition be like? What if anything does philosophy contribute to such an account? These questions should be construed as analogous to questions like: What does a scientific study of living creatures look like? We cannot be sure that a unified science of cognition is possible. There are two reasons for this. First, as we saw, cognition involves various achievements, and these in turn involve, in as yet poorly understood ways, mastery and manipulation of abstract structures. Perhaps accounts centring on the achievements and the structure of the objects mastered or created will not mesh in any simple way with the study of the physiological processes and psychological states that make up actual cognition. Secondly, we saw that actual thought is the result of many different factors, and we cannot be sure *a priori* that the accounts of these facts will make up a unified picture. Finally, there is the issue of how to link what we know on the basis of common sense about cognition with what a future science might teach us.

Recently, some philosophers proposed that there could be a unitary science of cognition, but it would throw out most of our common sense beliefs and concepts in terms of which we interpret our thinking life. One eloquent expression of this view is to be found in Stich (1983). Stich thinks that we should be willing to pay this price, on the ground that in the past there have been clashes between common sense and science, and science shows itself to be right in these cases. Stich thinks that all of our mentalistic concepts would have to go. This includes not only the concepts of the dualist such as thought, belief, etc., but also the content or object specifications of the philosopher in terms of concepts or propositions. He notes, however, with somberness, that this will threaten our conception of humans as responsible moral agents.

In assessing such a proposal we should keep several things in mind. First, it is not clear that all mentalistic terms are dualist in their ontology. It may be that terms like 'fear', 'learning', etc. as used in common sense are ontologically neutral between materialism and dualism, i.e. they specify ranges of application without this question being resolved. There are many other examples of such ontological indeterminacy in everyday language, e.g., how precisely is the ontology of the denotation of 'electricity' determined in everyday use? Secondly, the fact that perhaps none of the current theories of 'object' or content fits current speculation about the physiology and psychology of cognition is not a good ground for thinking *a priori* that these notions cannot fit into a scientific account of thought.

We need to take also a closer look at common sense. Is it true that common sense encompasses only the superstitions of the past and some contemporary broadly shared empirical hypotheses with weak supporting evidence? Some of past common sense, like belief in the flatness of the earth, or the geocentric view, were like this. But what about the layer of common sense G.E. Moore used to invoke, such as belief in an external world, the reality of the past, thinking of ourselves as decision-making creatures, etc.? Are these just superstitions? Has any science really sought to undermine these, or is physics not rather intent on accounting for these things – among others – by placing them into larger contexts? It might be advisable to distinguish between 'basic common sense' and 'peripheral common sense' (Moravcsik, 1987). 'Basic' common sense is a culturally invariant layer of thought without which human conception of human nature is not conceivable. Peripheral common sense comprises the many historically and culturally variant hypotheses that people come to share at one time or another, and discard when more thorough rational investigation shows them to be unjustifiable. The ontologies of both may be quite indeterminate. But more importantly, the relation of science, at least in the past, to these two components may be quite different. In the second half we shall go into this matter further, and in arguing against Stich's picture draw more on analogies to what happened in the development of the more established sciences.

One cannot help but conclude this survey on a somewhat somber note. Our review of ontology in the first part of the book showed that though basic disagreements persist, there is a general agreement on methods to be used and the main facts to be accounted for. In our survey of philosophic views about cognition, however, we see that there is widespread disagreement even about what the fundamental facts are, and on what types of programme philosophers should attempt to carry out. Naturalists and non-naturalists, and those wishing to throw away common sense versus those who want to preserve it, are further apart than nominalists and realists. At least the latter pair agree that one of the key testing grounds is the analysis of the foundation of mathematics. We saw also that it is one thing to expect a detailed, millisecond-by-millisecond analysis of what actually goes on when cognition takes place, and another to try to draw conclusions, no matter how incomplete, about the human mind in terms of some of its salient achievements. In the second half, we shall see proposals for how to deal with some of these matters, but these will be made against the conceptual back-ground of keeping the possibility in mind that perhaps the understanding of humans by humans has certain inherent limitations.

CHAPTER III

Language

Wittgenstein is reported to have said that we, humans, have great difficulties getting a proper perspective on things that are so close to us, so much part of us, that we almost cannot help but take them for granted. The phenomenon of language should be a prime candidate. The use of language is so much a part of our life that it is difficult to step back and attempt to view it as just another natural phenomenon. Yet viewed that way, language is very puzzling. On the surface, what one observes is humans making noises at each other. Somehow, out of this emerges a Shakespearean sonnet, a proof by Godel, and hypotheses by Einstein. How is this possible? As a first step we can say that the 'noises' we emit fall into patterns. These patterns enable the 'noises' both to be intelligible to humans and to describe parts of reality.

We find this way of viewing language articulated first by Aristotle. In chapter 1 of *De Interpretatione*, 16a3–8, he writes:

> Spoken sounds are symbols of affections in the soul, and written marks are symbols of spoken sounds. And just as written marks are not the same for all humans, neither are spoken sounds. But the affections of the soul, of which the spoken sounds are the signs, remain the same for all, and so do the elements of reality of which the affections of the soul are likenesses.

This passage introduces fundamental relations between language and the mind, and between language and reality. Aristotle likens the former to the relation between spoken and written language, and he also claims that some of the relations he invokes are universally constant, while some vary from culture to culture. Bypassing some of the details, we can see in this passage two basic relationships, linking up the triangle of language, mind, and reality. The one between reality and the mind is interpretation and conceptualizing. The other, between language and the mind, has two aspects. Language embodies or expresses some of the contents of the mind, and the mind in turn can understand language. To complete the triangle, Aristotle introduces yet another basic relationship between language and reality. We shall call this 'designating'. (For further evidence see chapter 4 of the *Categories*.) This relationship allows language to express truths and to contain parts that are descriptive of reality.

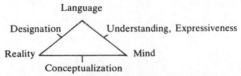

We have been wrestling with these notions ever since. They seem to escape definability, and are in perpetual need of elucidation. Thus our basic questions remain: 'What is language understanding?' 'How can language express thoughts?' 'How can the human mind conceptualize or represent reality?' 'How can a natural language express truths, falsehoods, and other elements that purport to be descriptive of reality?'

In the early part of this century some philosophers sought through the study of language and logic to uncover the most fundamental structures of reality. (Some outstanding examples are Russell, 1918; Wittgenstein, 1922.) Both Russell's logical atomism and the puritan ontology of Wittgenstein's *Tractatus* represent efforts to show what ontological configurations must be constituting reality if certain uses of language are possible. On the other hand, some of Strawson's writings represent efforts to link very general features of languages to general features of 'conceptual frameworks', that is, mental structures (Strawson, 1959). According to Strawson certain general features of language enable us to sketch parts of the basic conceptual framework that we share. Thus we are led from language to certain features of the communal mind. In both of these approaches the interest in language is only instrumental. We study language in order to arrive at some other structure. More recent approaches to meaning and grammar take natural language to be a topic of interest in its own right, and work towards adequate conceptual frameworks within which empirical study of language can take place.

A natural language has three components. These are studied by phonology, syntax, and semantics. All three raise important questions, but philosophers have been mostly preoccupied with the third, with some attention paid to the second. The reason for this is that for a philosopher semantics, or a theory of meaning, is the component that helps to answer questions about truth and reality to which semantic structures are relevant.

Language and Reality

The part of the philosophy of language that deals with relations between language and reality is concerned with how language can describe and be assessed from the point of view of veracity. The following are the key points concerning the expressive power of natural languages. Parts of language can express both what is true or false, both what is general and what is particular, and both what is an assertion and what is a question. Furthermore, there are rules for combining elements of language in such a way as to be able to form the appropriate units to express anything with the characteristics just mentioned.

In view of these facts, philosophers divide the theory of meaning into the following components. First, there is the distinction between theories of meaning for the basic descriptive parts of the language and the compositional rules that combine the more simple units into phrases and sentences. Within both of these components we distinguish between theories of meaning, or intensions, that are concerned with criteria or conditions of application, and theories of extension and reference that are concerned with relations involving veracity between language and reality. This gives us the following cross-classification:

theory of meaning, intension	e.g. sentence and proposition	e.g. word meaning
theory of extension, reference	e.g. sentence and truth	e.g. name and reference
	compositional	non-compositional

First we shall consider the non-compositional component. The philosophical theory of intension and extension to which we referred briefly in chapter 1, would posit for a term like 'human' as an intension conditions that under idealized circumstances would delineate the class of all those entities to which the term applies, and the related extension is the class of entities thus singled out. Under the more narrow interpretation the extension includes only all actual – past, present, and future – elements, while under the modal interpretation it includes also all possible entities to which the term truly applies.

There are other theories of meaning. One of these attempts to capture the meanings of various units of language as the set of conditions that specify what is needed for the success of such linguistic acts as saying, asserting, promising, etc. (Alston, 1964; Searle, 1969). These conditions apply primarily to whole sentences used in performing these acts. The meanings of the parts of the sentences are construed in terms of their contributions to the meanings of the larger, sentential, units. Such theories can be taken in two ways. A less ambitious view construes these as presupposing a theory of meaning in terms of extensions and intensions, and adding to this conditions accounting for the possibility of appropriate performances of promising, warning, questioning, etc. The more ambitious version has speech act theories actually replacing, not just supplementing, theories of intension and extension.

While speech-act theories see meaning as an aspect of certain acts, Paul Grice's theory attempts to define meaning in terms of speakers' intentions. In short, it attempts to replace intensions with intentions (Grice, 1957). There have also been in recent times interactions between lexical semantics and artificial intelligence. Out of this work came the proposal to identify the meaning of a word with the set of routines or procedures which one is called upon to follow as a response to commands in which the word plays the key role. These can include verifying something, initiating actions to change the state of the agent, affecting the audience, etc. This effort usually starts with determining meaning for languages designed for robots with clearly defined properties and sphere of activities (Suppes and Crangle, 1988).

Just as with regards to the study of animals we can distinguish the biologist from the naturalist, we can draw the analogous distinction for semantics. The naturalist wants to describe the many peculiarities of observed animals. The main interest of the biologist is in those phenomena whose explanation yields an insightful theory about the general features of species and genera. The 'naturalist' lexical theorist might be guided by the motto that 'natural language has no exact logic' (Strawson, 1950, last sentence), or he may simply do the 'spadework' and leave the possibility of general theorizing to others. Detailed accounts of interesting peculiarities of some English words have been given by members of what is, misleadingly, called the Oxford 'ordinary language' school (e.g. Urmson, 1952; Austin, 1956).

Choice between different theories of meaning depends on what one takes to be the fundamental facts to be explained, and which notions seem unproblematic. For some the notion of an intension seems to be a good starting-point for explaining everything else, while for others the notion of a linguistic act seems to play that role. There are some questions that can be raised about all of the theories. For example, if questions about individuation are raised about intensions, they should be raised also about linguistic acts and about extensions. If linguistic meaning is to be defined in terms of psychological notions, we should ask if there is any reason to suppose that psychological entities are ontologically more respectable than Platonistic ones.

After this brief survey of theories of non-compositional meaning, we turn now to theories about extension and reference. General terms apply to a whole class of entities, singular terms apply to a single entity. Hence the notions of extension and reference. Singular terms are either proper names or definite descriptions. We cannot define definite descriptions as descriptive terms that apply to only one entity. For on the one hand, there may be general predicates that – the world being what it is – happen to apply to only one thing, and again there may be many definite descriptions that purport to apply to one entity but in fact fail to do so. For example, 'the only human over 8 feet tall in Chicago' probably does not identify anyone, not even a basketball player, while a term like 'honest politician in Chicago' could very well turn out to apply to only one person. So we need to say that singular terms purport to refer to only one entity.

They accomplish this in virtue of their semantic and syntactic structures. How they accomplish this has been a source of puzzlement for philosophers over the centuries.

Some singular terms refer to an entity in virtue of their descriptive meanings, while others refer to single entities directly, in virtue of other kinds of conventions to be explained. In addition to this distinction, we need to separate the claims that a given expression refers to an entity and that a speaker using a term refers to a single entity. Reference can be seen as a relation between words and elements of reality, or as a relation between speaker, word, and reality. If we acknowledge the need to treat both of these relationships in a semantic theory, we can raise questions of conceptual priority between these.

We need to distinguish also different uses of definite descriptions. We use some, e.g. 'the smartest lawyer in town', in many ordinary contexts to focus primarily on descriptive content. Thus in this use this expression picks out different individuals under different circumstances, or what we called in chapter 1 different projections, depending on who happens to be the smartest lawyer in town at a given time or in a given possible context. There are other expressions such as 'the man there, to your right' which we use mainly to direct the hearer's attention to a particular individual. In such cases the descriptive content has as its primary role leading us to one particular entity rather than providing us with criteria that pick out a specific kind of entity from among all actual and possible ones. Many descriptions have both uses, giving philosophers an opportunity to try to characterize the conditions under which we interpret a definite description in one way rather than the other.

We shall now consider two influential proposals for analysing singular reference. Some of the key data concern sentences expressing human beliefs. As chapter 2 has shown, our having beliefs is a part of basic common sense. We could not suddenly conceive of ourselves as not having any. Awareness of ourselves as believers need not imply direct introspective access to all of our beliefs. But it does imply our reflecting on our beliefs. This self-reflective aspect of human belief-systems must be covered by any adequate semantic analysis.

Human beliefs are also projective in character. They are not mere representative copies of reality. This can be seen in two ways. The formation of a belief involves a preference or ranking among alternative projections of what will be, must be, or ought to be. In coming to believe *p* we normally come to favour *p* over alternatives *q*, *r*, etc. Furthermore, since there is no guarantee that the favoured belief is true, all beliefs should be construed as projections of reality, not copies of it. Beliefs can be understood prior to their assessment as true or false.

The projectivity of belief has its counterpart in the projectivity of reality. One can look at reality as the totality of entities and their relationships. Alternatively one can view reality as the totality of entities with their potentialities, developments, essential functioning, etc., thus interpreting all of reality as including not only what there is, or happens to be, but also what must be and can be. On this view reality is projective. Our ordinary interactions with nature conform to this view. Whether it is the education of the young or the growth of trees in our gardens, we try to make arrangements for the living in view of their potentials and limitations. Words like 'healthy', 'grow', 'become', 'develop', etc., reflect this view, and they are notoriously resistant to any non-modal analysis.

In view of these considerations we can insist that an adequate semantics for singular terms should reflect both the projective nature of reality and the projective nature of belief. The two phenomena as encoded in semantics have as a key common feature 'opacity', namely the fact that both in modal and epistemic contexts substitution of merely co-extensive terms will not preserve truth-value. But this technical similarity might cover up deep philosophical differences. This point will be taken up later. We shall start with a sketch of Frege's account of belief and identity.

Frege's account is not designed as an answer to the general question of how to analyse sentences expressing identity. Frege's main interest lies in explaining the interesting fact that some of these statements are informative (Frege, 1892). Being informative, unlike being abstract, is not an attribute that an entity can have or fail to have in isolation. To be informative is to be informative to some actual or ideal reasoning subject. This suggests a psychological interpretation. Could not the same sentence express something that is informative to one person and uninformative to another? If informativeness can be thus relativized to individuals, it becomes a topic for psychologists and not for semantics. Frege is, however, against the 'psychologizing' of semantic questions. Thus it is reasonable to interpret him as dealing not with actual but idealized subjects. We can restate his question as: 'How is it that some sentences expressing identity will be informative to a rational mind that has full knowledge of the language to which the sentences in question belong, but is not considering any other, extrinsic, information?' Thus one of our questions should be whether this idealization is useful. As we shall see, we need it also for accounting for other aspects of linguistic competence, such as our knowledge of grammar and the compositional rules of semantics. Thus there is a *prima facie* case for the notion introduced implicitly by Frege.

Whatever is informative is informative to some creature with beliefs. For to be informative is to make a difference to the beliefs of some reasoning subject. If something is informative, it provides new possible material for belief. If it is not, then it makes no difference to our beliefs. In this way Frege's puzzle about identity is linked to analyses of belief.

Frege's solution involves two steps. First, he shows that certain sentences of identity can express what is contingent and empirically discoverable. Secondly, he shows how the introduction of sense and reference can lay the foundations for an adequate analysis. Senses relate to concepts, and reference to the object under consideration. The informative sentences have the main identity sign flanked by singular terms that have the same reference but not the same sense. And while attaching the same sense, or meaning, to singular terms is a matter of the knowledge of the language, knowing which entity is picked out by a singular term via its sense is a separate empirically discoverable matter.

This brief sketch requires qualifications. Frege does not hold the view that all sentences of the form 'a=b' – in contrast with 'a=a' – are informative. In cases in which 'a' and 'b' have the same sense, something of the form 'a=b' is just as uninformative as something of the form 'a=a'. Furthermore, there will also be necessary truths of identity that are informative, since not all of these express identities between expressions with the same sense.

One might raise at this point the question of how we know what the various senses are. Frege is not committed to the view that sense must be expressible linguistically. He assumes that semantic competence with respect to a natural language will yield the appropriate intuitions. Thus he is also committed to the view that under ideal conditions the competent speaker-hearer knows all of the synonymy relations holding in the language. Hence if, for example, someone believes something about the Greeks but not about the Hellenes, and 'Greek' and 'Hellene' are synonymous, then this shows only that this person does not have full command of the language.

Recently, Frege's account has come under attack, and Kripke's writing on identity, necessity, and singular terms is seen by some as an alternative to Frege's views (Kripke, 1971, 1972). At first glance some of Kripke's proposals do seem like genuine alternatives to Frege. He claims that some sentences express true identity and are at the same time both informative and necessary, and that we can explain these facts without positing senses for definite descriptions and proper names. Kripke's proposals introduce some new notions. For while the notions of necessity and possibility are explicated in terms of truths holding in 'possible worlds', i.e. in different modal projections of the actual world, the distinction between the necessary and the contingent is separated from the dichotomy of *a priori* and *a posteriori* (Kripke, 1972, pp. 304ff). This enables Kripke to claim that a statement may be necessarily true and still be known empirically. Kripke, like John Stuart Mill, claims also that a name can refer directly, without the reference being mediated by a sense. In such contexts, a definite description may be needed to lead someone to the referent of the name, thus 'fixing' the reference, but the descriptive content of such a singular term need not be tied analytically to the name of the referent.

On the basis of such considerations Kripke proposes that certain singular terms, including many expressions that we call ordinarily names, should be construed as 'rigid designators' (Kripke, 1971, p. 145; 1972, pp. 269–70). Rigid designators pick out the same referent across all modal projections – or possible worlds – in which the referent exists. Furthermore, Kripke claims that they can accomplish this without the mediation of sense.

On the basis of these notions Kripke provides an alternative to Frege. On his view a sentence like 'the Evening Star is the Morning Star' expresses something both necessary and informative. What is expressed is necessary in the sense that it holds in all possible worlds in which the referent, i.e. the star, exists. Its informativeness can be accounted for without assigning senses to the appropriate expressions. For on this theory the informativeness is due to the fact that the reference of the two naming expressions in the sentence has been 'fixed' in different ways. It is informative, then, to discover empirically that the expressions whose reference was fixed in different ways do in fact pick out the same entity, and thus can form elements of a necessary identity statement.

Constancy of reference is accounted for by Frege with the positing of senses attached by rules to referring expressions. Kripke has an alternative device. According to his view, people use certain names with the same reference in virtue of the fact that the people in question are related through appropriate causal links (involving also the intentions of name givers and users) to the same introduction of the name in question. Thus while for Frege understanding the descriptive content of all relevant expressions of a language gives us also mastery of the singular terms, for Kripke the latter ability is assigned to a separate component.

There seem to be disagreements between Frege and Kripke. First, certain sentences expressing identity are construed by Frege as contingent while for Kripke these are necessary. Secondly, Frege assumes that there is a certain kind of informativeness which he explains by the positing of senses while Kripke thinks that the relevant notion of informativeness can be explained without invoking senses. On closer examination, however, the disagreements turn out not to be straightforward. Kripke is introducing a new sense of necessity. One might call this metaphysical necessity. A predicate is metaphysically necessarily true of a subject if it holds of that subject in all possible worlds in which the subject exists. This is different from pure logical necessity which holds in all possible worlds, without any existential limitations. Kripke is not claiming that statements of identity of the sort under consideration are necessary in Frege's sense of necessity. Thus the real issue is whether we need to posit metaphysical in addition to logical necessity. The argument for the additional posit is that we need it in contexts in which we assert that, e.g., rationality must be a property of a certain individual under all modal projections. Such essential patterns are required to describe phenomena of growth or development for many natural kinds. We do not want to construe such ascriptions to individuals as carrying logical necessity, since that would make the existence of these individuals logically necessary – a conclusion clearly to be avoided.

The disagreement concerning informativeness is not straightforward either. Frege has a notion of informativeness that is best explicable by linking it to the ideal speaker-hearer. Kripke is not saying that statements of identity are informative in Frege's sense. Rather, he relativizes informativeness to speakers who may or may not have complete command of the rules of the language, and for whom reference for singular terms is 'fixed' in a variety of ways. Thus the real issue is: Which notion of informativeness should we employ in characterizing semantic competence?

Still another important difference concerns the data that the two philosophers analyse. Kripke's main concern is a metaphysical projective picture of reality and the semantics that are needed for the description of reality under such a conception. Frege has nothing to say about the essential characteristics of members of natural kinds. He is interested in the semantics of belief. It is clear that the same semantic device cannot handle both types of phenomena. One alternative would be to add Kripkean components to a Fregean system, or the other way around. But other alternatives are open as well.

One of these is to deny that we have clear and consistent sets of intuitions on the basis of which one could construct a semantics for sentences expressing beliefs that would carry uniform rules, apart from the varying data-bases of the members of the linguistic community (Kripke, 1979). Another way out is to accept the metaphysical picture but to deny that it maps in a straightforward way into our system of beliefs. For while it is true that Aristotle would still be Aristotle even if he had not done any of the things for which he is remembered, such as being the student of Plato, inventor of syllogistic logic, etc., this might not be so represented in our belief system. As we saw in our previous discussion, neither the notion of belief nor the notion of its content can be precise. Perhaps if one took away all the properties which we associate with Aristotle, and asked whether the competent language user would still have an adequate object of belief, the answer would be: 'we don't know what to say.' Having certain properties remain attached to entities across possibilities when these entities are objects of human belief seems to be one of the conditions that makes the transmission of thoughts from person to person and generation to generation possible. Thus the Fregean view can explain certain modes of communication. At the same time one should keep in mind that certain metaphysical truths about individuals may not be communicable across large linguistic communities, construed both synchronically and diachronically. As to the many 'local' names that we give to children, pets, boats, etc., it may be that these items are only syntactically, but not semantically, part of a natural language. Their semantics may be governed by local conditions that are not part of the general linguistic competence, required for the mastery of a language.

These reflections suggest that it is a mistake to see as the clearest case of language being related to reality the case of name and bearer. The semantics of singular terms is no more simple or clear than the semantics of general terms. As we shall see in our survey of lexical semantics, the relation between predicate expression and the ranges to which it applies is mediated by intermediate levels. Our consideration of the views of Frege and Kripke suggests that one might need complexities of the same order if one is to write a semantics for the whole range of uses of singular expressions. To delineate the interactions of the metaphysical with the epistemic is a task still to be completed.

We shall turn now to a review of the most standard conceptions of compositional semantics. The most original recent suggestion is that natural languages can be treated as 'formal languages' in the sense defined by Alfred Tarski. Tarski himself did not intend this notion to be a tool for analysing natural languages. He thought of a formal language as embodying in a clear and conspicuous way scientific theories, without the burden of the so-called semantic paradoxes (Tarski, 1936). A formal language is defined by Tarski as having the following features: there must be a characterization generating all meaning-bearing elements. There must be thus formation rules deriving syntactically the complex elements out of the simple ones. There must also be a list of the semantic primitives and rules for defining the complexes. There must be a way of delineating the class of all sentences, conditions of assertability, rules of inference, and a systematic way of assigning to sentences conditions of truth, and to predicates conditions of satisfaction, the latter being approximately the equivalent to what we called within other systems extensions. A number of philosophers thought that, in spite of what Tarski himself said, this framework could be used to present a semantics for natural languages. Donald Davidson's version attempts to do without intensional notions, while Montague's uses those as well as higher-order logics. There is yet another version that features a new treatment of indexicals and a viewpoint within which those making assertions have only partial information about the world (Davidson, 1967; Montague, 1974; Barwise and Perry, 1983). We shall consider later arguments attempting to show that natural languages cannot be formal languages, in Tarski's sense.

We should note the limitations on what formal languages are meant to explicate. The semantics will yield conditions of satisfaction and truth. But 'truth' in this context is a technical notion. It is defined within a theory and applied to sentences within a formal language. Truth in Tarski's theory is not meant to explicate the meaning of the word 'true' in ordinary language, nor is it meant to adjudicate among rival philosophical accounts of truth such as the correspondence, coherence, or pragmatic theories of truth. (For more details, see Soames, 1984a; Moravcsik, 1975a, pp. 28–30.)

In a formal language syntactic structure and inferential structure go hand in hand. That is to say, if two sentences have different semantic properties, then they should have different syntactic structures. This seems in some cases counter-intuitive. As Etchemendy points out, the sentences 'Benjamin is healthy' and 'someone is healthy' have different logical properties, but they seem to have the same syntactic form (Etchemendy, 1983, pp. 319–20). Whether one will attempt to posit different syntactic structures in such cases will depend on whether one thinks that a doctrine of 'logical form', in the sense of close tie with syntax, is justified, and this in turn depends partly on whether one thinks that syntactic ways of dealing with logical properties are likely to be successful.

In Tarski's theory truth applies to sentences, but one can

extend the treatment to propositions. We shall review now some considerations leading to the positing of propositions as either the meanings of sentences, or as what sentences express and the bearers of truth-values, or both. Frege called the sense of a sentence a thought, and remarked: 'By a thought I understand not the subjective performance of thinking, but its objective content, which is capable of being the common property of several thinkers' (Frege, 1956, p.52). Fregean thoughts are roughly what people later came to call propositions, and they are what is primarily true or false. There are many ways of showing why this must be so. First, a sentence is a series of sound-tokens or character-tokens, and these are not the things we judge to be true or false. Furthermore, a number of different sentences can express the same truth or falsehood, and what we assert or believe too can be expressed by different sentences. These are fairly obvious observations. Philosophers who want to eschew the use of propositions in their theories do so because of metaphysical suspicions about the legitimacy of propositions. We dealt with this topic in chapter 1, where among the proposals we have seen arguments defending the legitimacy of intensional notions. Furthermore, such reductionistic programs have yet to be proven successful. (For a recent effort, see Field, 1978.)

Frege saw that for sentences expressing beliefs, the condition for preserving truth-value is not a substitution of merely co-extensive expressions but expressions with the same intensions. This applies both to singular terms and general predicates. And yet there are belief reports for which an extensional reading seems appropriate. Contrast

(a) Sam believes that all humans are mortal.
(b) Sam believes that all of the students in this room are clever.

Under normal circumstances one would give (a) an intensional reading, i.e. for 'humans' and 'mortal' we would accept only synonyms if we want to preserve truth value. But for (b) an extensional reading seems more plausible. It is unlikely that anyone would have some 'global' or conceptual reason for linking the attribute of being a student in this room and the attribute of being clever. If someone does make this assertion, it is more likely that he has some information about the particular humans who happened to be students in this room. Thus even a conjunction of their names in place of the expression 'students in this room' would preserve what Sam believes. One of the challenges of semantics for belief reports is to delineate the conditions that call for intensional and extensional readings respectively.

This concludes our review of philosophical views about language and reality. We shall now turn to another part of the Aristotelian triangle.

Language and the Mind

The relation between language and the mind has two aspects. On the one hand, language can express some of the contents of our minds. For example, it can express concepts such as those of justice or a constitution or triangularity. It can also express our sentence-like cognitive units which we might call judgements. Indeed, without committing ourselves to the view that all thought must be explicitly or implicitly verbal, we might entertain the thesis that language is the primary access that we have to mental contents.

On the other hand, language can be understood by the mind. What seem on the surface only inkmark or typed symbols on paper are interpreted by the mind as expressing important information or messages. We saw in the previous section how philosophers think meanings might be attached to parts of language. But even if some of these proposals turn out to be adequate, that would still leave the question of how the mind comes to understand these meanings.

On the lexical level, one might try at first a simple solution. Consider the meaning of the word 'job'. Why not posit a correspondence between the meaning of this word and the concept that we have in our minds of what a job is. Understanding such words, then, would amount to matching concepts with the meanings assigned to words.

We must be careful, however, in assessing such a proposal. For it certainly could not be a conceptual proposal. That is to say, it is not an *a priori* truth that our concepts should correspond to meanings. The meaning of 'job' gives us conditions for the application of the word. These conditions, however, can be conceptualized in a variety of ways. Perhaps humans conceptualize the notion of a job in different ways, or perhaps all those who do grasp this notion conceptualize it in the same way. In any case, it is *a priori* possible to have a number of different conceptualizations converge on the same conditions of application. There may be many factors having to do with the way the human mind, or brain, functions that affect the mental representation of various notions.

In considering this issue it is important to keep apart what are psychological entities and what are, given our ontology, Platonistic entities. Meanings are Platonistic entities. If the only criterion of adequacy for constructing meanings is that they should yield conditions for the right range of entities, then it is certainly possible that an 'adequate' theory of meaning and an adequate theory of the mind will not result in items that can be matched one-to-one. We had occasion to refer to the notion of a proposition. This, too, is not a psychological entity, though since we understand sentences one assumes that propositions have corresponding mental representations. Thus it is not rational to argue against proposals according to which propositions can have particulars with spatio-temporal dimensions as constituents on the ground that such constituents cannot 'fit into our heads'. It is true that Jumbo the elephant cannot fit into our heads, but a representation of him can. The same applies to propositions in general. They, being abstract entities, 'cannot fit into our heads', but representations of these can.

Having made these conceptual points, let us return to possible empirical hypotheses. While there is no *a priori* reason why an 'adequately' specified meaning should correspond to one of our concepts, neither is there *a priori* reason why such a match could not take place. In fact, one can make such a match a *desideratum*, and build it into the adequacy conditions for both semantics and cognitive psychology. Evidence for success may be always indirect and partial, but this is also true of most empirical hypotheses in fields other than semantics and psychology.

It is possible that from the point of view of such conceptual criteria as economy, elegance, etc. two theories that do not present ideal matches between concepts and meanings but are separately well founded fare better than a unified theory. But, as we saw in other contexts, there is more to the insightfulness of theories and their explanatory power than mere economy. Thus theories assuming that the picture of meanings matching concepts is sound should be attempted. Later, an outline of such an attempt will be sketched. There is no *a priori* necessity forcing all humans to form concepts in the same way, but our common biological nature suggests that such uniformity is most likely to obtain. We see, after all, this kind of uniformity with respect to many of the human functions; why should it not hold for concept formation?

Similar considerations apply to compositional semantics. Its rules will specify, for example, ways in which the meaning of an adverb is applied to the meaning of a verb in order to obtain the correct interpretation of the resulting complex verb phrase. Thus from the meaning of 'slowly' and the meaning of 'swim' we need a rule to give the meaning of 'swim slowly' in such a way as to show how the right, and only the right, inferences follow. For example, from someone swimming slowly it follows that someone is swimming, but not that someone is simply 'slow', whatever that would mean. But if this is our only condition of adequacy, then there is no *a priori* reason why such meanings could not be constructed without these corresponding to the modes of composition that one would discover if one could get at the structure of our mental representations. Still, in this sphere, as well as in the non-compositional sphere, the same considerations apply. One can aim at the psychologically relevant, even if the link between the semantic and the mental is only a contingent one.

These considerations suggest that we can look at the semantic and the mental as mutually constraining factors. Our hypotheses about mental representations of the semantic structures should be constrained by the properties of what we take to be semantic structure, and when we have choices among what seem equally adequate semantic posits, their possible relevance to cognitive organization should be a decisive factor. One might construct a semantics for a natural language that would be impossible as an object of cognition for a child learning his or her first language. Such hypotheses should be rejected in favour of psychologically more plausible ones. On the other hand, there may be theories about how we process language that are backed by psychological evidence, but break down when asked to represent the full semantics of a natural language. These too need to be abandoned in favour of semantically and logically adequate models.

These remarks should help us to see that one can agree both with Frege's 'anti-psychologism' and Chomsky's claim that in a broad sense the study of language can unearth important attributes of the mind. Frege's point is that we cannot substitute for work on semantics empirical work on how people seem to process human communication. Chomsky's point is that if we can construct semantic and syntactic systems that are constrained also by general facts about human cognition, we shall obtain important partial characterizations of the human mind.

Among the proposals concerning thought and language in this book there is an outline of an 'objectual approach' to cognition. If that approach is sound, then the mutual relevance of the study of cognition and the study of linguistic structures becomes that much more imperative, since according to that view our main access to cognition is via its complex objects.

The study of the mind in relation to language takes place on different levels. First, there is the question of how we actually process language in ordinary everyday contexts. Clearly, this will involve many rules of thumb, heuristic 'short-cuts', etc., since we do not need to bring to bear our full mastery of a language on the limited fragments whose speedy interpretation is our main daily task in language use. Secondly, there is the competence that we could bring to bear upon linguistic input, no matter how complex and unusual. Finally, there is the representation of that competence under idealized circumstances. The sequence given here is from the most observable to the most recondite. But from the point of view of what is central to a theory of language understanding, the sequence has to be reversed.

Finally, we need to mention the fact that the considerations adduced so far deal only with the relation of the understanding mind to language. But, as we pointed out before, humans are acting agents. Much in our communications is designed not only for intelligibility but also for action. This applies also to our thoughts about ourselves. Thus a full theory of the relation of language to the human agent should deal not only with how we understand, but also with how interpreting language can lead us to action. For this aspect of the work the most relevant part of semantics is that of personal pronouns and demonstratives. Correspondingly, in the study of cognition from the point of view of understanding how language can lead to action, we would have to get a grip on how demonstratives and personal pronouns are represented in our minds. This task still lies ahead. The closest approximation is the work on robot descriptions mentioned above.

In view of the discussions in chapter 2 on thought, it is worth stressing in conclusion that this brief discussion was completely neutral between such alternatives as materialism and dualism. Thus this is yet another illustration of the thesis that many of the central issues concerning language and the mind can be discussed fruitfully, and empirical hypotheses formulated on the basis of these discussions, without having to choose between these ontological alternatives.

Can Lexical Theories Link Language, Mind, and Reality?

As noted, meanings identify, under idealized conditions, the class of all actual and possible elements to which the term in question truly applies. The extension of a term is constituted by that class. Since intensions determine extensions, they link language to reality, thus accounting for one of the Aristotelian links mentioned at the outset. Having adequate representations of intensions in one's mind constitutes understanding, thus accounting also for the relation between language and the mind. Communication is described within this framework by the elements of the communication evoking the same mental representations in the minds of the communicants. This conception, originated by Frege and elaborated by Carnap, has economy, elegance, and explanatory power (Carnap, 1956). In spite of its attractiveness, this conception has recently come under attack by Putnam and others (Putnam, 1955). One felicitous way to explain the criticisms and proposed alternatives is to consider a number of facts that lexical semantics should explain, and see how the various proposals deal with these.

1. *The fact of incomplete understanding.* While we learn more

and more about natural substances, the meanings of the names of these remain constant. Hence even if there is an ordinary meaning for a word like 'water', and this can be formulated as an intension, this does not correspond to the series of scientific definitions that physicists through history offer of this substance.

2. *The fact of continuity.* While our understanding of natural kinds changes, we continue to investigate and describe the same kinds and substances. Thus it seems that as our understanding changes the intensions change, but the extensions remain the same.

3. *The fact of homogeneous use.* Scientists and non-scientists use the same language and talk about the same natural kinds, even though they possess different degrees of understanding. We need, then, a semantics that accounts for the different uses without positing sheer ambiguity between ordinary and scientific uses of words.

Since the intensional model posits a series of different intensions corresponding to the different definitions, it has difficulty in accounting for the constancy of use underlying incomplete understanding. In more general terms, this model has difficulties with diachronic phenomena. Furthermore, it does not explain what assures us of the continuity mentioned in 2, even though it is compatible with it. Finally, since it posits a different intension corresponding to every definition, this model must posit ambiguity between lay and scientific uses of words designating natural substances and other figuring both in lay and scientific discourse.

The above includes the gist of Putnam's criticism of the intensional model. Let us see now how his own proposal fares when recast so as to serve as explanations of the facts mentioned. In its original form, Putnam's proposal is designed only for words introducing natural substances. According to Putnam, such words have no intensions; rather, they function as 'rigid designators' in the sense introduced already, picking out the same entities across modal projections without the mediation of intensions (Putnam, 1955, pp. 231–4).

This proposal accounts for 1 by saying that scientists and non-scientists use the relevant terms with the same reference but with different degrees of understanding. The same purely referential force also accounts for the continuity mentioned under 2, and it avoids positing ambiguity between scientific and lay uses by claiming that scientists and non-scientists use these terms with the same referential force. The fact that they have different degrees of understanding is not represented in the semantics. It does not matter that different things are in the heads of scientists and non-scientists since what determines reference is not a function of what is in their heads. Frege thought that intensions are transmitted from generation to generation; Putnam thinks that reference, via various causal chains, involves speaker's intensions, without the mediation of senses.

Putnam's proposal construes semantics as dealing almost exclusively with the relation of language to reality. It leaves the explanation of understanding either to cognitive psychology or to a philosophical verificationist theory.

In order to have a more complete background for a comparison of the two conceptions, let us consider two more facts:

4. *The explanatory role of natural kind terms.* Construing the words introducing natural kinds as name-like rigid designators seems plausible as long as one concentrates on their role in subject position. We need, however, to consider also the fact that these words play an important role in predicate positions. In this role their use points to the nature of the substances which then helps to explain some feature of the subject which is in some way a part of one of the substances. For example, 'this is red' is in an ordinary context a mere report of what something looks like, but 'this is made of iron' helps to explain why the subject has certain properties. Natural kind terms have this role explicitly when embedded in 'because' clauses. For example, 'because it is made of aluminium' typically explains why the subject is light yet solid, durable, etc. This is not true of ordinary names. An introduction like 'this is Joe' only gives us a label, not something that will explain why the person is what he is. Even later, when we got to know the person, a sentence like 'because Joe did it' explains only in view of contingent associations of properties to an individual, not anything that follows from the introduction and use of the name.

5. *Developmental facts.* We learn the use of proper names like 'John' and 'Mary' and the use of indexicals like 'this' and 'that' in one jump. But we learn the meanings of natural kind

terms, as well as the meaning of many other types of expressions step by semantic step. For example, children learn to use the expression 'father' for someone with certain functional characteristics, and learn only later what a father is in biological terms. The same applies to a word like 'sun'. We learn first those layers of meaning that pertain to some of the causal properties of this celestial body, and we find out only later what it is in terms of our overall conceptions of planets and solar systems. This suggests that the use of such a term should be explained by positing layers of intension, and that accounts of non-criterial reference fixing will not be of much use in accounting for these facts.

From this brief enumeration of some of the relevant facts pertaining to semantics we see that while Putnam's proposal seems to account for facts 1, 2, and 3, it has difficulties with facts 4 and 5. The intensional model, on the other hand, seems either to capture 4 and 5, or at least provides some of the basic tools for dealing with these phenomena. It seems, then, that the two proposals capture different facts. The proposal to be presented in the concluding chapter is designed to account for all five of these facts.

In order to explain the relationship between lay and scientific uses Putnam introduces the doctrine of 'division of linguistic labour' according to which the layperson uses natural kind terms as rigid designators without intensions, and leaves to the scientist the fixing of the boundaries of the referents of these terms.

The contrast between lay and scientific use should be placed in a wider context. First one might explore the relation between it and the uses that link children's talk with that of adults. Children leave many referential matters for adults to fill in. There are also cases, such as that of the wine taster or the chicken-sexer, in which not the determination of criteria but simply the ability to identify and pick out a specimen is left by the layperson to the expert. In these cases observational ability rather than theoretical knowledge separates the expert from the layperson, and yet we communicate successfully.

The division of labour applies also diachronically. There are terms whose exact reference the scientist of today leaves up to the scientist of tomorrow. These observations lead one to the view that beneath Putnam's dichotomy we can find a number of important distinctions. These do not coincide, and it is arbitrary to single out any one of them as a key fact to be explained by semantics. Some of these distinctions are: the essential and accidental, the theory-laden and non-theory-laden, the unobservable and observable, and the lay and scientific uses. Some items like colours wear their essences on their sleeves, that is to say, the essence can be specified in terms of observables. There are also unobservable essences like that of reading; an activity that includes the underlying state of understanding, but whose name is not a theory-laden term. Still other words like 'health' or 'illness' are defined by the layperson primarily in functional terms, and detailed scientific definitions do not affect this use.

These cases show also once more that understanding should not be identified with the ability to identify members of the extension of a term, as the verificationists would have us believe. The competent speaker understands the word 'disease', but it usually takes a medical expert to be able to pick out elements of the range of application. Similar considerations hold for a word like 'money'. Competent speakers understand the word, but it takes local non-linguistic information to be able to pick out in various countries the entities to which the word applies.

Let us consider further differences between natural kind terms and proper names. One of these is that natural kind terms can form parts of quantified phrases, as in 'he drank some water', or 'we ate many oranges', but quantified phrases cannot have in the corresponding places proper names. We cannot say 'many of Mary', or 'we met some of Smith'. Quantified phrases including natural kind terms require that the natural kind terms they contain should be linked to principles of individuation and persistence. There are no such demands on proper names. One might argue that they should be linked to sortals with principles of individuation, but that is very different from a demand that the entity to which the word applies should have some of its internal structure represented in the semantics. We may need to know that 'Susan' is a name for a human, but in the case of 'gold', it is not enough to know that it is a metal; one must know whether it is a count or mass term, and whether quantitative assessment can be applied to it or its parts directly. Principles of individuation and persistence, however, are parts of intensions. Hence a consideration suggesting that natural kind terms have intensions after all. The explanatory power and the principle of individua-

114

tion both suggest that we should posit something like intensions for natural kind terms. Furthermore, these intensions, needed for understanding and the referential apparatus, must be conceptually linked. We cannot find satisfactory a conception of mental representation that leaves these representations divorced from our referential intentions. For this would involve not only referring to that which we do not understand, but also to the positing of situations in which our psychological right hand, forming referential intentions, would not know what our psychological left hand, forming intensional modes of representation, was doing.

These considerations suggest that perhaps one could look into lexical theories that do link language, mind, and reality, that is, deal both with meaning in the sense of what determines reference and meaning in the sense of what makes understanding possible. But such a theory would have to be different from the standard intensional model that we sketched in this section. In the section on proposals an attempt to construct such a theory will be made.

Distinctive Features of Natural Languages

The meaning of 'odd' as applied to numbers is 'not divisible by two'. This specification requires no reference to time, place, context of the speaker, or any other such non-qualitative feature. Hence we can regard words like this as constituting the qualitative semantic core of a language. Since Frege deals primarily with this part of language, we shall call it the Fregean Core. In contrast, a word like 'now' has in its meaning both a qualitative specification – in this case, roughly, 'time of utterance or other contextually defined point' and a procedure for repeated re-application considering the time of utterance and communicational situation. We can label words with this kind of meaning structure as parts of the indexical layer. Indexicality may not be marked explicitly in a language in all instances. Putnam (1955) suggested that the meanings of natural kind terms contain hidden indexicality. In our earlier review of 'naturalism' it was suggested that according to that conception there should be an indexical element of the meaning of every expression. This contrast raises important questions: How large is the Fregean Core in a natural

115

language? How essential is it for a natural language to have a Fregean Core, or to have an indexical core? Will answers to these questions affect different ways of viewing what is allegedly distinctive about the semantics of natural languages? To enable the reader to begin to form approaches to these questions, I shall contrast here two fundamentally different conceptions of what is distinctive about natural languages.

Let us look first at what will be labelled the 'Fregean View'. According to this view the most fundamental fact about natural languages is that they can encode thoughts like those of Euclid, Plato, or Newton, and that these can be transmitted from generation to generation, without knowing who said it, where, when, and why. These sentences encoding the appropriate thoughts will have as their descriptive constituents members of the Fregean Core. Thus according to this view our main task is to account for the semantics of the Fregean Core, and then explain all else as derivative from this. Thus all else will contain a qualitative, Fregean, specification and then various rules for relativizing this to times, speakers, etc. The parameters of the relativization are left in the semantics as primitives. Their analysis is left to other disciplines such as sociology and psychology. Thus according to this view, in the semantics of natural languages there is a separable component that corresponds to the understanding of purely qualitative notions. This is presupposed in the analysis of other parts; hence in that sense it is more fundamental than the other parts. Within this framework we represent most of the links between language and spatio-temporal reality as indirect, mediated by senses or intensions. This means that the link between language and action is also indirect. This need not be a disadvantage. One would have to view in detail complete theories and see if the Fregean, 'two-layer' approach is in fact less elegant, insightful, etc. than the more pragmatically oriented alternatives. It might be a real mistake to think of paradigmatic language use as involving speaker, hearer, and objects for reference that are visible to both. According to the alternative, 'Fregean' conception, communications systems evolved into languages having the basic structures of human natural languages only after our ancestors got into tall grass so that they could not see each other, and 'language had to speak for itself'.

116

The alternative conception starts at the other end of the spectrum, and takes direct person-to-person communication between speakers who are visually in contact with each other as the basic fact that semantics should explain, and all else within this conception becomes derivative. The basic task is to construct a formalism for expressing the principles of the use of language in person-to-person communication, and other uses are to be explained by systematically relaxing the conditions on the intended audience in terms of time, place, and causal contact with the speaker. Thus, for example, the US Constitution could be viewed as somewhere between extreme examples like 'Eat this!' and '2+2=4'. The Constitution has authors but their exact specification is not pertinent. There is an intended audience, but its nature is not fully specified. Roughly, it is the class of all American citizens for some, unspecified, time to come. Within this conception we deal with the mathematical sentence quoted by relaxing the speaker–hearer specifications even more. We can regard this as a kind of 'limiting case' of communication, with constraints on speaker and audience quite indeterminate. Within such a conception of language the notions of the semantic intentions of speakers, and available modes of ostensions play more important roles than within the Fregean model. This conception represents the relation between language and action in a more direct way, with demonstratives like 'this' picking out contextually objects of desire or objects to be manipulated. Thought, based often on only impartial information, is attached to these semantic 'pegs'. (For an interesting attempt along these lines, see Barwise and Perry, 1983.)

There is still another way in which one can contrast these two views about natural language. The 'Fregean' conception stresses what is purported to be unique about natural human languages, while the other conception stresses the evolutionary continuity with other communication systems. Thus in assessing the rivals, a key factor should be the exploration of whether the jump from the indexically 'infested' parts of a language to the Fregean Core is indeed a 'quantum jump', or should be viewed as a series of moves along a continuum, or a scale admitting merely matters of degree.

There are many theories of indexicals available. The following are some of the questions we should raise about these. First, should we treat most indexicals as rigid designators without attached intensions, or should we analyse these expressions in an extended Fregean way? (For such an attempt, see Peacocke, 1983.) Second, are we to interpret phrases like 'this man', or 'that manuscript' always as referring to objects as wholes, or at times as referring only to what we call stages of entities? For example, one could interpret a sentence like 'The man in front of me is the person I met at the bar yesterday' as 'The person-stage I am confronted with is a stage of the same man as that whose stage I was confronted with yesterday at the bar.' Within such a theory every stage is necessarily a stage of the object to which it in fact belongs, but the objects in question could have been composed of different stages. Finally, we need to explore different ways of representing the indexical meanings. Let us suppose that according to some theory there is no Fregean Core. How should this be reflected in our representations? Currently, indexicals are represented as 'the entities having property F relative to parameters x, y, z, of indexical assessment', where these parameters can be time, place, speaker, cultural context, etc. But this mode of representation suggests that there is a qualitative core which we relativize. Why should there not be lexical items which have such qualitative cores as meaning without the relativizations? Alternatively, if there is no Fregean Core, maybe there is a way of representing indexical meanings in which qualitative core is not presupposed.

We shall turn now to different ways of viewing the grammars of natural languages, and see to what extent the differences there have analogues to the distinctions we have drawn so far.

We had occasion to refer to the attitudes of Russell and Wittgenstein towards language in their respective metaphysical quests. Since they were interested in a 'real' structure of language on the basis of which ontological conclusion can be drawn, the ordinary syntax of natural languages seemed to them only a hindrance; something to get away from as one uncovered logically or ontologically important structures. The positivist school adopted by and large a similar attitude, since they were interested in reconstructing natural languages or a least parts of these so as to forge a framework suitable for the clear and transparent presentation of scientific theories. For Russell the main 'culprits' of ordinary grammar were the treatments of definite descriptions like 'the first man on the moon', and quantified phrases like 'all humans'. Both of these appeared as distinct units in ordinary syntactic analysis, while they were broken up and integrated in a variety of ways into the syntax of the sentences in which they were embedded on the Russellian analysis.

A different view emerged in the writings of Richard Montague. He maintained that the syntax of a language like English could be reconstructed to be formally similar to the grammars of what Tarski called formal languages. That is to say, within such treatments the syntactic structure mirrors the logical and semantic structures (Montague, 1974). Thus the significance of this work is not merely the technical achievement of assigning appropriate semantic interpretations to traditional syntactic categories – including treating 'all humans' as an integrated noun phrase – but the philosophically significant claim that the grammatical rules of a natural language can be seen as serving primarily semantic interests and being motivated by these. Within such a conception 'syntax is but a slave of semantics'. We posit syntactic rules wherever the semantics demands these.

The third view arose out of Chomsky's early work (Chomsky, 1957). It views the syntactic component of linguistic structure as a conceptually independent element, and demands empirical syntactic evidence for the positing of rules of grammar. Apart from empirical questions strictly within the domain of linguistics, there are philosophical considerations why one should support the view that the grammar of a natural language has a 'life of its own'. For the syntax of a natural language is shaped by a number of factors other than semantic convenience. There is the need of the phonological component, biological human constraints, and constraints that emerge from the fact that one of the uses of natural languages is person-to-person communication, with the need to condense rapidly the processing of much information. One of the differences between the view of Montague and the third view is that Montague was interested in articulating what grammars in general might have in common, whereas those working in Chomsky's tradition are interested in delineating what might be distinctive about the grammar of human natural languages (Kasher, 1975).

In view of these contrasts it is appropriate for us to review arguments purporting to show that natural languages are not formal languages in Tarski's sense. For the purposes of this review we shall regard as a natural language that which can be learned by a human or cognitively sufficiently human-like creature or machine as his or her first language under normal circumstances. This characterization contains some vague terms like 'normal circumstances' and 'sufficiently human-like', but at least it serves so as to allow questions like: 'Is esperanto a natural language?' or 'Could one invent a computer language that is a natural language?' as sensible empirical questions.

The first argument supporting the thesis that natural languages are not formal languages concerns the semantic paradoxes. Starting with the intuitive version of the well known liar's paradox, and building this into the appropriate formalism, Tarski has shown that formal languages can contain this paradox, and that the way out is to construct a hierarchy of languages such that the semantic properties of one of these languages are described by the language above it in the hierarchy. But natural languages do not seem to contain such hierarchies of languages. Thus anyone thinking of a natural language as a formal language has to show how he can avoid the semantic paradoxes. There may be other ways of doing this besides positing hierarchies of languages (e.g. Kripke, 1975).

Another argument concerns proper names (Black, 1948). A formal language must have all of its meaning-bearing elements specified, and interpretations for these given. This includes the class of individual constants, the analogues to what are proper names in a natural language. Thus if English is to be a formal language, all of the proper names that belong to it must be listed with their interpretation. But it is not true that knowledge of English requires knowing the referents of all of the names, such as those in the New York telephone book. There may be various replies to this argument. One of these is not to treat proper names of the ordinary kind as belonging semantically to a natural language like English, but only syntactically. On this view English is like a formal language except that it leaves syntactic 'slots' for proper names, to be filled in locally and contextually by subsets of the linguistic community.

A philosophically more substantial objection points out that formal languages were devised in order to encode theories of, e.g., mathematics or physics within them. But a natural language does not have a detailed theory of the world encoded in it. Rather, it is that elastic vehicle of communication that allows people with very different views about the world to communicate with each other. It allows us to retain the same language while changing our theories about the world. A possible reply to this is to insist that the merely competent use of a natural language does commit us to a rather vague and sketchy theory, but still a view, about the world. We saw, however, that what we called basic common sense is not a theory about reality, but only a few conceptual links concerning a few of its features.

A more elaborate argument starts with the observation that the natural languages in currency are historical and biological phenomena. As such, some of their features, including some of the semantic ones, should be determined by functional needs of the human organism, and not solely by the formal considerations that lead Tarski to his kind of semantics. Let us consider the following empirical claims.

1. A natural language is a spoken language. One of its main roles is for it to be used in person-to-person communication. (This is not incompatible with the Fregean view, or the claim that there is a Fregean Core.)
2. A natural language is a biological phenomenon. Its structure is constrained by biological mechanisms such as our acquisition 'device'.
3. A natural language is a historical phenomenon. Its structure must facilitate change and development.

Though these are obvious empirical claims, their acceptance would support strongly the claim that natural languages are not formal languages. 1 and 3 together suggest that complete explicitness of the semantics – a key feature of a formal language – would not be a virtue in a natural language. A formal language is not an historical process. It cannot postpone difficult questions for the future. Its semantics must legislate over all possible cases for all times. In a natural language this would be both impractical and not feasible. For example, we are in no position to determine for all future technological developments and changes what should count for all times as a vehicle, or as a computer. We simply cannot envisage what possibilities technology may or may not open up.

Consideration of 1 also suggests that too much explicitness would be dysfunctional in a natural language. Typical person-to-person communication takes place in environments in which there are many non-linguistic clues for filling in details of reference and meaning, and a certain background of shared information can be presumed. 1 and 2 suggest also that given the limitations on human capacities for attention and perceptual input, brevity and perceptual conspicuity should character-ize both the syntax and the semantics of a natural language. These considerations, however, are irrelevant for formal languages.

One way in which semantics is 'filled out' in context is provided by the interaction between scope and stress in negation. For example, 'Mary did not walk into the house' admits of three different interpretations depending on whether we stress 'Mary', or 'walk', or 'the house' (Gabbay and Moravcsik, 1982). Another example of contextual determination of the semantics is the interpretation of tensed sentences in English. In tense logics the past indicates merely some time prior to the production of the utterance. In a language like English the context provides more information. For example 'he used to live there' does not mean just any time prior to the utterance, and 'I will make a payment' does not leave the future completely open, but is meant to apply to an acceptable part of this.

Interactions between humans also cut down on explicitness. For example, for 'give me the screwdriver' as uttered by a man working on a car to his helper, the nature of the relative positions of the two workers determines which screwdriver is being referred to.

These facts suggest that in natural languages meanings are only partially determined, and much of the determination of the referential force is left to non-linguistic context. This suggests the following principle: in the semantics of natural languages the principle of least effort holds. In this respect, then, these languages are quite different from formal languages.

For a natural language the maxims are: do not do today what you can do, on the basis of better information, tomorrow, and do not do by rules what typical non-linguistic context can do for you.

These are functional arguments. The following argument suggests that, unlike in formal languages, in natural languages the syntax will not mirror semantic considerations.

Only on a certain level of generality do functional explanations have any force in biology. They may work on a level exemplified by 'why do we have fingers?' but surely not on the level of 'why five instead of four or six fingers?' In fine detail anatomical explanations are autonomous in the following sense. Structural accounts cannot be replaced by functional accounts, nor are the latter always available to correlate with the former ones. Furthermore, once we reach a certain level of specificity, all of the explanatory power rests in the structural accounts. Once we have specified the functional needs that a biological mechanism serves, we still need to explain exactly how it serves these needs, and at that level further functional explanations are neither needed nor expected.

Applying all of this to semantics and syntax, we can suggest the following. There will be certain features of syntax that are free from the demands of the semantics and of functional needs. In this sense they have a life of their own. There will be also features of the semantics of natural languages that will service neither the requirements of truth and satisfaction, nor of functional requirements. Thus these too have a life of their own.

All of these considerations suggest that grave conceptual obstacles lie in the path of those who would assimilate natural language to formal languages.

There is still another way in which natural languages are different from the formal languages constructed by logicians and philosophers. This is their interaction with non-linguistic context. We shall now review various considerations suggesting that the sentence is not always the basic unit of semantic interpretation, and that in many cases non-linguistic factors enter into language understanding. This has been suggested by some of the more general considerations adduced above, but we shall now look at more specific evidence.

First, let us consider the kind of evidence that indicates the need to consider larger segments of discourse on some occasions before we assign meaning to one of the sentential components. The following is an excerpt from a conversation involving a West Coast philosopher. 'There is no such thing as a mouse,' he said.

In most contexts this would raise eyebrows. We need not wait for the verdicts of experts to know that these little furry creatures are very much with us, and thus the evidence against the sentence quoted is overwhelming. The philosopher, however, went on; and I shall quote the relevant part of the discourse in its entirety. 'There is no such thing as a mouse. If you have seen a mouse, that means you have got mice.' Once we see the whole discourse, the first sentence makes perfectly good sense. If we add the information that this discourse was part of a conversation involving people who had just moved into recently purchased houses, the interpretation is easy and unambiguous. Worry about rodents is one of the things on the mind of someone who moves into a house in the country. In this case it would be quite useless to look at the first sentence in isolation, try to determine its meaning on that basis, and then just add it to the conversation. Other examples of this sort can easily be produced.

Another problem confronting those who want to provide a semantics for natural languages without looking at extra-linguistic context is that of the semantic categories. Carnap is said to have thought that the sentence 'this stone is thinking about Vienna' is not necessarily false but meaningless. For, one could argue, it is ruled out by the very specifications of the meanings of the constituents. Something in the semantic category of a stone could not be the subject of a statement ascribing or denying thought to something. We cited the distinction about terms with individuation and those without as a legitimate purely semantic distinction. At the other end of the spectrum one could cite a piece of advice given to pet owners, 'Don't use that laxative which did wonders for old Aunt Jenny on your cat.' This is clearly empirical and not linguistic advice. If, miraculously, the laxative that brightened up Aunt Jenny's days turned out also to bring relief to your kitty, medical and veterinarian advice might have to be rewritten, but not the rules of English.

So there are biological categories as our last example shows, and purely conceptual ones such as those dealing with individuation and persistence. In between we seem to have a continuum, and increasing extra-linguistic information can change our conceptions of what should or should not be ascribed to the meaning structure.

Still another type of case showing the need for contextual

interpretation is exemplified by an advertisement that appeared in the *Mariposa News*, the newspaper for a small community in the foothills of the Sierras in California. It read: '1982 Fiat. In good condition. Needs engine.' For some of us – admittedly not car aficionados – this ad seems rather bizarre. Even without excessive metaphysical and ontological commitments one might hold the view that having an engine is an essential prerequisite for a well-functioning, or even simply a functioning, car. If, however, one takes the pragmatic context into consideration, the discourse makes sense. The advertisement appeared in the 'Cars for Sale' section of a small town newspaper, the advertiser pays by words printed, money in the community is rather scarce, etc. In short, brevity is at a high premium. And indeed, taking all of this into consideration, one could argue that the Fiat in question might be a not too disastrous buy for the amateur mechanic who likes to put engines together from parts found in scrapyards.

At other times, knowing about the outlook and mannerisms of a person or persons in certain walks of life seems essential in order to interpret the intended communication. A classic case of this is the message sent home by a British naval officer to his family in one of Arthur Ransome's books, *Swallows and Amazons*, as the reply to a request to allow his children to go out for a week or two, without adult supervision, on a boat to an island, and camp there. The telegram read: 'Better drown than duffers, if not duffers, won't drown.' The family surmised, correctly, that this was meant as an affirmative. One could not possibly come to this conclusion if one tried to interpret the message on the basis of starting with the constituents of the sentence and then constructing a proposition expressed by the whole. And yet, once the pragmatic context is filled in, every reader of the book will find the message self-explanatory.

This is just a small sample of the kind of phenomena that need to be dealt with by a component of language interpretation – call it discourse analysis or pragmatics – that is outside of the semantics we considered so far. Furthermore, there is good evidence for treating this as a separate component. Some people are good at understanding English in the narrower, semantic sense but less good at getting the pragmatics. With others, it is the other way around. Thus a full study of language understanding and the structure of natural languages requires the treatment of this component as well (Kasher, 1976, 1977).

This survey of problems shows the inherent difficulties in constructing anything that could reasonably be called a full theory of natural languages. We saw that there are crucial decisions to be made about the appropriate framework for compositional and non-compositional semantics, their resemblance to formal language structure, their significance for studies of cognition, and the role of grammar in all of this. Hopefully, some day one can add also a philosophical treatment of phonology, and the intriguing epistemological questions that it raises (Halle, 1978).

In view of the vastness of a complete project, it should not be surprising that among the proposals in this book the ones on language will be limited to lexical semantics. But the proposal in question will deal, at least within that restricted context, with questions covering relation of language to reality as well as language to mind, and to non-linguistic context.

In conclusion let us recall the Aristotelian triangle with which we started this survey of problems. We saw there a few basic notions: terms having extensions, language being understood, and the mind conceptualizing reality. The work surveyed in this chapter shows that we have today a more detailed understanding of these phenomena. But the notions resist definition in terms of something else. They remain basic, indefinable terms for us as well. Chomsky once suggested that some of our problems are problems in a genuine sense; i.e. admitting, in principle, of solution, while others could be regarded as mysteries in the sense that for reasons not known to us now, they may be permanently beyond the pale of human understanding. The basic elements of the Aristotelian triangle seem to be good candidates for this lofty status.

PART II PROPOSALS

CHAPTER IV

Ontology

In the survey of ontology in Part I of this book we covered a number of distinctions that are needed as the background for our study of thought and language. These were the contrasts between universals and particulars, among particulars between events and material objects, and the opposition between realists and sceptics concerning the modalities: an opposition that also yields different views on persistence and individuation. We considered the advantages and disadvantages of construing one or the other of these contrasting pairs as ontologically fundamental. It is time now to lay out our own proposal. The following claims will be supported. First, both universals and particulars are equally fundamental ontological categories, and neither is clearer in ontologically relevant ways than the other. Second, we can draw a non-circular distinction between universals and particulars, but only if we rely in our analysis on the modalities. Thus one should be as much of a realist about the modalities as one is about universals. Third, one should be a realist about principles of individuation even if the ones we use at any given time are only approximations of the ones in fact governing reality. Furthermore, principles of individuation apply to both particulars and universals only kind by kind. There are no all-inclusive general principles of this sort for either category. Finally, events are as fundamental an ontological category as that of material objects, and principles of individuation apply to both events and material objects only kind by kind, thus mirroring the situation obtaining for the categories of universal and particular.

The Mystery of Universals and the Two Circles

Perhaps even if we did not live in an age in which the most visible successes have been technological and hence focused on spatio-temporal entities, we would have more of a feeling of immediacy in connection with particulars than in our contacts with universals. After all, we humans are particulars. Our actions and interactions seem to involve primarily items from that category. Our contact with these entities is at least partly empirical, while no such contact is possible with universals. Nevertheless, in ontology, as in any other serious theory, we should overcome these superficial first impressions and attempt to view matters in a more detached way.

As a result of the influence of powerful writers like Quine, universals had a 'bad press' in the Anglo-American philosophy of the past three decades. The campaign reached its climax in the 1960s, and the effects are still lingering on. One way to counteract this is to bear down on the theoretical problems linked to the nature of particulars.

To regard particularity as problematic is not to deny that from a common-sense point of view, spatio-temporally scattered 'stuff', with some qualitative differences, is given. But, as we saw in our survey, the thesis that particulars are an ontologically fundamental and intelligible category implies much more than that. For we saw that the world of particulars cannot be built up solely from spatio-temporal scatter and qualitative difference. Being scattered in space is in some cases not enough to account for individuation and in some cases it is even an obstacle. Furthermore, qualitative difference permeates all particulars, at times separating and at other times uniting them. Particulars persist through time, keeping as well as losing some properties, keeping as well as losing some parts. Once we come to see these as basic facts about particulars, Wang's trenchant criticisms of this category, surveyed in Part I, can be fully appreciated.

The notion of a part seems clear in some contexts, especially practical ones. We know what the parts of engines, cars, furniture, trees, and animals are. But once we project this notion globally, asking about the parts of particulars as such, our intuitions founder. What are parts of particulars? 'Give me a more limited context, and I'll tell you' our common sense seems to whisper. The point of raising the theoretical difficulties is not to claim that we don't know what trees, mountains, or celestial bodies are, but that their particularity is problematic. Which is not to say, of course, that we think particular trees to be universals.

We mentioned the projects of semantic reductionism. To show once more why these, even if successful, are not decisive for ontology, let us imagine that an extreme realist reduction is possible that leaves in our ontology no particulars. Humans are treated as constituents of complex properties and the same is done with other particulars. I have no argument to show that this is not possible. But it seems clear that even if this programme appeared well executed, in a leading philosophic journal, it would not convince many of us that we are not in some sense particulars.

We shall now place worries about universals and particulars into proper perspective by considering an argument by Quine designed to cast doubt on the legitimacy of universals (Quine, 1953b). Quine's argument is couched in terms employed by semantics, or the theory of meaning and denotation. Herewith a brief and informal sketch of the relevant notions, and their link to the ontological categories that we considered. A sentence like 'some rabbits are brown' is reasonably taken to be about rabbits. It says nothing interesting about the nature of the universals of being a rabbit and being brown, except that the two are compatible and in fact have common instances. The latter fact could not be gleaned from a mere understanding of the descriptive terms contained in the sentence. On the other hand, if we understand the terms 'rabbit' and 'animal', then the sentence 'all rabbits are animals' should provide no new information, and does not say anything about the world that the mere understanding of the sentence has not provided already. The following framework of a semantic theory seems to account for these facts (e.g. Carnap, 1956).

Predicates like 'is a rabbit', 'is brown' have as their meaning conditions of their application. These are called within semantics intensions. They contrast with the ranges to which the predicates can be truly applied, called extensions. We can think of intensions in a number of ways, e.g. as idealized instructions, or simply as properties that members of the extension must have in order to qualify. In any case, the intensions are universals of some kind. If we think of that part of language that describes spatio-temporal reality only, then we can construe the members of the extensions as particulars. We shall have occasion to discuss intensions, and the whole theory within which they play a key role, later in the third part of our proposals. For our task at hand, all we need to note is that in invoking intensions to explain meaningfulness, this theory adopts a realist stand towards universals. According to the theory a sentence like 'all rabbits are animals' expresses a necessary truth that rests solely on the relation of meaning inclusion between the intensions of the two predicates. A sentence like 'some rabbits are brown' expresses a contingent relation between the extensions of the two predicates. It says something that happens to be true, but could have been otherwise even if we keep the intensions of the two predicates constant.

Quine attacks this framework, and thus also universals, by claiming that he does not find the notion of intension clear. Furthermore, he charges that intension together with the notions that within semantic theory are invoked to explain it, form a circle. Each member of the circle can be explained only in terms of the other members of the circle. We shall label this the Intensional Circle. It can be illustrated in the following way.

Let us consider the sentence: 'Writing is an activity.' This sentence is regarded by competent speakers of English as expressing a necessary truth. It could happen that if all children start using computers from a very early age, then there will be no more writing done. But as long as people do write, an activity is performed. That writing is an activity is not a contingent matter; it has to be that way, it could not be otherwise. But these remarks so far are only on the intuitive level. How do we know that the sentence expresses a necessary truth, and what facts make the proposition expressed necessary? The notion of necessity has been controversial among philosophers, but these controversies do not affect this argument. Quine is arguing against those who believe that there are no informative necessary truths; all such truths simply spell out what mere understanding should have given us already. This understanding is given by knowing logic and the semantics of the language we speak. We would have to complicate this reconstruction of the argument in order to cover synthetic, informative necessary truths, but these ramifications do not affect Quine's main claim.

According to the proposal at hand, we have the rules of language and logic on the one hand, and facts in the world on the other – facts that could have been otherwise. Information about these facts is synthetic, while the information following from what is already contained in the rules of logic and semantics is analytic. Thus we can account for the necessity of the content of the sentence by showing that it is analytic. Analyticity explains necessity.

But what makes the sentence analytic, and in virtue of what is it true analytically? It does not say anything informative about the world that it describes. It is true either in virtue of the rules of logic or those of the semantics of the language. In this case, we have a truth in virtue of semantics, i.e. of the meanings of the constituents of the sentence. The meaning of 'writing' includes the meaning of 'activity'. This relation determines the truth of the sentence, and hence renders it analytic. Thus apart from truths of logic such as 'if all A's are B's, then all A's are B's', analyticity depends on relations between meanings.

Meanings, as we saw, are analysed in terms of intensions. Two expressions can have completely different intensions, or one can be included in the other, or the two can be identical. The rules of meanings for items in a language are explicated in terms of these relations between intensions. Intensions, which constitute a subclass of universals, are the ontological basis of the theory. In cases of sentences in which the intensions of the predicate expressions stand in relations of identity or inclusion, what the sentences express is analytic. So we explain analyticity in terms of logical truth – a detailed discussion of which is omitted here since it does not bear directly on our project – and sameness of intensions and its consequences. But what does it mean to say that two predicates stand for the same intensions? What are criteria for this? How do we individuate intensions?

Sameness of intensions is a technical term in semantics. Those favouring such a theory use our ordinary notion of synonymy in attempting to explicate the technical notion. Let us consider a sentence like 'all altruistic nurses are unselfish nurses'. Assuming that 'unselfish' is synonymous with 'altruistic', the sentence in question is trivially true since its truth rests on a relation of synonymy in our language. Thus we explain the rules for intensions in terms of the notion of synonymy.

But how do we know that a relation between two predicates is that of synonymy, and in virtue of what facts is this true? It has been claimed that a competent user of a language has intuitions about synonymy relations in his or her language. It is also claimed that competent speakers of languages converge in their judgements about synonymy. Thus perhaps we have arrived at a way of grounding the whole family of concepts after all.

There are, however, no behavioural or other observable ways of determining whether a speaker is in fact expressing intuitions of synonymy. Furthermore, apart from what one may think of behaviourist or introspectionist psychologies, it is a plain fact that our introspective judgements as to whether two terms in our use are synonymous are subject to error.

We can link, however, our intuitions about synonymy to our intuitions about necessity. A sentence expressing synonymy relations expresses something that, given the rules of the language, cannot be otherwise. Thus judgements of synonymy are a species of the judgements of necessity. Non-contingent facts, assuming the rules of the language, determine the truths of these sentences. This account seems clear enough. The only problem we face now is that we have come back to necessity, the very notion whose explication started us on this sojourn. We arrive back at full circle. From necessity to analyticity, to intensional relations, to synonymy, to necessity. This is the Intensional Circle.

Our reply to Quine is not to attempt to break out of this circle. I do not know of a way of doing that. On the other hand, one can point out that the notions Quine favours, the extensional notions, also form a circle, in the same way in which the intensional terms do. It is not easier to break out of one circle rather than the other. We said earlier that both universals and particulars seem to have some problems of individuation. Now we claim that they are also in the same boat when it comes to definability. Parity rules supreme. This favours the realist who argues for both particulars and universals having equally fundamental and legitimate ontological status.

Let us trace the extensional circle. We started the intensional circle with necessity, thus we shall start the extensional circle with contingency. We must not confuse the question of what gives a proposition the status of contingency with the epistemological question of how do we verify or disconfirm most of these propositions. Thus we cannot use the concept of empirical knowledge to explain contingency. There may be necessary propositions that are also known empirically, and nothing in the concept of contingency rules out the possibility that some of these propositions are not known empirically. A sentence or proposition is contingent because it describes a state of affairs that could have been otherwise. As in the case of necessity, here too, we should supplement this characterization by an answer to the question: In virtue of what is a given proposition contingent? A general reply is that a truth is made contingent by a configuration of elements of reality that need not have been related in that way. The typical case is the kind of sentence whose predicates have as their extensions ranges of particulars. Thus 'some rabbits are brown' expresses something contingent because of the relation between the extensions of 'is a rabbit' and 'brown'. Thus we can explicate within semantic theory the notion of contingency in terms of certain relations between extensions. The relevant relations will hold and at the same time the correlated intentions do not exhibit identity or inclusion. By 'contingency' we mean simply 'mere truth', and not the notion of contingency that contrasts with necessity within treatments of modalities.

But how are we to explain extensions? As was pointed out above, the best way is to illustrate this notion with reference to first-order languages in which the predicates range over particulars. Thus extensions are collections of particulars related to language via the relations of reference and range of application. For example 'tigers no longer live in Israel' is contingently true because it expresses a certain relation between those particulars that are tigers and those that live in Israel; a relation that happens to be true and does not follow simply from the rules of our language.

In passing, one should note that basically the same explanation can be given even if one considers languages in which some of the extensions contain also non-particulars and contingent truths are expressed concerning universals. Since we are considering the whole issue in the context of Quine's objections to universals, we need not tarry over these complications.

So we explain contingency in terms of relations between extensions, and we explain extensions by reference to particulars. But what is a particular? We did not confront the analogous question about universals head on. Instead, we turned to linguistic criteria for identity and distinctness of the linguistically relevant kinds of universals, namely intensions. Thus we posited sameness of intension and inclusion. The analogous notions in the case of particulars are those of co-extensiveness and co-referentiality. Under certain circumstances two predicates are co-extensive and two singular terms co-referential. We have co-extensionality when the particulars making up the extension of one predicate are the same as the particulars constituting the other extension. (This would need some qualification in a more precise statement. The particulars have to be related in relevantly similar ways, etc. But these matters do not affect the gist of the argument.) The same holds for co-referentiality. Thus 'Napoleon is the husband of Josephine' expresses a truth based on co-referentiality. This co-referentiality holds because the two phrases refer to the same particular. In this discussion we take particulars to be what adherents of physicalism or of Goodman's nominalism would accept. If we take classes as particulars, different arguments would have to be given.

But how are we to explain the co-referentiality of two singular terms or the co-extensiveness of two predicates? A judgement of co-referentiality or co-extensiveness is in this framework just a judgement that certain extensions happen to coincide. It need not have been that way, but the world being what it is, it turned out that way. The link between the expressions involved is contingent. It cannot be derived from the rules of our language. We arrive in this way back at the notion of contingency, thus completing the circle. To summarize: we moved from contingency to information about extensions, from that to the notions of extensions and particulars, and then back to the notion of contingency.

Someone might try to break out of this circle by claiming that the notions of a term being applied truly, or a singular term being used to refer to something are closer to the observational level than the analogous notions in the intensional circle. But the evidence for this is very dubious. Attempts to relate reference closely to behaviour have failed. (See Quine, 1960, who does not

In schematic form:

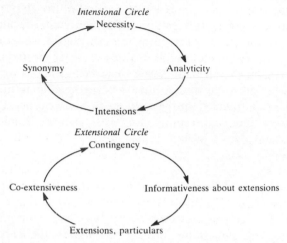

Intensional Circle

Necessity

Synonymy   Analyticity

Intensions

Extensional Circle

Contingency

Co-extensiveness   Informativeness about extensions

Extensions, particulars

interpret his data that way, but casts doubt on the traditional notion of reference.) Reference involves, as a notion relating speaker and object, attention, individuation conditions, application, and many other attributes whose realization cannot be tested by mere observation.

Each member of each circle can be explained only with reference to other members of the same circle, or by contrast to their 'opposite numbers' in the other circle, and the two circles can be explained only by contrast with each other. There is no 'neutral background' against which one could describe the two circles and compare them, in a non-committal way. As far as circularity of definition is concerned, the universals and their friends are no worse off than Quine's semantic friends.

One might try to break parity by invoking the notion of immunity to revision. Thus on Quine's view no sentence is immune to revision on the basis of new evidence. In reply, however, we should note that this is also true of the friends of the intensions. They too believe that no sentence is immune to revision. But they also believe that there are two kinds of revision; those based on discovering more contingencies, and those involving conceptual revision of logic or the intensional structures linked to the descriptive elements of the language. The difference between these 'unitarian' and 'pluralistic' views about revision cannot be explicated without going back to our two

137

circles. Thus this way does not help us out of the two circles.

We see, then, that when we look at the universal–particular distinction by relating it to traditional semantic theory, we get only circles and contrasts. Let us return to ontology as such. Is there a non-circular way of distinguishing universals from particulars, or is any attempt to tell them apart already presupposing what we want to explain? We saw in our survey of problems that merely concentrating on the primitive notions of 'part' and 'instance' will not do. In the next section we shall criticize some modern attempts and then present a solution to this problem.

Universals and Particulars: a Non-circular Differentiation?

In Part I we were introduced to intuitive ways of telling universals from particulars, and in the last section we saw a way of separating out two circles of notions, one of which rested on an ontology of universals and the other on the positing of particulars. We shall now look at attempts to arrive at a theoretical non-circular characterization of the two categories.

One approach, practised in antiquity, involves the use of spatio-temporal locatability. We can trace a tradition from Plato's *Timaeus* to the writings of Russell and Moore according to which particulars must have spatio-temporal location, while universals lack such locatability (Russell, 1912; Moore, 1923). This suggestion can be backed by certain intuitions. For there are true answers to such questions as: 'where is Mount Tahoma?' or 'where did Napoleon fight his last battle?' while questions like: 'where is triangularity?' or 'where is the property of being divisible by two?' are nonsensical. Similar examples can be adduced using temporal location. Such intuitive data are, however, not sufficient for clinching the case. For the distinction to have non-circular bite, we must show not only that we do not, but that we cannot make sense of assigning spatio-temporal location to universals. If we see that such assignments are possible, then one must show that the difference between the ways in which particulars and universals have such locations can be explained in other ways than by arguments that already presuppose the respective modes of being that lead us to form these intuitions.

With regards to spatiality, our options are represented by the following schema. One can take any of the following three positions concerning the spatial location of universals. *S1*. Universals do not have spatial location. Courage, triangularity, the property of being a motion, etc. have a mode of being that excludes spatial location. One can certainly construct a theory of universals with this feature included, but the question remains: other than initial intuitions, what justifies this move? We cannot justify it by claiming that universals cannot have spatial location assigned to them, because as *S2* and *S3* will show, such assignment is possible, i.e. is not incoherent. Furthermore, if we say that universals are outside of space, we still have to account for the fact that they interact with entities in space, namely with some of their instances. In reply, one might insist that the 'interaction' is utterly unlike the normal causal interaction between events or objects. In fact, it is the unique interaction of instantiation. But such a defence would presuppose the very notion we are trying to explain. The concept of instantiation no more explains universals than non-spatiality.

These considerations show that *S1*, as simply an axiom about universals, is arbitrary. It is one way of theorizing about universals once one has already understood the notion, but we are not forced to accept this as a starting point.

Let us now turn to another view, *S2*. Universals have as their spatial location the sum of the locations of all of their instances. Thus they have a scattered spatial location. But of course, the same is true of many particulars. In Goodman's nominalistic scheme 'red' is the name of a particular that is scattered over space and whose parts are all of the red surfaces. Furthermore, we can find such examples even on a common sense level. Germany between the two world wars was a discontinuous particular, not to mention present-day Indonesia, or Oxford University. So even if we do accept *S2*, it does not differentiate universals from particulars.

As our final try, let us consider *S3*. Universals have more than one spatial location at any given time, while a particular has only one such location. This view construes the location of any one instance as also the location of the universal as a whole. Russell earlier pointed out difficulties with this view (Russell, 1912). For example, we shall be forced to say that universal U' is located at time t' at spatial location s', and that U" is located at t' at s", and nevertheless U'=U". For example, unselfishness is located now at s', and altruism at s", but unselfishness = altruism. One might insist that we revise our standard views about the relation between location and diversity in order to accommodate this view, but the only conceivable ground for such a radical conceptual revision could be the effort to account for the *sui generis* mode of being of universals, which is the notion we are trying to explain. One could also revise the notion of recurrence so that it does not apply to universals; but then have we not blunted the distinction between the two in its original sense? These reflections show that none of these three ways gives us a non-circular way of differentiating universals from particulars.

What if we point to uninstantiated universals? These do not have spatial location, so why is this fact about some universals not sufficient to draw the distinction? In considering the claim that some universals have not instances we must distinguish between saying that some universals cannot be instantiated from saying that some are and always will be uninstantiated. There are no necessarily uninstantiable universals in the sense of logical necessity, for such entities would correspond to self-contradictory concepts. At most there can be contingently uninstantiatable universals. In singling out this subclass of universals we rely on modal properties. We posit universals that can, but possibly will never, be instantiated. But those who are sceptical about the conceptual legitimacy of universals will be sceptical about this kind of property as well. Later in our own proposal we shall invoke the modalities but in such a way as to apply both to particulars and to universals.

Let us now try to draw the distinction in terms of temporal location. There are two fairly obvious options. *T1*: Universals, unlike particulars, are not in time. *T2*: Universals, unlike particulars, are omni-temporal. If we opt for *T2* which says that universals like justice or triangularity exist at all times, then we have a view on location that does not distinguish universals from particulars. For various proposed particulars such as God, space, time, or matter could also be omni-temporal or eternal. Eternity may be excluded for particulars by a theory of physics or cosmology, but nothing in the notion of particularity excludes this possibility. So we fall back on *T1*. This seems intuitively more plausible in any case. But once we lay aside initial plausibility, we see the same problems surfacing as in connection with *S1* above. Once we understood the universal–particular distinction, we might opt for *T1* as a 'theorem' of our realist ontology, but as a starting point it is arbitrary.

We might try the analogues of the other two options surveyed in connection with space. *T3* would say that the temporal location of a universal is the sum of all such locations of its instances, while *T4* claims that a universal is 'all there' at any one location of one of its instances. It is easy to see that the difficulties of these proposals would parallel the ones surveyed in connection with spatial location. Hence we shall not pursue these options any further.

Thus we must conclude that in spite of its initial plausibility, the strategy of trying to give a non-circular, distinguishing account of universals and particulars in terms of either spatial or temporal location is not successful. One can point to differences, but understanding and appreciating these involve understanding the universal–particular distinction. Once we understand this distinction we can say that universals and particulars differ in their ways of relating to space and time.

We shall now turn to a very different strategy. It is based on a certain way of interpreting standard predicative structure. The upshot of this interpretation is supposed to be that there is an asymmetry between universals and particulars with respect to predication. The view admits of complex presentations, but its gist is that universals can be predicated of particulars, but particulars cannot be predicated of anything. (This is the view adopted by Strawson, 1974.) Thus, for example, the property of being a human can be predicated of Plato, but Plato – or, for that matter, the Pantheon – cannot be predicated of anything. This view has been implicitly adopted by many philosophers without any clear defence, and thus it is not surprising to find it challenged already in writings in the earlier part of this century. The most penetrating challenge was formulated by Ramsey (1931). Ramsey ascribes the asymmetrical ontological interpretation of the subject–predicate structure and its alleged fundamentality to intuitions having more to do with being impressed by technical achievements in logic than with genuine ontological insight. We can summarize Ramsey's key points in the following way. He points out the analogy between the subject–predicate form and the argument–function scheme, and says that taking the latter to be basic has proved to be very convenient for modern logic in its task of encoding mathematics. But surely from this alone no ontological conclusion follows. Secondly, Ramsey does not see why someone should view the subject–predicate form as the basis for locating some ontologically fundamental ground-level domain such as those of particulars. According to his view there is nothing intrinsic to the subject–predicate form that would prevent us from treating the alleged basic level, i.e. material objects, 'adjectivally' to use his felicitous phrase, and see these related to the events making up their life history in a way that is analogous to the relation between a universal and the particular of which it is predicated. (Ramsey rightly credits Whitehead with having worked out this view in some detail.) We can interpret properties such as wisdom as characterizing Socrates, and Socrates as characterizing a series of events, namely the Socrates-events, the ones constituting his life history. Unless we already assume the fundamentality of the distinction we want to explain, what would prevent us from extending the notion of 'predicate', or 'apply' to these levels as well?

For example, one can take the series of events that makes up the life history of a tree, and predicate 'treeish' of these. The fact that we do not find such constructions in a language like English may be only the reflection of the pragmatic interests of those who used this language throughout its history. In such a scheme properties are 'applied' – to use a neutral term – to material objects, and these in turn are applied to another species of particulars, namely events. Ramsey is not saying that the two questions are exactly the same. But he challenges a non-question-begging answer to the question of why one should regard either of these 'applications' metaphysically more fundamental than the other. And what reason could there be for saying that only one of these is really predication, except the intuition we are trying to explain, i.e. that universals have their own unique mode of being?

An alternative to the Whiteheadian scheme and still within the spirit of the Ramsey proposal is to construe material objects as constituted by stages. (For details see Gabbay and Moravcsik, 1973.) For example we can think of the planet earth as constituted by its spatio-temporal stages s', s'. . .s^n. Individuation and persistence conditions govern the kinds of stage sequences that can make up a planet, mountain, etc. Thus we have two relations: 'is an instance of' and 'is a stage of'. The two are ontologically different, but can we say in a non-question-begging way why both should not count as underlying the linguistic relation of predication?

To buttress this argument, let us look briefly at the ontology of stages. As we said, a particular like a mountain is interpreted as made up of a sequence of stages. Many changes pervade the sequence. Depending on the individuation conditions linked to the kind under which this particular falls, in this case that of a mountain, some changes help to maintain existence while others lead to destruction. Persistence conditions account for the changes from baby to adult to be life-sustaining conditions, while ruling out the possibility of adult humans turning into eagles.

This framework does not posit stages as the fundamental building blocks of the universe. There is a two-way dependency between stages and material objects composed of these. This can be illustrated by considering a person, Jones. A stage of Jones could not have been a stage of another human or other kind of entity. We do not have a world populated with independent human stages that can be coupled or uncoupled at will. Thus a stage of Jones is necessarily a stage of that entity. On the other hand, it is a contingent fact that this human, Jones, has this particular stage s' as one of his stages. Jones' life could have taken a different turn, and he might have had a partly different collection of stages. Still, Jones' existence depends on his having a sequence of stages determined by the relevant individuation and persistence conditions. Thus the stages of Jones depend on Jones, for they could not be stages of someone else, and Jones depends on having some stages, even though not necessarily the exact sequence that he happens to have.

The modal relations between Jones and his stages are the following. Any of his stages s' is necessarily a Jones-stage, but it is only contingently true that Jones has s' as one of his stages. This interesting asymmetry is not unique to this situation. On a reasonable interpretation the same holds for humans and their parents. Given what we know about genetics, etc., it is reasonable to say that Jones has necessarily X and Y as his parents, but it is a contingent truth that X and Y have offspring.

There are roles that the objects have rather than the stages, and again some roles are best ascribed to the stages and not the object. For example, the most natural way to interpret responsibility is to ascribe it to the object, i.e. the human, and not to stages. There are, however, other truths that are best interpreted as being about stages. For example, 'the baby I saw here fifteen years ago became that young woman whom I see over there' says that a human stage that was the baby I saw, and another stage that is the young woman I see now, are stages of the same human. Or to take another example, on confronting a human one might say 'this is not Wagner', meaning by that that the stage I am encountering is not a stage of Wagner.

To be sure, our basic scheme: 's' and s" belong to the same individual' can be expressed also in an alternative framework that does not posit stages, but only objects. It replaces the stages with complex temporal properties. Instead of saying that those two stages belong to Jones, it says that Jones has two temporal properties, i.e. of having been a baby at t' and being an adult banker at t". But even if such reductions can be carried out, we should ask if these are ontologically illuminating. (The reduction might run into trouble accounting for stages in connection with aspectual relations.) There are considerations in favour of the stage ontology, even if the reduction could be carried out. First, there is the analogy with spatial parts. One can spot the tail of an alligator behind a hut, the head of an alligator on the other side of the hut, and wonder whether tail and head belong to the same alligator. Shall we translate this into a framework in which instead of spatial parts we talk only about animals and their complex properties replacing the 'part talk'? What Russell called a 'robust sense of reality' should convince us that tails and heads are as much parts of the world of particulars as the alligator. It seems that the same should hold for babies, octogenarians, or lion cubs. Reference to such stages is referring to elements among particulars as much as when we refer simply to the human or the lion. An alligator is more than a mere sum of spatial parts, and humans are more than mere sums of stages. This creates no mystery. It is a part of the framework within which we understand processes of growth and development and decay. From seal pups to seals, caterpillars to butterflies, and enthusiastic recruits to fading old soldiers. Secondly, it seems that babies, octogenarians, etc. are what we are, not just something that we have as properties. Being tanned, or educated, or kind are properties that we have. In contrast, being a baby, being an adolescent, etc. describe what we are. Intuitions are not the last word in philosophy, but it is good to have a coherent theory that, by positing stages, can account for such intuitions without introducing anything mysterious.

The adoption of a framework like the one we sketched does not necessitate treating objects 'adjectivally', but at the same time we are not prevented from doing so. One can represent objects as functions ranging over stages, and properties as functions ranging over objects. This yields a function hierarchy. The mere form of predication does not force us to regard the distinction between object and property as a fundamental ontological cleavage. For example, we can interpret the relation between Socrates and his stages as a basic, primitive, 'constitutive' relation. But we can also interpret it as analogous to the object property relation, and say that the stage is 'Socratish'.

Ramsey warns us not to draw from convenience of logical notion ontological conclusions. We are not doing this here. Rather, we argued that several alternative notations are available, and none of these can be singled out as the only one that is ontologically revealing, without begging questions.

These reflections lead us to the view that within an ontology that does not include the modalities of necessity and contingency as ontologically fundamental, there is no non-circular way of distinguishing universals from particulars. At this point the ingredients of the basic propositions – atomic ones – posited by Russell and Wittgenstein respectively in the early periods, might come to mind (Russell, 1918; Wittgenstein, 1922). Do these entities help us to illuminate the dichotomy at issue? The ingredients of these propositions are by definition very different from both universals and particulars. As Ramsey said, we are in no position to say that the distinction between universals and particulars must be relevant to the analysis of atomic propositions.

In Part I we reviewed realism and scepticism with regards to the modalities. Here we shall sum up, briefly, the considerations favouring realism, and then take this stance. We saw that the modalities are at the very core of human reasoning. There is no practical reasoning without them, since practical reasoning involves planning, and this requires projections. There are no explanations without the modalities, since a genuine explanation must do more than relate what is the case. It must tell us what has to be the case, or at least would be the case even if circumstances were different from what they happen to be. While one cannot infer from this fact that the modalities have an ontologically fundamental role, we can follow the lines of reasoning advocated by C.S. Peirce (as discussed in Chomsky, 1980, p. 136), and say that the fact that the kinds of human reasoning involving the modalities have been so successful in so many contexts throughout the centuries provides us with a reasonable ground for claiming that unless serious conceptual obstacles are in our path, the modalities should be assumed to be part of our ontology. We saw that some philosophers did raise what they took to be conceptual problems with the modalities, but the arguments advanced turned out to be inconclusive. We found that arguments involving the modalities and essential as well as accidental ascriptions of properties can be cast into a form that makes perfectly good sense of these. We then adopted the maxim, true for metaphysics in general, that as long as key notions can be made intelligible in terms of a natural language, we should not dispense with these just because they do not fit into what some logicians might opt for as their favourite symbolism.

To sum up, we cleared the modalities of charges, we found them fundamental for human reasoning, and – to turn to the last consideration – they are involved in the individuation principles that make reality an ordered and intelligible collection of items. We saw reasons to suppose that even if some of our pragmatic interests affect to an extent the individuation and persistence principles we use, it seems very implausible that the whole network should be just a way of meeting practical human needs. On the basis of these considerations, we shall adopt the realist stance, and utilize the modalities in drawing a non-circular characterization of the universal–particular distinction. A universe in which the modalities are acknowledged to have an ontological place will be called a dynamic universe. Two arguments show that in a dynamic universe there are non-circular ways of distinguishing universals from particulars.

The intuitive heart of the first argument is that possibilities affect universals differently from the way they affect particulars. For the purpose of explicating the argument we shall distinguish two notions of possibility. One of these is mere logical possibility. This is a rather 'thin' notion. It allows everything to be possible that is not self-contradictory. Thus it admits far more than what the laws of nature and the dynamics of organic growth and perishing would allow. In the account distinguishing universals from particulars we shall make use primarily of the more restricted notion of natural necessity, i.e. that which corresponds roughly to what the laws of nature, and in particular the laws of the sciences dealing with the organic, would admit as possible. For example, this enables us to deal with the potentialities that we ascribe to members of natural kinds. Within this conception, then, naturalistically possible entities are those that could have come into existence if some of the causal links that in fact relate actual particulars were different. Examples are houses that might have been built, or children who could have been born of couples with child-begetting capacities. Some particulars have the causal capacity either to bring into being or prevent from coming into being other particulars. Universals, on the other hand, are not causal agents. They cannot bring into being particulars, for they do not have the kind of causal power encoded by laws carrying what we called natural necessity. Also, universals cannot be caused, in the same sense, to come into being. We can cause only instances of universals to come into being, but not universals. Universals provide the metaphysical background for coming into being and perishing. For members of this realm, namely certain properties, are instantiated by some particulars, and it is this instantiation that enables the particulars to generate others.

Drawing attention to this difference is not to deny that one can make sense of a description of certain universals as possible entities. One might describe uninstantiated universals in this way, i.e. the ones that are not instantiated but could have been. But the causal network of reality applies to universals only indirectly through their instances. For example, heat causes ice to melt. This is so in virtue of certain relations between the property of being heat, of being ice, and of melting. But the causal processes involved range over particular instances of these properties, not the properties themselves. Thus the difference between the way universals are linked to causal correlations and the way particulars are affected by causality admits of a straightforward description that does not presuppose the intuitive notion of a *sui generis* mode of being for universals.

This way of differentiating universals from particulars does not imply that no abstract entity could come into being at some specific time. Types are abstract entities, and someone might think of these as having a temporal origin. We mean by 'type' here one half of the type–token contrast introduced by C.S. Peirce. Elements of various symbol systems, such as either the spoken or written elements of an alphabet, have the type–token structure. And we do say that certain languages or alphabets were invented at a certain time. This issue comes up only to show that the account we are giving of universals has the following implications. First, the type–token distinction is not the same as the universal–particular distinction. Criteria for what count as instances of the same universal are not the same as what determines the ranges of tokens for a type. Secondly, our account of universals and particulars leaves the question of whether types have temporal beginnings open. Some have also argued that species are not particulars, and that they come into being at certain times (Almog, 1986; and in conversation). This too is compatible with the claim we make here. For biological species are not, within the conception under consideration, universals. They have their own mode of being, just as types do.

It would be also misleading to restate the distinction argued for here as the claim that particulars have potentialities and possibilities while universals do not. For if we mean by having potentialities simply having modal properties, then both universals and particulars have potentialities. For example, justice might have been instantiated in Sparta at a certain time, but was not. Kindness might have been instantiated by Napoleon, but was not. Still, within these projected states of affairs only particulars are affected directly by causality. Neither the lack of instantiation by Sparta nor the one by Napoleon can be sensibly described as a causal effect on the two universals involved. Some sentences might be misleading in this respect. For example, some complain that there is less justice today than there used to be. But here we are talking about justice as a scattered individual whose parts are acts and people, not about a universal. We find a similar situation when considering the claim that there is less ice in the world today than there used to be. This is hardly a statement about the property of being ice; it is about the 'mass' we call ice. Particulars and universals are different in this respect. You take away some of the mass from Mr Churchill and he is still the same human. But if you take away too much, he will not survive. Justice and kindness as universals – perhaps fortunately – survive any decrease.

We called attention before to the fact that we can truly describe states that do not obtain in the actual world but only in some projections. For example, there could have been more rain this year in Michigan. This is because there is a universal, the property of raining, which was not sufficiently instantiated in Michigan this year, but is instantiated in that way in a possible projected state. We need the sameness of universals in order to compare the actual and possible states in question here. For what would it mean to say that it is not raining in our world but it is raining in a projection, unless the property of raining remains the same across actuality and projections? If properties could change across projections, what would be the basis for judging these to be the same or different? Certain possibilities at least require the sameness of universals across possible states. There may be other needed conditions for veridical comparisons, e.g. conditions on space and time across projections. Since this is a matter for physics, we shall leave that issue aside. This account is also neutral with regard to the philosophical utility or lack of utility of talking about projections in terms of 'possible worlds'.

The argument is, however, incomplete. For there are also possibilities that require that particulars remain identical across possibilities. This is illustrated by 'Mt Tahoma could be smaller'. The truth of this statement requires that the mountain remain the same entity across the actual and the possible. It is the same mountain but with a smaller size. There are many examples of this sort: 'Socrates could have been more diplomatic', 'If Plato had lived later, he could have suffered from writer's cramp', etc.

We started with the intuition that when we consider causal links, we can see differences between the modal involvements of universals and particulars. We then saw that both have modal properties, and now we see that possibilities require some kind of fixity across projections from both. We shall now turn to the final point that does give us a clear differentiation; namely the ways in which sameness or fixity is achieved.

Identity of universals, or property-identity, is a basic primitive metaphysical notion. For example, the property of being a

149

triangle remains the same regardless of where and how it is instantiated, and what place it occupies in geometric theory. Our conceptions and definitions of triangularity may change, but that does not affect the universal itself.

The identity of particulars across projected states of affairs has a different status. When we ask whether Socrates is the same in two distinct projections, we assume that we are asking this question about a human. For we need to apply some individuation and persistence condition; merely being Socrates will not give us any. If Socrates can be a human here, a mountain there, and the number 13, elsewhere, then there is no fact in virtue of which he could be the same or different across projections. Even if, by some miracle, our theories changed so much that it would make sense to talk about an entity that is first a human, then a mountain, etc., this would not change the situation. For in such a world there would be no Socrates. There would be a different entity a stage of which would resemble Socrates, and we would be asking the question of sameness about the new kind of entity.

Thus for projectibility to make sense, Socrates must be a human, Mt Tahoma a mountain, etc. This remains true even if we move from modal to temporal projections. If we strip away all of the properties from Socrates and Mt Tahoma, we may be left with a mysterious substratum, an 'I know not what', but hardly with something about which questions of individuation or persistence can arise. We would not even be able to say whether it is one or many things; thus it would not even qualify as the 'coat-hanger' in what Russell called the 'coat-hanger theory of predication', in which the properties are the coats. Russell himself believed in no such coat-hanger, thus embracing what I call the 'onion theory' of predication, since once you peel away all of the leaves from an onion, nothing is left.

These reflections show that while universals keep their identity across projections without depending on items from other ontological categories, particulars retain sameness across projections only in virtue of some link to some universal remaining constant. Comparisons of possibilities are primarily qualitative. This is possible only if the qualitative background has stability.

The stability of particulars, on the other hand, depends on their having certain stable, or if you care essential, relations to some universals. (There are degrees of essentiality, and the thesis advanced here need not commit itself to any specific strong thesis about essences; some stability across projections is all we need to show the proposed asymmetry.)

In this sense, then, universals do not exist contingently. We need them across possibilities. We could, however, compare two projections with totally different 'particular populations'. Thus both in terms of independence and required stability across projections, universals and particulars have different ontological roles. This can be spelled out in the following. First, there is an asymmetry in terms of dependency. Particulars depend on universals for existence across possible states, but universals do not depend on particulars for existing across possibilities. Secondly, there is a property, namely the property of x requiring entities other than itself such that those are universals, in order for x to remain the same across projected states and this property is shared by all particulars, even God if he exists. This property is not shared by universals.

Someone might object and say that universals also depend on other universals for their stability, for redness has to remain a colour, justice a virtue, and so on. But these propositions expressing second-order property instantiations just spell out what the first-order universals are. They are not more fundamental than the property identity of the the first order items. It is not as if we had red, blue, etc., and then could consider whether these are colours or not. The property of being a colour depends on its instances. It could not have different instances. We have said that property identity is a fundamental notion. The statements we just mentioned are not more fundamental. Red is a colour because it is the property it is; there is no separable fact over and above this, that could be expressed as red's also being a colour.

Herewith a more precise summary of the non-circular account. If we assume that universals and particulars make up two distinct ontological categories then for a distinguishing mark separating the two classes we have two open sentences to do the job.

The open sentence:

x is such that for its identity across projected states x does not depend on relations to elements in another ontological category
is true of all universals and false of all particulars.

The open sentence:

x is such that for its identity across possibilities it depends on some element other than itself and this element is a universal is true of all particulars and is not true of any universal.

The second open sentence contains a reference to universals. Thus someone might suspect circularity after all. There is, however, no circularity. The reference to universals in this open sentence is not to any unique mode of being of these entities. It refers to universals in the pre-theoretic intuitive sense in which this notion was introduced at the outset. Unlike in the case of the attempt to draw the non-circular differentiation in terms of spatio-temporal location, within the proposed contrast we need not assume anything about the *sui generis* nature of universals, but merely that we can pick out intuitively long lists of items that are universals. If infinite conjunctions were possible, we could substitute one of those in place of 'universal' in the open sentence under consideration.

The non-circular differentiation and the other proposals concerning the nature of universals defend realism and show that universals and particulars are equally fundamental in ontology. We have reached, however, also another conclusion. Since the modalities are conceptually coherent and play an indispensable role in the differentiation of universals and particulars, these too are an ontologically fundamental category. Without the modalities we cannot draw the universal–particular distinction in a satisfactory way. Thus we would have to fall back on the monism of the Eleatics like Parmenides, or that of F.H. Bradley. That, of course, would make the task of formulating an adequate account of thought and language a simple task, one might say: 'a one-line task'. Nevertheless, we shall embrace the ontology of realism, and press on with the more complex but also intellectually more satisfying task of proposing an account of thought and language for a universe made up of a plurality of at least partly intelligible entities. As our final steps towards that task, we shall look at the individuation of universals and then distinguish among particulars the two kinds, event and object.

The Individuation of Universals and Particulars

Grammatically, 'particular' is a count noun. It admits of pluralization, and thus purports to divide its reference. As soon as we try, however, to carry out the individuation procedure, we encounter obstacles. For there are an indefinite number of equally good answers to the question: 'How many particulars are there in this room?'. We can count pieces of furniture, or cubes of wood, or molecules, atoms, etc. The meaning of the term 'particular' does not tell us which is the 'right' way. One could take the bull by the horns and say that all of these together answer the question. On this view the correct answer to the question above is: 'An infinite number'. This, however, invites further objections. There are different kinds of infinite collections. Some are well ordered collections such as the set of positive integers. In such cases there is a procedure generating for any member x in the sequence, the next one x'. But the collection of particulars is not like that. Two people can count particulars in the same spatio-temporal region, and come up with different results, having taken different units of counting. There is no non-arbitrary way of settling on 'basic' particulars. Spatio-temporal continuity, as we saw, will not do. It is not sufficient for the individuation of particulars in general, and it is not necessary either, since we can find spatio-temporally scattered particulars. Furthermore, what is true of the spatial diversity of particulars is also true of their persistence. The notion of particularity does not determine what we should take as a particular persisting through time.

As soon as we subsume particulars under kinds, the situation changes. Questions like: 'How many animals, celestial bodies, lakes, etc. can we find in region X?' have non-arbitrary, true answers. Similarly with persistence. Particulars under various kinds are governed by persistence conditions, dividing the spatio-temporal world into distinct entities persisting through time. It is reasonable to assume that some kind will cover any particular. There are, after all, kind-terms formed by phrases like 'piece of', 'fragment of', etc. that individuate the stuffs mass terms cover.

Our conclusion is not that particulars cannot be individuated, but that they cannot be individuated *qua* particulars. Particulars form an orderly and intelligible plurality of entities that are individuated and are governed by persistence conditions, because they are instances of a variety of kinds. Thus particulars meet Quine's demand that members of an ontologically respectable category should be under individuation principles, but they do so indirectly via their links to kinds. Particulars as such can be conceived of as a gigantic mass, like physical matter, providing a domain for varieties of individuation and persistence conditions.

Brief reflection should convince us that universals are in the same conceptual boat. There is no non-arbitrary way of counting all of the universals that are instantiated in St Paul's Cathedral now. If we say that their number is infinite, we encounter the same line of reply that was developed above in response to the similar move made about particulars. Once, however, we see how universals are also structured under kinds, the mystery disappears, and we have as much order and intelligibility as in the case of particulars. A question like: 'How many biological kinds are instantiated in this cage of the zoo?' admits a non-arbitrary true answer. So do questions like: 'How many positive integers are there between 5 and 29?' And just as in the case of particulars, where 'lump of', 'piece of', etc. help to create kinds, so in the case of universals, 'kind of', 'sort', etc. help out where more articulate scientific classification lags.

Thus to the same extent to which particulars admit of order and intelligibility from the point of view of individuation, universals, within kinds, also constitute orderly pluralities. This point, then, together with what was argued previously in this chapter, completes our defence of realism. As we shall see, this ontology is necessary as the background for any viable theory of thought and language.

Events and Material Objects

The proposal about events to be articulated in this section rests on two theses established in our ontological survey of problems. First, there is no conceptual barrier to regarding events as a legitimate ontological category, on a par with that of material object. Second, there is no general conceptual reason for regarding any of the sub-categories of the class of events such as subjectless events, mental ones, physical ones, etc. as having ontological priority over others. Our account will also rely on realism with respect to universals. It will posit both event universals and event particulars. An adequate account of events has to answer the following questions:

1. What are events?
2. How do they differ from material objects?
3. How does the distinction between essential and accidental properties apply to events?

4. In what ways do events have spatio and temporal location?
5. What is the significance of events having an aspectual nature?
6. What is the nature of individuation and persistence conditions governing events?

Our use of 'event' is wider than the ordinary use of this term. It includes changes, processes, states, motions, and what one might call plain occurrences such as sounds. We saw in our review of suggestions by other philosophers that there is disagreement on whether events are individuated by intensional or extensional conditions. We shall now see that this dichotomy, when applied to either ontology or semantics, needs considerable expansion. The traditional intensional–extensional distinction is usually illustrated by examples such as the following. If Jones believes that cougars are wild, and 'cougar' is co-extensive with 'the most feared animal in Arizona', it does not follow that Jones believes that the most feared animal in Arizona is wild. Thus beliefs of this sort are individuated intensionally. This involves also the fact that from my believing that cougars are wild, one cannot infer that cougars exist. Intensionally individuated belief states are described by sentences that have no existential import, and into the embedded clause of which one cannot substitute co-extensive terms while guaranteeing truth preservation. In contrast with such cases, a sentence like 'Smith kicked the mule' does carry existential import, since Smith cannot kick a mule that does not exist. Furthermore, co-extensive expressions can be substituted in the object position, while preserving truth value. For if Smith kicked the mule, and the mule is the only domesticated animal in the barn, then Smith must have kicked the only domesticated animal in the barn.

On the basis of these examples one might want to rest with a dichotomy. In the case of intensional contexts we have two marks, lack of existential import and substitutivity on the basis of sameness of intensions, not co-extensiveness. For the extensional contexts we have the marks of existential import of the relevant referring expressions and substitutivity on the basis of co-extensiveness. On closer inspection, however, we find more than just these two types of context, and this has bearing both on semantics and on the ontology of events. What follows presents schematically all four kinds of cases.

1. There are events such as kicking a mule, kissing Molly, and other useful and/or enjoyable activities whose object must exist and can be specified by any of the appropriate co-extensive expressions. In these cases it is also reasonable to suppose that the principle of individuation for events of this kind will be along extensional lines, i.e. that phrases co-extensive with 'kick' or 'kiss' will pick out, respectively, the same event.

2. Events such as someone building a house, or writing a letter, or a seed growing into a flower. In these cases the final object such as the house, letter, or flower, cannot exist during the event or process. Thus we do not have existential import. On the other hand, the object can be characterized by co-extensive terms. If Jones is building the house at 12 Elm Street, and the house at 12 Elm Street will be the ugliest building in the county, then Jones is building the ugliest building in the county. The object in these cases is 'in the offing', one might say, and is expected to be realized in the normal context. Finally, the event individuation may proceed along either intensional or extensional lines; one intuition does not cover all of the cases. Building or growing are partly teleological or functional notions. Thus one might claim that these processes require design or function. But if this is so, we must interpret these notions very broadly, so as to allow for such obvious truths as: 'Beavers build dams.'

3. Events whose object must be identified by intensional criteria of substitutivity and need not be actual. Some examples are: worshipping Zeus, praying to Oziris, hunting the Yeti, etc. In these cases the event itself needs to be individuated along intensional criteria. The events of worshipping or hunting are not identical with other co-extensive property instantiations.

4. Events whose objects need to exist, but are individuated by intensional criteria. In these cases the event itself is individuated intensionally. Obvious examples of this type include: to know, to have the concept of, to understand.

This fourfold classification shows that existential import need not go with extensionality, and lack of existential import need not go with intensionality. It also shows that in addition to the above facts needed for a successful verb semantics, we need to take these matters into consideration when considering event individuation. As our examples show, some events require objects as participants, others do not. Some are individuated extensionally, some intensionally. The most general thing we can say is that events are property instantiations at times, with varying temporal structures, kinds and number of participants, and conditions of individuation that can amount to property-identity-related facts or facts related to co-extensional substitution. We shall expand on this issue later.

This survey shows that events have a closer conceptual relation to time than material objects. For the difference between state, mere event, and process is a matter of the property instantiation ranging over different temporal configurations such as points, intervals, and various combinations of these. (For details see Gabbay and Moravcsik, 1980.) Spatial location may or may not be a requirement for all events. Even if it is, and we insist on locating, e.g., thoughts at the place at which their subject is, differences in spatial locations are not crucial factors for determining individuation for events. In the case of material objects, it is the other way around. Their essential locating is in space and various spatial configurations. To be sure, all material objects are also in time, but this fact has less bearing on their individuation.

Thus we characterize events as property instantiations essentially in time, with a variety of individuation conditions. This characterization not only fits the elements of the category, but for reasons given above, also differentiates events from material objects in other than just the rather trivial way of linking the latter category to three-dimensionality and its components, while not requiring this of events. One might be tempted to opt for a criterion based on a common-sense intuition; namely that since time is continuous, events are ontologically 'dense', while matter being scattered over space, objects are partitioned by this scatter, and are thus not ontologically 'dense'. We should reject this alternative proposal, for it takes a contingent fact, namely the alleged non-density of matter, as the basis for a metaphysical distinction. Physics can posit 'scattered' matter one day, and on another day matter that is 'dense' throughout.

Our distinction helps to differentiate events also from other kinds of particular such as energy. For these too do not have the intrinsic tie with time that events do.

We have now answered two of the questions with which we started. We shall turn next to event individuation. The considera-

tions adduced so far in connection with the general characterization of what an event is set the stage for the thesis that though
'event' is grammatically a count noun, it, like 'material object', is
semantically really a term without conditions of individuation.
Thus both events and material objects are individuated by the
kinds that they fall under. For events some of the individuation
conditions are tied to the number and kinds of participants that
they require. Some events are economic transactions. Let us
consider the event of John selling a cow to Jeremiah for ten
pounds. The four participants, John, Jeremiah, the ten pounds,
and the cow occupy four essential argument places for sale to
take place, namely a seller, a buyer, something to be sold, and
the object to be given as price. These have to remain fixed for the
persistence of the event. If a different cow is being sold, or the
same cow resold, or someone else becomes the buyer, etc., then
a different event replaced the original one. There are, of course,
also other conditions of persistence. It is worth noting that
temporal continuity is not one of these. A sale can take place
over several days, with interruptions. This kind of event also
requires completion. There is no sale until the selling is done. In
the case of other types of event like battles, concerts, etc.
sameness of participants becomes a much more complex matter.
In a concert there may be a soloist who does not play in the
second half, and in a battle there is a steady supply, and
unfortunately also a steady demise, of soldiers. There are also
still other types of event, like sounds that do no require
participants at all. Science may supply from time to time a variety
of candidates as participants in sound, but the concept cannot be
rested on these changing hypotheses. Thoughts are individuated
in a still different way, requiring both intensional individuation of
event and of object. Thinking of Napoleon is not necessarily the
same as thinking of Josephine's husband.

We see, then, that both in terms of individuation and in terms
of persistence events are governed by different conditions
depending on the kind under which they fall. The same is true of
material objects. Their individuation and persistence depends on
the kind under which they fall. Different conditions apply to
lakes, mountains, humans, collections of body cells, artefacts,
and so on. Thus the two categories are analogous in this respect.
Semantically and ontologically we should think of 'event' and

'material object' as mass terms, without conditions of individuation or persistence. What falls under them constitutes the 'mass' which is then individuated in a variety of ways by kinds.

This analysis should serve as an antidote for the temptation, shared by philosophers of language and metaphysicians, not to acknowledge particular events. For without this acknowledgement, there is uniformity of semantic structure in simple sentences of subject–predicate form. 'Socrates is wise' has a relation between a particular and a universal making it true. Without positing particular events, 'Socrates is walking' has the same structure. It too is just a statement made true by a relation between a particular and a universal. According to our analysis, the two sentences have different configurations making them true. In the first case, it is indeed a relation between a particular and a universal. But in the second case we have two particulars, Socrates and an event of walking, related to universals. Thus our ontology and semantic analysis requires more primitives than the standard account. But parsimony is not always a virtue. Within the ontology proposed we can represent in a more natural and ontologically perspicuous way propositions involving aspect, temporal modifiers, and the mixtures of these. (For details see Gabbay and Moravcsik, 1980.)

We shall now turn to the examination of the essential–accidental distinction as applied to material objects and events. All that will be shown is that this distinction is as clear when applied to events as it is when applied to material objects. Thus we need not go into complex issues such as the precise way in which the distinction is to be drawn, whether it admits of borderline cases, whether its applications can be verified empirically or in other ways, and similar concerns.

For our purposes it is enough to show some clear cases of application. Thus, for example, being a human is a necessary property of all humans. If an entity that is human stops being that, it is replaced by a new entity, even if there is continuity. On the other hand, being a bartender is an accidental property of some humans. Even if they changed profession and became spies, they would remain the same human and same entity, and would be treated by our society as such, e.g. retaining social security number, family obligations, and, from a metaphysical point of view, above all falling under the same individuation and persistence conditions.

One aspect of essence and accident has to do with properties, as we illustrated. The other related aspect is the question of how much of an entity can be taken away or destroyed, or replaced, and not destroy thereby the entity at a time or over a period of time. In the case of mountains, chairs, and similar medium-sized objects it is clear that mere gain or loss of a few parts will not destroy the individual. A chair with a few scratches is still the same old chair, and similar losses – or in the more usual case, gains of a few pounds – will not destroy the human individual either.

Do the same considerations apply to events? Would the baptism that took place yesterday be a different event if Uncle Joel had not fallen sick and would not have had to leave early? Would the tank battle at Caen have been a different event if a couple of tanks had got lost at Bayeux and would not have put in an appearance?

What might pull one in the direction of saying that the chair with the chip and the gentleman with a few more pounds are still the same entities, while in the case of an event even the absence of one soldier, tank, relative, etc. would make this not the same event? Some might have an intuition that events are more deeply enmeshed into the network of causal links than material objects. But this is a superficial view. If it is reasonable to believe that historical necessity placed all of the tanks that happened to take part in the battle of Caen on that plain at that time, then it is also reasonable to say that the entire previous state of the universe determined causally that the old rocking chair should have at any given time exactly the chips it has, even if the causes for this seem less accessible to us than in the case of the tanks. Thus asymmetry is not justified.

Historically, the question of retaining sufficient number of parts for survival has been put in terms of sand piles. But the example of a sand pile is atypical. For unlike in that case, in the case of tanks, humans, weddings, etc. it is not the number of parts that matters, but the kinds of constituent whose presence is essential for the object to function as a member of the kind under which it falls. Sand piles are not functioning wholes. But engines, baptisms, trees, and earthquakes are complex structures; some are material objects and some events whose persistence requires some elements much more than others. This is true of both of the subcategories of particulars under consideration.

So far we looked at the parallel between events and material objects with respect to gains and losses of parts. Let us return to the other aspect of essentiality, namely to the division of properties into essential and accidental ones. We saw earlier some clear cases of the distinction applying to material objects, such as humans. We shall consider examples showing that the same is true of events. For example, an event of walking is essentially that. It cannot change into flying or calculating and remain the same event. Of course it is logically possible that we shall discover new kinds, under weird circumstances, that require stages of what are now regarded as walks and flights, for their persistence. In that case, we have a new kind, a new collection of events, and if everything that is now an event of walking is absorbed into the new activity, then there will be no more events of walking. The same holds for material objects and new possible kinds for these.

We see, then, that events have essential properties. A walk is necessarily a walk, a calculation a calculation, thinking thinking, etc. Events have also accidental properties. A walk could have been slower or faster and still be the same walk. A political speech could have been more or less effective and still be the same speech. Someone's reading a book has the accidental property of its being a careless reading. The same event could have had the property of being a more careful reading. These examples parallel the case in which a house can have an extra floor added on top and still retain its identity. We can illustrate this phenomenon also in terms of temporal projections. The walk that picks up speed and then slows down is still the same walk, and the reading that becomes more attentive is still the same reading.

The seeming density of events might lead one to think that all of the properties of an event are essential. But this is linked to views about determinism and indeterminism, and not to the very notion of an event. Different conceptions of nature and different scientific theories impose different types of determinism on the phenomena. Our account does not rule out the possibility of some science imposing a heavy essential structure on a theoretically distinguished subclass of events. But we cannot rest our concept of an event, needed to specify foundational features of thought and language, on fluctuating views about how much of the causal network is essential to events. This issue is empirical. Our interest is in a core notion of events that can be used in other parts of philosophical analysis.

We turn now to the spatial location of events. We need to consider at least two questions. First, is specific spatial location necessary or only an accidental feature of events? Secondly, do events differ from material objects with regards to spatial location? It is obvious that at least some events have spatial locations. Otherwise we would not name events as the Battle of Waterloo, the Congress of Vienna, the Yalta Conference, etc. These locations, however, show neither that all events must have spatial location, nor that the ones that have, must have very precisely defined spatial occupancy. We can locate the Battle of Waterloo outside of Waterloo, or the Congress of Vienna in Vienna, but there seems no non-arbitrary answer to the question: 'Where exactly were the spatial boundaries of these events?' In this respect, however, events do not differ from material objects. Some of these too have only inexact spatial boundaries. Countries, mountain ranges, or prairies cannot be given precise location. There are, of course, material objects, especially the small ones dealt with by physics, that can be given very exact location. But this is also true of some events. Certain explosions, for example, can be given exact locations, and the same is true of collisions of small entities in a laboratory setting. Furthermore, for most events exact spatial location is not essential, even when available, unless we build this into the specification of the particular event. For example, 'the heat expansion in such-and-such a region of a controlled space in a laboratory equipment'.

Locating and relocating events admits of some flexibility. The Battle of Austerlitz could have been a few hundred metres to the east. But it is difficult to conceive of drastic relocation of events. It is not true that the battle between Montgomery and Rommell could have taken place at the North Pole. They could have met there, but it would have been a different battle. Nor can an avalanche have taken place a few hundred miles south. It seems, however, that the reason for these limitations is not something about spatiality itself, but the causal network that is spread over space and within which we locate particular events. This, however, holds also of material objects. One might think it to be a matter of accident that the chair on which I am sitting happens to be located at that exact spot. But it would be absurd to suppose that the chair could right now be in Singapore, without drastically changing the whole causal network within which the history of this chair has taken place. If that collection of matter were now in Singapore, many other things would have to change as well.

Still, someone might use the same gambit that we used above, and try to separate the notion of material thing from cosmological assumptions about the amount of determinism in the universe, and claim that this particular material object, namely the chair on which I sit, could be located anywhere in space as long as conditions in a region do not lead to solids not holding together. And events as such cannot be taken out in such a way from the causal context. Thus we find here a lack of analogy. From a strict ontological point of view spatial location for material objects is necessary, but their relation to the place that they happen to occupy at any given time is not necessary. Since events cannot move as easily in and out of the causal network, there is a difference in this respect between them and material objects. We covered on pp. 41–3 the difference exhibited in some events not requiring spatial location at all.

Let us turn to temporal location. Our initial intuitions are similar to those with regards to spatiality. Events can be moved temporally, but not too much. A birth, a battle, a revolution, the coming of spring, grandfather's walk, etc. can all be conceived as having taken place a bit earlier or later than these in fact have taken place, but wholesale relocation causes conceptual problems. We saw that this is primarily because of the place of an event in a network of causal development, and various – often implicit – assumptions that we make with regard to determinism and the nature of temporality, e.g. can it have gaps, is it absolute, like a container, etc.

In the case of material objects we find the same situation. These can be 'moved' temporally, but not too much. Notre Dame of Paris could have been built a little earlier, but not much earlier. A mountain range could have developed a bit later, but not much later than it in fact has. Perhaps these intuitions are less tractable in the case of material objects, because of the illusory conception that just imagining an object and then placing it into some place in the flow of time are separate mental experiments. This is misleading, because regardless of what images we can form, for most kind of material objects causal ancestry is important. If this is so, then the relation to the history of the world is also more fixed than simple images might suggest. In the case of organic entities this is quite obvious. A child could not be just anyone's child, even on the most permissive and informal conception of biology. But similar considerations apply to other types of material object. A continent comes into being because of certain causal interactions; it is not just some 'stuff' that could have come into being in any way at any time. The same consideration applies to islands, veins of gold, etc. We are discussing cases of natural substances, for these are the most difficult ones for the view that matter too is bound within certain temporal constraints. The case of artefacts, depending on design, creative intention, etc. is more obvious. Furniture of a certain kind can be manufactured only under certain conditions of technology.

It seems, then, that as far as location is concerned events and material objects are similar with respect to time. There is, however, the difference alluded to earlier; the structure of kinds of events depends on temporal structure the way the structure of material objects does not, and temporality, but not spatiality, is necessary for all events; material objects need to be locatable however in both.

We have seen that aspect is a feature of temporality; in particular the aspects of ongoing happenings and of completion. It is true that aspect affects verbs denoting events, while we do not have a part of the grammar of nouns and noun phrases devoted to aspect. Still, closer inspection shows that there are interesting analogies between the main aspects of verbs denoting events, and the semantics of certain nouns denoting material objects. We pointed out that certain events are processes culminating at a point marking the end of the interval in which the process took place; such as building a church, growing into an adult tiger. It seems, however, that there are material objects with analogous structures. Let us consider a specimen of a biological species, such as a bear or a human. There are persistence conditions articulating the sameness of the bear throughout his lifespan. But the object itself, the body of the bear, undergoes alterations, from cub to reaching adulthood. The bear is not a 'real' or adult bear until the body reaches a certain stage. Thus the body of the bear over time resembles the general features of what we called processes requiring completion. The aspect of the perfect takes verbs or verb phrases and makes phrases denoting quasi-processes out of these. We have no such syntactic device for nouns, but the two types of entities resemble each other.

We find the same situation holding for the progressive. In the case of events we saw that this aspect enables us to refer to ongoing activity or series of changes within a larger interval within which a whole event takes place. For example, 'While he was crossing the street, a car came.' Street crossings, like other events, admit of various kinds of interruptions without these destroying the persistence of the event itself. A walk, a period of reading, or even a street crossing admit of sub-periods in which activity comes to a halt. The whole event is a series of activity intervals interspersed possibly but not necessarily with periods of inactivity. The progressive enables us to pick out a contextually given period of activity. Interestingly, we can find analogues to this in the structures of many material objects. A cathedral, for example, is a combination of matter with empty space in between. There are spaces between the flying buttresses, there is the nave, etc. This is also true of specimens of biological species. Events are not just solid uninterrupted activity, and material objects of the more interesting kinds are not just solid matter.

We are now in a position to answer the six questions posed at the outset. According to the proposal articulated here events are property instantiations over time, with the temporal structure of points and intervals interacting with the properties to carve out different types of events. The lack of a conceptual link to three-dimensionality and the sole necessary locatability being temporal, as well as the interaction with temporal structures, separate events from material objects and other types of particular.

With regards to the essential–accidental distinction we saw that it cuts across the dichotomy between events and objects. The distinction is as clear and as applicable in one case as it is in the other. Doubts on this matter seem to be related to different conceptions of determinism.

We saw some differences between events and material objects with regards to their links to particular spatial location, but these were difficult to disentangle from larger, and for our purposes irrelevant, cosmological considerations.

We saw also much similarity between the temporal location of events and material objects. Once we admitted the difference between conceptual interactions between event structure and temporal structure on the one hand, and material object structure and temporal structure on the other, we found many analogies, including even some aspectual structure.

Finally, with regards to individuation and persistence we reached a conclusion similar to what we reached in the case of the categories of universal and particular. Individuation and persistence conditions are linked to kinds that are more narrow and specific than these ontological categories. And once we looked at the various kinds, individuation is no more or less clear for events than for material objects. This completes not only our answer to the key questions, but also the argumentation for the claim that events are as legitimate an ontological sub-category of particulars as material objects. Our little friends, the events, are no worse off than their more prestigious big brothers, the material objects.

None of this should be taken to embrace a relativistic conception of identity. Identity for all of these types of entity is the same. Two entities are the same if and only if they have all of their properties in common. Only individuation and persistence are tied to kinds.

In conclusion it should be stressed again that we dealt only with those aspects of ontology that will play important roles in our proposals about thought and language. There are many other important issues concerning non-existence, sets, facts, etc. that we bypassed. We shall see, however, that different proposals about how to analyse thoughts or how to treat the mental, make different assumptions about the realist–nominalist controversy, and that the same holds for arguments for and against physicalism; in the latter case the event–material object contrast and the defence of these categories enters the picture. Finally, our analysis of language will depend heavily on realism with regards to universals, modalities, and events.

CHAPTER V

Thought

The proposal to be aired touches on many issues raised in our survey of problems. Though articulated in four separate sections, it is a unified treatment of the ontology, salient properties, and methodology of the study of thought. It starts with a view about the relation between science and common sense that sees no sharp break between these either in terms of concepts or in terms of ontology. It introduces a way of looking at the ontology of cognition, both in common sense and in science, that exempts us from commitments to either materialism or dualism, or any of their rivals. The proposal shows why we should reject behaviourism as a philosophic dogma even if one might want to retain some of the empirical results. It shows also why functionalism and its presuppositions do not provide the right conceptual framework for understanding thought. The proposal culminates in a sketch of an 'objectual' view of cognition that stresses the unique sense in which cognition has objects, and construes the characterization of cognition in terms of its objects as primary, leaving the links to phenomenal experience, and the processing mechanisms, as well as analyses of these components, indeterminate. Finally, within this proposal we can make conceptual room for aspects of cognition such as understanding, and the articulation of explanations, that cannot be analysed as complexes built solely from propositional knowledge and know-how. This gives us one more building-block to an eventual development of the conception of humans as *homo explanans*, rather than as a primarily information-processing creature.

Given the sweep of this proposal and the confines of this book, it is not possible to argue for each claim in great detail. Many of the papers mentioned in the bibliography deal with more specific topics than this essay. But in this age of specialization – if not overspecialization – it is important to see from time to time the forest and not just the trees, especially when what is presented is a new way of looking at the forest, right or wrong.

Common Sense, Science, and Ontology

In our survey of problems we encountered a radical proposal, exemplified by Stich's writings, according to which a viable science of cognition would have to do away with most of our common sense concepts and beliefs concerning cognition. Our starting point will be a critical assessment of this thesis. How much precedent is there for such a radical break in the histories of the other more mature sciences?

In answering this question we shall avail ourselves of the distinction sketched briefly before, between basic and peripheral common sense. Basic common sense is that set of concepts and principles which we find indispensable when we think of ourselves, other humans, and the environment in our everyday interactions. This layer of common sense is invariant across cultures and history. It includes, for example, the belief that there are causal links between some parts of nature, that these links can connect objects and events, and that objects and events are in space and time. It includes the belief that humans have beliefs and emotions such as fear or joy, that these emotions can take parts of nature as their objects, and the conviction that we cannot help but make decisions about how to interact with other parts of reality. It makes no sense for someone to say something like: 'As of this afternoon, in view of recent discoveries, I can no more be said to have beliefs and emotions,' unless the speaker is announcing his impending demise.

It is beyond the scope of this work to document the universality of basic common sense, but a few guide posts can be provided. We need not and should not claim that every language has a word with exactly the same meaning as our 'cause,' or 'thought', or 'belief'. One can, however, look at whole families of words centring on the notions we label in the ways mentioned, and see these spread across natural languages. There are also practices and institutions that seem universal, and point to basic common sense. For example, societies seem to have institutions for deliberations and council, even if the structures of these vary considerably. Furthermore, since arts and crafts constitute a cultural universal, we can see in this a universal recognition of some causal links between human actions and parts of the material world.

Basic common sense can be divided into concepts, beliefs, and explanations. We have covered above some of the concepts already. These include that of a human, of the difference between me and others, belief, decision, and emotion. Some of the beliefs of basic common sense are quite general. These include belief in the external world and our own existence. Others relate to more specific aspects of our existence, such as our loving and occasionally hating others, and our being able to render some parts of reality unproblematic by the use of our reasoning processes.

Basic common sense also consists of some low-level explanations. Examples of these would be: 'He did this because he was afraid', 'She completed the task because she knew the solution', or 'He could solve the problem because he understood it.' We can admit this type of explanation as a part of basic common sense without construing it as a monolithic theory, or for that matter as a theory in any reasonably sophisticated sense.

It is also important not to confuse what we call basic common sense with what in the philosophy of science is called the observational level, even though the extensions of the two notions might overlap. Basic common sense takes certain facts for granted, but not all of these can be reasonably interpreted as being on the observational level. For example, could one regard the belief that humans make decisions in councils observational; or is this already a mixture of the observational and conceptual? Again, we take it for granted that certain experiences cause joy in humans, but it is not beyond dispute whether one could interpret this as an observational statement.

Another important characteristic of basic common sense is its indeterminateness. We have been talking about concepts, beliefs, and explanations. Someone might take this to mean that we attribute to humans at this level concepts and beliefs with sharply defined objects, characterizable as such in terms of modern logic and semantics. On this view the convictions of basic common

169

sense could be expressed as well-defined propositions. Indeed, Stich seems to have this conception in mind when he character- izes the relevant part of common sense as 'folk-psychology'. Stich's folk-psychology seems to be the fusion of what we call basic and peripheral common sense, construed as a monolithic theory about the mental; a theory which – like most other older theories – we need to discard. The concepts, beliefs, and explanations of basic common sense as we are defining this notion, are indeterminate. We shall take some time out to explain this indeterminateness. Some concepts are vague in the sense that their borders shade into those of others. The colour terms are good examples of this, with no sharp lines between green and blue, red and orange, etc. Other concepts are open- ended in the sense that we cannot fix now exact boundaries for all future applications. Such concepts include many technological products, e.g. the concepts of a vehicle, since we do not know and cannot envisage in precise terms what kinds of artefact technology will produce that will require legislation covering applications of such terms. The indeterminateness invoked in our discussion is different from both vagueness and open-endedness. A concept is indeterminate in our sense if it does not have conditions of application for all currently envisaged logical possibilities. For example, religion is viewed by anthropologists as a cultural universal. Accepting this hypothesis we can assume that every culture contains religious practices. It seems absurd, however, to suppose that in each of these cultures the notion of a deity is defined in terms of powers, attributes, etc. for all logical possibilities. Given the concept of a deity in any one of these cultures, there will be many questions – different ones for different cases – which cannot be answered by invoking the relevant concept. The same applies to the notion of a human being. Our ordinary notions of a human being are not such that in terms of these we could decide within each 'logically possible world' whether this or that fanciful creature is or is not a human. Our ordinary notions do not stretch that far. (I would argue that this is true also of most of our scientific notions, but this would take us too far from our main topic.) In chapter 6 we shall see a proposal of how to present in semantics indeterminate concepts. For the present we shall leave this notion on the intuitive and informal level. It will suffice to keep in mind that in claiming that everyone has a concept of the self one need not – and should not – claim that common sense comes equipped with elaborate theories of personal identity.

Someone might accept our sketch of basic common sense, but wonder if there is a constant conceptual core, or if there may be constant change and only continuity as the defining thread. The proposal is that there is a constant conceptual core, but this is made up of indeterminate elements, and does not amount to a monolithic theory. My suspicion is that the developmental view emerges mostly in cases in which it is thought of as the only viable alternative to the monolithic theory view. Needless to say, the claim that there is a constant core is not incompatible with claims that there are also some minor changes even in our most basic concepts. This is a matter for empirical historical and psychological work. Furthermore, our conception leaves room for a certain kind of development in any case. For as cultures develop and affect human cognition, some of the indeterminateness of the concepts or beliefs might be eliminated. Questions that were not answerable gain answers. Yet this kind of development does not reduce indeterminateness in an absolute quantitative sense. For along with answering the previously unanswerable, we gain new conceptual ground that enables us to pose questions that a century earlier would have been inconceivable. Thus new dimensions of indeterminateness also arise. For example, basic common sense has nothing to say about problems of identity raised by genetic transplants, etc. Furthermore, this question could not have been raised two hundred years earlier, since the conceptual tools for raising it were lacking. Conceivability, like so many of our other cognitive powers, is a historically conditioned phenomenon.

This completes our characterization of basic common sense. It contrasts with peripheral common sense, i.e. concepts, beliefs, and explanations widely shared at some points in history within a culture or several cultures, but not invariant across history and culture, and not such that at any stage of history humans could not conceive of themselves and the environment without this conceptual paraphernalia. Peripheral common sense changes – at least to some extent – from time to time, and context to context. In western thought it included at various times the flat earth thesis, the geocentric view, and claims such as lisping children being merely stubborn, and certain mental illnesses being signs of an evil character.

The list of examples just given suggests that peripheral common sense is always suspect, and is likely to lead to falsehoods, at times very harmful ones. This would not, however, be a fair characterization. Peripheral common sense includes also a kind of wisdom; the sort that is exemplified in an American classic like *The Old Farmer's Almanac*. Changes in peripheral common sense do not prevent even its ephemeral parts from being at times of value. There may be also cross cultural folk wisdom that remains constant, is of value, but is not required as a part of a necessary set of concepts in terms of which we think of reality.

In summary, it is a mistake to think of peripheral common sense as just a collection of past mistaken scientific theories seeping into common consciousness. Some parts of peripheral common sense come from previous science, some from everyday reflection. Some are useful for a time, others are not. Some may be with us through history, and these may not be true ones. In any case, all of peripheral common sense has to be kept distinct from basic common sense, especially with respect to relations to the sciences and claims for preservation. Science occasionally clashes with peripheral common sense. This is no cause for concern. But we should ask the following questions. Does science 'clash' with basic common sense? Should the preservation of basic common sense be required for good scientific explanations?

'Clash' and 'break' in this context are at best suggestive metaphors. We shall attempt to unpack these by dividing the issue into several sub-topics. First, it is obvious that the sciences add a great deal of information and understanding to that supplied by basic common sense. They do this both by giving better explanations for everyday phenomena and by unearthing new phenomena and providing information for that too. This point hardly needs belabouring, and has no bearing on affirming or denying any 'clashes'. Secondly, the sciences provide new concepts. Some of these, for example, Darwinian or Freudian concepts, seep into peripheral common sense. To understand this, we should reflect on the fact that the concepts of a science fall roughly into three categories. Some, such as that of a living thing, or space, are simply taken over from common sense. Others are taken from common sense and then refined to suit theoretical needs. Some of these are the concepts of force, matter, and time. Many scientific concepts start as common sense concepts, then are turned into metaphoric ones, then become calcified metaphors, and eventually technical notions. The history of the notion of force illustrates this nicely. In these cases there are no 'breaks' or 'clashes'; on the contrary, we see development and continuity between common sense and science. There are also cases in which entirely new concepts are added by science, e.g. those of quanta, neutron, etc. But even in these cases it makes no sense to talk about clashes. For these technical notions are forged to deal with phenomena that are not part of everyday observations. Concepts dealing with different ranges of phenomena cannot clash.

It is also true that the sciences can add new modes of explanation. For example, the kind of precise probabilistic models of the behaviour of certain parts of nature that the modern sciences can provide cannot be found in basic common sense. The same holds for complicated mathematical proofs. But even in the realm of explanations there is a core of simple models that are parts of basic common sense and are preserved also in the sciences. These include induction by enumeration of samples and simple *modus ponens*. Science has not discarded these, but expanded them and refined them so as to allow for more explanatory power in theories. Once more, there are no clashes here.

Science can also affect basic common sense by placing some part of it within a larger theoretical framework within which it does not have a central place. Thus physics, for example, does not deny our common-sense conceptions of solid, medium-size material objects and the causal relations between these, but within its theories these concepts and correlations are not the most fundamental. Basic common-sense concepts, beliefs, and explanations do not constitute what in an axiomatized version would be the foundational core of either physics or chemistry. It is also true that the common-sense observations that are parts of our everyday conceptions of the physical world are not the basic facts that physics or biology strives to explain. But this amounts only to a conceptual dislocation of basic common sense. It does not lead to clashes if we interpret this notion in the strong sense of incompatibilities and contradictions.

We have now surveyed various ways in which science interacts with common sense, without finding any breaks or clashes. To be sure, continuity is not uniform. But to show what Stich and some of his cognitive science friends claim, we would have to show either that science contradicts basic common sense, or that it renders some of the basic commonsensical notions as useless and illusory as those of ghosts and witches, or that its modes of explanation lead to the rejection of some of those contained in basic common sense. It would take a detailed examination of the histories of the mature sciences to show that these things never happen. But the burden of proof lies with those who see clashes where we, on the basis of these general reflections, see continuity. It is natural to see clashes between science and common sense if one thinks of the latter as merely a series of older discarded theories. We have shown, however, that this is an inadequate and simplistic conception of common sense.

Let us push the matter a little further and see if there are philosophical considerations supporting the claim that clashes between science and common sense should not take place. The following arguments support this claim. What is intelligibility? What is explanatory force? Is it merely predictability and the subsuming of what we know under generalizations with wider scope or more formal power? Is it enough to have a deductive structure with statements describing the observable at the 'lower end'? Or do we also require that the unfamiliar should be explained in terms of the familiar, or at least related to concepts that we have and that cover familiar facts? If we opt for the second option, then we have strong reasons for saying that though science brings new concepts, beliefs, and explanations, and can lead to the dislocation of common sense mentioned above, ultimately it must have some links to familiar concepts and facts if it is to provide intelligibility. Puzzlement and the problematic start at the common sense level, and if science is to have genuine explanatory power for humans, it must be able to return to this level as well.

These reflections lead to the following two theses.

- *Thesis I.* Historically, there has been no widespread clash

174

between science and basic common sense.
- *Thesis II.* One of the aims of science should be to reduce or link the unfamiliar to the familiar, and thus clashes with basic common sense should be avoided or at least minimized.

Much more needs to be said in order to establish these theses securely. But at least an alternative to Stich's position has been spelled out, it has been made clear what it takes to refute it, and that the more articulate conception of common sense that it contains should provide a challenge for those who would want to defend the view of many clashes between science and common sense.

Someone might, however, agree with our analysis and with Theses I and II, but still insist that in the case of a study of cognition everything is different. What reasons could there be for saying that a science of cognition provides a unique conceptual challenge? The following is a possible reply. The elimination of concepts like belief, intention, etc. and the reduction of a science of cognition to a physiological base would not be a matter of eliminating common sense in favour of something quite different, but rather of shifting a range of phenomena to explanations in terms of the material. Materialist concepts themselves are or are based on some of the concepts of basic common sense.

In reply to this move, we should point to historical precedents. In attempting to reduce biology to chemistry, the basic biological notions are not eliminated. Rather, they are accounted for within a larger framework within which they are no longer central. This is very different from the drastic conceptual surgery that the friends of Stich advocate. There is also a normative reply. It points to the unprecedented conceptual crisis into which the proposed move would place us. We would be in the schizo-phrenic position of using the concepts of belief, decision, etc. in our everyday lives, and at the same time thinking of these as no less illusory than the concepts for ghosts and witches.

In conclusion, we sketched ways in which science and common sense interacted in the past. The burden of proof lies with those who think that in the case of cognition things will be quite different. In the meantime we shall press on and present a conception of cognition within which science and common sense can peacefully co-exist in the same way in which they co-existed

175

during our past history. The reflections supporting my stance can be seen as a much weakened and historically oriented version of the 'unity of science' thesis. For my position is to assume that relations between the various sciences and basic common sense, though admitting of some variation, remain fundamentally the same, and there there is no reason to suppose that it will be different in the case of cognition. This is not just a matter of induction, but also a demand on science if we adopt as part of the criteria of intelligibility the tie to the familiar, articulated above.

So far, then, we defended the claim that there are good reasons to retain concepts like those of belief, understanding, deciding, etc. within a philosophical or scientific conception of cognition. This, however, does not resolve the ontological issue. Do science and basic common sense clash with respect to ontology? Will they in the case of cognition? If so, how do we resolve the conflict? We had already occasion to introduce the notion of indeterminateness as applied to concepts. Let us apply this notion also to ontological questions. Philosophers or scientists may opt to be materialists or dualists with regards to cognition. But it seems odd to force this option on basic common sense. Questions like: 'Are all aspects and constituents of human cognition material entities?' cannot be answered on the basis of basic common-sense conceptions, because these are not determinate for these possibilities. One can have conceptions of the self, of a human, of belief, that leave this particular choice open. We can live together, relate to each other, learn, teach, make decisions and cooperate, while making some assumptions about ourselves and each other, but without facing questions about the materiality or immateriality of entities and characteristics that we posit.

The same applies to a concept like reasoning. Neither basic nor peripheral common sense is prepared to regard this process as either necessarily material or necessarily immaterial. One can be sure that reasoning exists, without knowing how to categorize it in terms of these philosophic dichotomies. Thus I suggest that while basic common sense has some ontologically determinate concepts – e.g. the ones for material bodies and their parts – it also has some that are not. Cognition and its constituents fall into the latter category. Stich thinks that common sense has an anti-materialist ontology for cognition, but we saw that he also thinks that common sense has a monolithic theory of cognition. Once we see that the latter claims can be rejected, the former becomes dubitable too. Basic common sense can have an ontological commitment to belief, decision, etc. and fairly complex concepts of these, without taking a stand on the materialist–dualist controversy.

It is time now to extend this argument to scientific conceptions. We can study cognition in many of its aspects, we can give much of it detailed characterizations, without committing ourselves on the materialist–dualist issue. Two cognitive psychologists can study together cognitive developmental stages for the growth of language or arithmetic skills without agreeing on whether all of cognition is on a purely materialist basis. Only some research projects assume a definite ontological commitment, and even in those cases the results – e.g. examinations of the neurophysiological basis of cognition – can be reinterpreted also in other ontological schemes.

The same considerations apply to the notion of 'content' or object of thought. One can study these and articulate definite proposals, while leaving the question of an eventual success of nominalistic reductionist schemes open. At the present time, our study of cognition resembles in some ways the earlier stages of astronomy. People held a variety of views about the ontology of the celestial entities, but they could study these in great detail from the point of view of paths, and even suggest ways of accounting for these paths by invoking various sorts of theoretical entities.

On the basis of these reflections we reach:

- *Thesis III.* Both science and common sense, with respect to cognition, can be ontologically indeterminate enough not to have to choose between materialism and dualism. The contrast between science and common sense does not correlate with the contrast between materialism and dualism.

Thus we can make this sort of ontological indeterminateness a part of our proposal, and leave issues of an eventual materialist or dualist account a matter of future empirical research rather than philosophical dogma. We saw in our survey of problems that materialism, physicalism, and dualism each has conceptual strengths as well as weaknesses. The notion of matter turned out to be so open-ended as not to be suitable as the foundation of philosophical ontological creeds. When shifting to the twin doctrine of physicalism, we found ourselves shifting to a sociological thesis of faith. Why make physics the ultimate standard of what is real in space and time? Why not geometry or biology? Answers to this question will fall back on themes canvassed already; physics is good because, unlike biology, it deals with everything and does so in non-teleological terms, and unlike geometry it investigates everything in terms of causal connections. But why should we make these requirements implicitly the key arbiters of metaphysical matters? Furthermore, how do we know that future physics will not include teleological notions or abandon the stress on causal correlations in favour of another, as yet undeveloped, basic notion linking entities together? Physics in our times is linked to technology. Hence it faces pressures of various kinds. Among these are moral considerations, matters of human convenience, and many others. How do we know that such factors will not affect its ontological choices? The unity and continuity of any of the sciences through history is a debateable matter. Thus departmental demarcations might not correspond to important conceptual divisions. This was well noted by Professor Quine, who in his lectures at Harvard used to say that philosophers tend to confuse the compartments of the universe with the departments of the university. Quine himself, however, has taken stands favourable to physicalism. But I have difficulties seeing why physicalism should not be a prime target of Quine's dictum, quoted here.

We saw that dualism faced problems with respect to the individuation of some of its key elements and with respect to interaction between material and immaterial substances. But it did link up with one of the important components of our concept of cognition, namely phenomenal experience. Is it fair, then, to suppose that its ontological posits are like the positing of witches? Positing entities on the basis of superstition is either a matter of theorizing on the basis of inadequate empirical evidence or reaching ontological decisions on the basis of considerations, such as those arising out of fear or political pressure, that should be irrelevant to rational empirical enterprise. But neither of these ways accounts for the positing of mental, immaterial entities. We saw three reasons for positing these, namely, intentionality, immediate cognitive experience, and the special relations to abstract objects that cognition has. None of these is a matter of inadequate evidence, or of fear, political pressure, etc. Dualist claims survive even if someone shows that the hypothesis that God created the universe and humans have immortal souls can be maintained on a materialist basis, with both the deity and souls analysed in terms of some rarified concept of energy. The same applies to the notion of a responsible moral agent. This is not to say that dualism could not be avoided or seem faulty. But a comparison to the posits of witches and ghosts seems unfair and places the alternatives in too good a light.

Our remaining non-committal with respect to an historically very influential dichotomy in philosophy, and seeing it as an empirical choice which we cannot make yet in good conscience, leaves us without any conflicts with views on freedom, determinism, and similar larger issues that we decided to leave aside at the outset. There are various conceptions of freedom, determinism, and indeterminism, and these do not require either a necessarily material or dualistic framework. Morality requires a notion of responsibility, but we saw already that this is a matter for theories of determinism and indeterminism and causality.

In summary, this section presents a certain view of common sense and its 'anatomy', and a certain view of the relation between science and the various ingredients of common sense. This view suggests that we come up with a notion of cognition that is philosophically viable, provides a framework for further empirical research of several kinds, and preserves what we called basic common sense. We then went on to argue for another part of the proposal, namely that a viable philosophical notion of cognition meeting our first condition can be, and should be, also ontologically indeterminate at least as far as the dualism–materialism debate is concerned. Before we present further positive ingredients of the proposal, we shall take a look at behaviourism and functionalism from the perspective gained so far.

Why Do We See With Our Eyes, and Hear With Our Ears, and What Does This Show About Cognition?

Some time ago, in a paper whose insights have not been

sufficiently appreciated, Paul Grice (1962) discussed some of the problems we encounter when we try to imagine what it would be like to recognize a new sense. We shall use some of this material in our proposal for what an adequate concept of a sense is. After that we shall see how much of this is transferable to a characterization of cognition. Utilizing this result and the conclusions reached in the previous section we shall move towards the core of the positive proposal by seeing why, in light of what we suggest in this section, neither behaviourism nor functionalism is adequate as either a philosophical or scientific notion of cognition, though much of the empirical work done within these approaches may be useful.

Though Grice does not put it in these words, one can sum up the gist of the problem by asking: 'Why do we see with our eyes and hear with our ears?' To many this will sound like an inane question. Is this because they regard the sentence 'we see with our eyes and hear with our ears' as analytic, and would regard the sentence: 'we could be seeing with our ears and hearing with our eyes' nonsensical? If so, on what interpretation does the above sentence prove to be analytic? It seems that we obtain the analytical interpretation if we take a completely functionalist position. For on that view the eye is 'whatever enables us to see'. Hence apart from very general constraints, it does not matter what the organ is like. As long as the result is seeing, it is an eye that did it. But this does not ring true, as Grice himself suggests. Would we really call an organ as different in structure and constituency as the ear is from the eye an eye as long as it gave us information about colour, etc? Could there not be other ways of sensing to gain the kind of perceptual information that we normally get via seeing? And yet, the sentence under considera-tion seems analytic in some ways. So perhaps we should try another reading. Suppose that we take a non-functionalist, let us call it a 'structuralist', stand, and say that as long as something is in terms of structure and constituency sufficiently similar to the eye, even if quite different in function, we shall call it an eye, and change the definition of 'see' accordingly. Once more the sentence proves to be analytic because we shall call seeing whatever it is that an 'eye', as defined, does. But that does not seem right either. If something were to be very similar to an eye but would not function that way, we would not call it an eye. Yet

180

Grice seems right in suggesting that the connection between eye and seeing, ear and hearing, etc. is not purely contingent. Where does this leave us?

Grice's paper is 'dialectical'. It makes a number of suggestions which show what the prolegomena to any future individuation of the senses should be. We shall not pursue that matter. Instead, we shall concentrate on the four factors that Grice considers as relevant to a characterization of a human sense:

1. Its proper objects, e.g. for seeing colour, etc., for hearing sound.
2. The proper felt experiences, e.g. the sensations of seeing, hearing.
3. The appropriate physical stimuli; for seeing light and surfaces, etc., for hearing whatever causes sound.
4. The appropriate organ in terms of constituency and structure.

We can now restate various alternatives within this scheme. A functionalist would say that 'eye' should be defined solely in terms of what leads to behaviour involving 1. A 'structuralist' would say that 'eye' should be defined solely in terms of 4. A materialist would give the definition in terms of 3 and 4. It seems that each of these proposals is deficient. We do need in our concept of 'eye' the inclusion of all four factors, including 2. Could there be hearing without any auditory experiences? Could there be smelling without any of the physical stimuli that cause olfactory sensations? It seems, then, that in our talk of eye, ear, etc., and seeing, hearing, etc., we assume that the four factors mentioned by Grice will go together. But there can be no law of logic or semantics that forces these factors to coincide in nature. It is logically possible that in some conceivable state of affairs they do not. It is plausible to suppose that under such circumstances semantics would be insufficient and we would not know what to say. (This can be interpreted in two ways. Either a claim that under such circumstances we would not know what to say, or the claim that we cannot know now what we would say then, i.e. under those circumstances. For our immediate purposes it does not matter which reading we adopt, but the issue will become important in the Concluding Postscript.)

Thus we can view the coincidence of the four factors as one of the very general facts that serves as a background against which our talk of the senses and perception takes place. Our conclusion is, then, that 'eye', 'ear', 'see', 'hear', etc. are not defined 'across all possible worlds': rather these terms are indeterminate in the sense we used this notion before. They apply only in worlds in which certain general conditions obtain, i.e. in worlds in which the possibilities are conditioned by the coincidence of the four factors. Our concepts of the senses are not logically sharp concepts. All four factors are relevant, and there is no precise way of determining how much variance semantics allows for each factor, or how much variance in one can be counteracted by precise correspondence to the 'normal' in the other factors. Thus as far as our ordinary concepts for the senses are concerned, neither functionalists nor materialists have the last word, since our concepts for the senses include, in not precise ways, structural, phenomenal, as well as functional factors. The range of admissible mixtures does not admit of a precise delineation.

What should we say, in view of these reflections, about scientific concepts for the senses? These, as we know, stress the ingredient least emphasized in the everyday concepts, namely the processes and the material base for perception. But one can place this focus within a scheme roughly the same as that provided by the everyday concepts. Indeed, given what was said in the last section about the presumption that science should incorporate basic common sense, one would strive for a philosophical and scientific concept that will leave room for the emphasis by science on one factor, perhaps by philosophy on another, and still leave us without a sharp break between the commonsensical and the theoretical. To be sure, basic common sense may be dislocated in the sense discussed above, and the 'anatomy' of the four factors be made more specific and detailed. But still, the empirical work on the details of the processing will sooner or later, at some level, have to account for the content or representational nature of a sense like seeing as well. We do not want to know only what the physiology and optics of perception are, we want to know also how we gain information from it (Marr, 1982; and Kitcher, 1988.)

Equipped with this rough outline of concepts for the senses, let us see how well we can apply this to cognition. Obviously, cognition is not one of the senses. But the basic structure in terms of the four factors is still applicable, though in need of qualifications. Cognition certainly has its proper objects, whether we describe these within naturalistic and pragmatic frameworks or within a framework more in tune with what is proposed here. In either case, the objects will include concepts and propositions or sentences, individuated in ways mentioned in our survey. There may be others, but we need not go into that here. Felt experience is also a part of cognition. Just as we have certain experiences of seeing and hearing, we have also characteristic experiences of thinking and believing, even if it is difficult to describe these precisely, and different people might stress different aspects of experience, such as imagery.

The third factor is more problematic. In the case of the senses, this is the appropriate stimulus, presumably identifiable in terms of physical factors. In the case of cognition, it is not clear what the appropriate stimulus should be. If one accepts the spontaneity of thought, then the stimulus may or may not be physical, but in any case it will not be something external to the human body. On a naturalist pragmatic picture, it will be something external. One might also hold the view that the only appropriate stimulus is a previous thought, and all else is accidental. This raises, of course, the problem of the first thought. In any case, it is part of our concept of cognition that there are some appropriate stimuli, even if we are quite unclear about their nature. Our everyday notion of cognition would hardly entail the emergence of thought, atomistically, out of nowhere.

The same lack of definiteness characterizes the fourth component. Humans today agree for the most part that this is the brain, but it is not clear that one would want this to be part of basic common sense, given the way we define this notion. Furthermore, it is unclear whether there might be other non-material aspects of the agency underlying thought. Thus, once more, we should say that there is a fourth factor, for we do think that humans 'think something', but its nature is left unspecified. Thus we have the four factors in the case of cognition too, but two of these are much less specific than in the case of the senses.

As in the case of the senses, our concepts of belief and thought and the semantic of the corresponding terms operate against the background assumption that the four factors coincide. Again, there is no logical or metaphysical necessity that will guarantee this coincidence. Thus belief and its conceptual cousins cannot be defined 'across all logically possible worlds'. Furthermore, even for the possibilities constrained by the conditions of coincidence, the concepts remain indeterminate. For there are no precise conditions specifying how far alleged cases of cognition can stray from the normal cases of meeting 1–4. What if the felt experiences are different? What if the thought/belief system seems to malfunction systematically for typical cases of decision-making or problem-solving? What if the creatures in whom cognition allegedly takes place do not and cannot envisage truth and falsity, but only weaker notions of acceptance?

Thus it is reasonable to propose both as our everyday concept and as the philosophical and scientific concept of cognition one in which we find the four factors mentioned, and in which the kinds of indeterminatenesses referred to prevail. Within such a scheme empirical work can flourish with regards to the phenomenal experiences, the physiological processing, and the material base. This can take place alongside philosophic analyses of the objects, with mutual constraints emerging from both kinds of work. Keeping in mind the dismal record philosophy has in predicting empirical matters, this conception does not make an *a priori* judgement on whether the various kinds of work mentioned will converge. Furthermore, this conception of cognition can remain ontologically indeterminate with regards to the dichotomy of materialism–dualism, and can leave the eventual resolution of the dichotomy, if not its overcoming, to be a matter of future empirical findings. This is especially appropriate given the open-endedness of the categories of the mental and the physical. 'Whereof one cannot be certain, thereof one should remain undogmatic' to borrow and rephrase a well-known pronouncement from a different context.

Having sketched this proposal, let us see what we can say about behaviourism and functionalism. We shall take up behaviourism first. We have seen various conceptual problems affecting this approach. In this section the key criticism of behaviourism will centre on the threefold distinction between evidence, fact, and explanation. This can be illustrated with reference to fatigue. There is the state of someone's being tired, the evidence for this state, and explanations for it. The evidence would normally include both introspective evidence such as the agent's feeling tired, as well as behavioural evidence, e.g. fatigued behaviour. The behaviourist would want to rule out the first type of evidence but this seems arbitrary. If even in the physical sciences we rely ultimately on someone's report of personal observation, why not also in the case of psychology? Of course, introspective evidence can be unreliable. A person's reports on feeling or not feeling fatigue are not decisive with respect to whether he is really tired. Behavioural evidence might clash with and overrule the subjective data. This is why baseball managers rely on performance behaviour rather than on the pitcher's subjective data ('I feel quite alright. I am just having bad luck, etc.'), when considering a change on the pitching mound. But the opposite can happen as well. If the subjective data clash consistently with what we take to be relevant behaviour, we might look for other causes of the behavioural pattern.

As to the fundamental facts to which we want to address ourselves, some of these emerge on the behavioural level while others do not. The key issue cannot be whether there are interesting behavioural facts, for this is admitted by all sides. But the non-behaviourist points to important facts to be explained by cognitive psychology that are not on that level. For example, a child moving from numbering elements of collections to the concept of numbers and the operations on these is an important fact for a theory of cognition to explain, but it is not on the observational level. The same applies to other aspects of learning. We cannot specify all of the facts of human learning on the behavioural level, yet an adequate theory of cognition should account for all of these.

We have argued that actual behaviour is a function of many diverse capacities and dispositions. This can be used as an additional argument for claiming that many of the important facts of cognition cannot be stated on the behavioural level, for we want to isolate the facts to be explained by a theory of cognition of some sub-field of this enterprise from other facts whose accounts will involve other branches of psychology or other disciplines altogether. Objects like chairs, tables, etc. have different aspects, and these will be studied by different disciplines such as geometry, physics, chemistry, furniture-making, etc. This parallels the multifacetedness of behaviour. Thus just as we have no unified science of chairs, tables, etc., we should not expect the emergence of such discipline for behaviour as such.

So far we have talked about two of the ingredients mentioned at the outset, namely evidence and fact. Turning to the third element, explanation, one should apply the general morals of the philosophy of the other sciences also to cognitive psychology. In all rational empirical disciplines we try to explain dispositions in terms of underlying unobservable structures or material substratum. This should be true also of cognitive psychology. Adequate explanations of language use, calculation, practical reasoning, etc., will not only correlate pieces of behaviour, but will try to account for these in terms of dispositions, and for these, in turn, by some underlying configuration of cognitive structure which may or may not be specified in ontologically indeterminate ways. We explain language interpretation by reference to dispositions, and these, in turn, by reference to operations on representations of linguistic structure, be these material or not. Thus the positive message of behaviourism seems to be at most: stay as close to the level of the observable as possible. Such a message would be compatible with approaches to psychology other than the behavioural. But apart from this, it is very doubtful that the message is really good advice for scientific methodology. Staying close or not staying close to the observable is an option that should be judged case by case, in terms of what we gain in any specific context when we move away from the observable. We might gain conceptual clarity, more generality in explanatory power, a better chance at mathematical models for the explananda, etc. Alternatively, moving away from the observational in some cases can lead to obscurity or pseudo-explanations. One needs to take all of these facts into consideration. The pull towards the observable is only one of the relevant factors. One shudders to think where, for example, physics would be today if it had stayed close to the observable. On the other hand, this by itself is not a reason to push determinedly, no matter what, to a state in which cognitive psychology is as remote from everyday experience as physics. There may be inherent reasons why one science yields illuminating explanatory structures that are close to the observational level while others do not. But as of now there are no general arguments showing that cognitive psychology deals with phenomena that are inherently suitable for theories that stay close to the surface.

In summary, an empirical science has the following fundamental ingredients: 1. observations, 2. facts to be explained, 3. evidence used, 4. explanations. The facts need not be wholly on the observational level. Evidence is used on different levels in different contexts. We use evidence for the positing of facts, then can use these as evidence for hypotheses, then use evidence to confirm or disconfirm hypotheses, etc. Explanations typically emerge on a higher level of abstraction than the facts to be explained or the evidence used in confirmation and disconfirmation, but this need not be always the case. In reflecting on the various relationships between the four ingredients, one should be prepared to see different configurations in different sciences, and in different sub-fields of the same science. Behaviourism as a philosophical or methodological creed places arbitrary restrictions on how the four ingredients should be arranged in cognitive psychology. Hence it should be rejected.

Let us turn now to functionalism in light of the above considerations. We saw in our survey of problems that functionalism emerges primarily as a way for some to preserve their materialist ontology while agreeing with a non-reductionistic way of specifying cognitive phenomena. On the basis of our reflections, however, this is not a sound motivation for a psychological theory, for we saw that a dogmatic commitment to materialism rests on shaky grounds. Furthermore, we saw that functionalism in its usual form comes burdened with the presuppositions of naturalism and the pragmatic picture. Once these presuppositions are stated, one can envisage plausible alternatives without giving up the idea that cognition can be a legitimate object of an empirical science. It is worth noting that linking some parts of cognition to a pragmatic scheme is more plausible than when one attempts this for other parts. For example, it is more plausible to do this for belief or inference and other parts of information-processing than for those parts of cognition that are not so closely linked to information-processing, such as understanding or gaining insight. Furthermore, functionalism rests on a translation scheme within which mental terms can be given translations into reference to functional states. We saw reasons to suppose that carrying out such a scheme is problematic. All of these considerations are grounds for exploring other conceptions of psychological theory.

Our defence of ontological realism in chapter 4 leaves the prospects of linking functionalism to a nominalistic representation of object or content rather remote. First, we saw that nominalism does not offer more clarity than realism, thus some of the motivation disappears. Secondly, the reductionistic programmes entailed by nominalism have not met with success even when attempted by first-rate minds. One can only speculate how much impetus would be left behind functionalism if its adherents were to admit that materialism is not as attractive as they thought it to be, and the prospects of nominalistic 'contents' were also rather dubious.

We have considered in the previous pages relations between scientific concepts of cognition and what we called basic common sense. Let us see how functionalism fares when we make the appropriate comparison. At first glance, it is clear that functionalist notions of the mental do not stay close to what we characterize as common sense. For in functionalism explanations of several distinct ingredients of the common-sense notion are squeezed into just one facet of the analysis of cognition, namely the functional states. Furthermore, even at that, one of the ingredients, namely felt experience, is left out altogether.

In reply the functionalist can say two things. First, that he never meant to stay close within the confines of common-sense notions. Secondly, his main focus is on providing certain kinds of explanations, and these should be judged on their own merit, not in relation of proximity or lack of such with regard to common sense.

If what was suggested in the previous pages is sound, then the closeness to basic common sense is a relevant factor in assessment, even when we consider solely the functional explanations as proposed pieces of science. But on the other hand, it is true that this is not decisive. If all else is equal, then closeness to basic common sense is important. But is all else equal? The answer to this question depends on how we assess, apart from considerations of philosophical worry, functionalist explanations as *bona-fide* scientific explanations.

The following seems to be the main shortcoming of functional explanations, considered simply as a type of empirical hypothesis. These explanations locate what we called object or content as ways of specifying functional states and not as separate components of cognition, to be studied in its own right. But by doing this, the functionalist rules out from the start that interesting correlations and mutual constraints can be found between, e.g., the study of the objects of cognition and the study of the physiological processing. In this respect the computer analogy, on which functionalism was originally based, is misleading. To be sure software and hardware can be designed and produced separately. But when we study human beings, we should not rule out the possibility that studying the human hardware will help us delineate feasible representations of the objects of thought. Likewise, we should leave open the possibility that an intense study of ways of representing the objects of thought places constraints on viable hypotheses about human processing mechanisms. Finding out about physiology cannot do semantics, but it can help us choose between different accounts of semantics. Or the other way around, careful study of some of the properties of the objects of thought can help us avoid pitfalls of positing too simple a physiological processing mechanism. Considering such interplays between components suggests a richer concept of cognition and a more multifaceted form of explanation than the functionalist seems to allow.

Finally, we shall take up the issue of the functionalist not having a place within his scheme of things for the link between the various ingredients of cognition and felt experience. Can we give considerations to show that this is a greater flaw than the gap in our own 'objectual' account in terms of explanations, between the objects of cognition and cognitive states and processes?

The adequacy of the reply to be given depends partly on whether one accepts what has been said about the need to relate the unfamiliar, and the desirability of having the same four ingredients in our philosophical and scientific conceptions of cognition as the ones we found in the concept of cognition of basic common-sense. For in terms of that view, there is a considerable difference between the two 'gaps'. The functionalist has no link between his explanation and the conceptual framework within which these are formulated on the one hand,

and one of the basic ingredients of the common-sense notion on the other. Within the objectualist view, all four common-sense ingredients are acknowledged and are parts of the philosophic conception. What is left open is a link that is left open by common-sense, namely the empirical relation between object and cognition. Leaving room for but being as yet unable to fill in an empirical gap is not the same as not representing within one's theory what is a conceptual link within the basic common-sense notion that we are analysing.

The functionalist would be ahead if he could show one of the following:

1. That his chances of linking functional organization and felt experience are greater than filling in the empirical gap between the cognitive processes and the objects of cognition conceived within a realist ontology; or
2. that filling in the 'gap' of the 'objectualist' is in principle an impossible empirical task.

I see no reasons for supporting either of these claims. What the mind can represent and how this might take place are at present questions of the most speculative kind. Thus a dogmatic stance like 2 seems unjustified. As to 1, any such comparison is speculation of the most dubious kind. We are comparing probabilities of successes of research programmes in light of essentially no evidence.

Nothing in this argument is meant to show that the functionalist cannot explain some day how the functionally organized mechanisms are linked to felt experience. On the other hand, while the presence of this gap is worth keeping in mind, we have given other philosophical considerations to support the claim that functionalism should be seen at best as a last resort conceptual move. In what follows we shall see if we cannot do better.

The Objectual Theory

In preparation for the presentation of the main point of the objectual view, we shall review considerations against naturalism and the pragmatic picture, and specify the unique way in which cognition is related to its objects.

The following considerations seem in my view to weigh heavily against naturalism. Our conceptions of the natural and natural relations evolve through history. This is not only a matter of increased information but also of emerging new explanatory patterns. Thus whatever we might regard as 'nature' and 'natural relations' is really a part of the science – and of the peripheral common sense – of yesterday. Restricting ourselves to explanatory patterns in this way is to adopt a very conservative point of view. The stand against naturalism says that we should remain open-minded with regard to new explanatory patterns and models. Above all, we should not regard the 'natural' of today a restriction on what basic common sense suggests as explananda. According to basic common sense, cognition has certain complexes of universals among its objects. This should not be ruled out from the start on the ground that no current natural relations account for it. Maybe we shall find such a relation, and again, it may also be the case that some relationships will remain forever beyond the pale of human understanding and explanations.

The following consideration is the basis of my stand against the pragmatic model. If we accept the spontaneity of thought, mentioned in our survey, then it seems arbitrary to think that cognition has as its primary function the the orientation towards action. For if thought must lead in some indirect way to action, would this not be a restriction on spontaneity? And if so, is it a reasonable and empirically supported constraint?

The denial of the pragmatic picture should not be confused with the rejection of two very plausible assertions. One of these is that in order for us to be thinking beings, we might have to be acting agents. This would not be incompatible with the rejection of the pragmatic picture. For this does not say what thought is; rather, it states that a necessary precondition of human thought is the capacity to act. The other claim is the epistemological point that we typically find out about beliefs and thoughts of others by observing their actions. This tells us something about our everyday methodology for finding out what is on someone else's mind. It tells us how we know what someone thinks; it does not tell us what thinking or having beliefs is. Thus the acceptance of this point too is compatible with the rejection of naturalism and the pragmatic picture.

The view I am advocating can be labelled 'realism', for its starting point is the claim that the analysis of cognition should be within what can be taken to be real, and not restricted to a subset of this realm called the 'natural'. As we saw, a rough informal and non-prejudiced characterization of the real is that it is whatever is a genuine subject of true propositions. This does not delineate reality in some informative way – nor is it meant to do that. Any further restriction on what constitutes legitimate elements for an analysis of cognition is, from my point of view, to take an unduly dogmatic position. Starting with this claim, then, we move on to see how the different parts of reality such as mathematics, art, cognition, the workings of the physical world, etc., are linked together. This is an empirical issue, and our conceptions of these links at any time historically conditioned. We locate, then, cognition as a part of reality, and make no dogmatic assertion as to how it relates to other parts of reality, except, as we shall see, the claim that it must be related to what are in a unique way its objects.

We include under cognition thoughts, beliefs, concepts, understanding, explanation, proof, and similar items. For purposes of facilitating the exposition of the proposal we shall concentrate mostly on thought and take this to be an articulation and representation of propositional content. Thus, roughly, to think that something is the case is to think that p, where the latter stands for a declarative sentence, can be assessed as true or false. This characterization says nothing so far about *human* thought. We shall take that notion to be thought as just characterized, with limitations imposed by various human biological and psychological factors. We shall also hold that the expression of thought by humans is typically a matter of simultaneous manifestation of thinking and many other factors such as intentions, emotional needs, etc.

The first important ingredient of the proposal is the claim that thought has a special conceptual involvement with its objects. In order to explain this claim, we need to survey various ways in which processes, activities, and states can have objects, Needless to say, we shall restrict the discussion to a few important types of cases.

The first type is that in which we can distinguish conceptually as well as in space and time between processes and states on the one hand, and objects to which these are related causally. Examples are: pushing, pulling, kicking, digesting, etc., as well as to be angry with someone or to be irritated or annoyed with someone. The first few items are examples of what we call physical activities, and the latter instances of what we call psychological processes. The causal relations are not always the same. The first two examples involve moving objects, the third involves exerting force on an object, the fourth involves transforming an object, and some of the others involve being affected by objects. For this type of case, in each instance we can specify a process such as moving or transforming things, or being emotionally affected by them, and independently specify objects, such as material things, persons, etc., that can enter into these relations. The two, i.e. process and object, are individuated independently of each other. Kicking is an event. Its individuation does not depend on the number of objects kicked. The same considerations apply to pulling or pushing. Furthermore, the types under consideration include not only physical processes. It cuts across the physical–mental distinction. Thirdly, the processes can involve either observed or unobserved entities.

These examples contrast with what we can call objectless activities and states such as walking, being ill, smiling, etc. In the case of these activities there are many causal interactions between objects while the activity or process lasts, but these do not figure in the semantics of the terms denoting the activities.

Our second type of case involves closer conceptual links between process and object. Examples of this class are: hunters of whales, worshippers of Zeus, carpenters, and architects. In all of these instances we have activities that are conceptually specified by links to objects. A hunter of whales is different from a deer hunter, worshipping Zeus is not the same as worshipping Baal, making chairs is different from building houses. In these cases the individuation of the activities is partly in terms of the specifications of the objects. Furthermore, the object need not be in a causal relation to the activity. This is particularly clear in the case of the Zeus worshipper, for here, as far as we know, there exists no object to relate to. It may be that a common element among all of these cases is that intention is necessary for them. A person making a table by accident is not a carpenter, a person sacrificing on the altar of Zeus by accident is not a Zeus

worshipper, etc. For our purposes these illustrations are sufficient. Looking for exact criteria for intention would take us too
far from our main topic. It is important for our investigation,
however, that in these cases the specification and individuation of
the activity does not require reference to the internal structure of
the objects in question. To understand carpentry we need to
know a lot about tables, etc., but we need not know much about
these objects in order to understand the term 'carpenter'. The
same holds for the understanding of phrases like 'hunter of
whales', 'architect'. To be sure, a worshipper of Zeus must know
in the relevant sense 'who Zeus is', and similar considerations
apply to the hunter of whales. But this requirement does not
mean that the practitioners must have knowledge of the detailed
anatomy of the objects to which they are related.

The point made here about the lack of necessity to be able to
manipulate conceptual constituents of the objects in these cases is
a semantic one. It is not a comment on the psychology of
intentions. One might claim, for example, that whenever
intentionality of the sort illustrated is involved, there must be
some mental representation of the object. The hunter looking for
whales must have some representation of whales in mind, and the
same holds for the architect or the worshipper. But the
representations need not go beyond including a few salient
properties of the objects represented. This holds also for
architects and carpenters. To be sure, such practitioners will
know a lot about specific objects they construct, but that does not
require some conceptual articulation of the 'anatomy' of objects
in general.

We have singled out so far two types of case in which activities
or processes have semantically required objects. We turn now to
the third class of cases which is the focus of our discussion. This is
the class to which the various states and processes of cognition
belong. Let us consider thought in general, and its involvement in
mathematical reasoning or language understanding in particular.
Like in the second type of cases, the objects need not be causally
related to the processes and activities. Let us suppose that
someone is entertaining the thought that koala bears are
marsupials. The object of the man's thought is the proposition
that koala bears are marsupials. This proposition involves
combinations of properties. We saw in Part I a realist defence of

194

interpreting the object in this way. Given our knowledge of cognition and of the constituents of propositions as well as our conception of causality, it seems that the link between thought and object is not causal. As of now, the exact nature of this link is not specified either by common sense or by science. This does not prevent us from seeing a number of important conceptual points.

First, the thoughts we have are individuated by their objects. Only in some cases can we point to important behavioural differences, as in cases like thinking that the approaching animal is a cow, or thinking that it is a lioness. Introspective felt experience also takes us just so far. There are many cases in which the only crucial difference between thoughts is in their respective objects. Thus, for example, the key difference between the thought that koala bears are marsupials and the thought that wallabies are marsupials lies in the difference between the objects. One might say, however, that this differentiation concerns primarily thought types. Thus we need to supplement the account and say that tokens of the same thought type are individual events. We defended having these as fundamental elements of reality in the part on ontology. So thought-types are individuated by objects, tokens are individuated by objects and by relation to subject and to time and place that individuates particular events of this sort.

We still have not reached what is unique about the way thoughts have objects. For someone might say that what we said so far is also true of whale hunters and Zeus worshippers. To consider a more realistic example, the only difference between the hunters of kangaroos and the hunters of wallabies is in the respective objects. In fact, for those ignorant hunters who do not know the difference between these two lovable animals, the two activities collapse into one and, for that matter, for these people the relevant chapters of Milne's fine book that are concerned with Kanga and her friends could be just as well about a wallaby.

It was said above that for the intentional cases it was not essential that the practitioner or the person understanding the meaning of terms introducing the relevant activities should be able to articulate conceptually the objects, but only to have some beliefs about them. This is, however, necessary in the case of cognition. For the thinking person to have the proposition that koala bears are marsupials as the object of thought, it is necessary that he should be able to decompose this into constituents, reorganize these constituents with the help of others into other complexes, etc. To have these abstract entities as objects one must be able to understand their internal anatomy. This applies also to the person who understands the meaning of 'think', 'explain', 'understand', etc. Some conceptual articulation into parts is necessary in order to have the right conceptions of the meanings of these terms. This applies not only to propositions but also to properties. We have concepts corresponding to properties, and these may be complex or simple. Having a concept of a complex property involves having some articulation of it into constituents, without any commitment to the concept being determinate, or it being decomposable into a set of simples. If someone believes that there are atomistically simple concepts, then the requirement is that one has to be able to build out of these complexes. In short, properties and propositions come in large organizations, and having their correlates in mind entails having some way of finding constituents for these.

Adding this requirement enables us to see how the way in which cognition has objects is indeed unique in so far as it is different from mere intentional objects, and from objects linked to processes in spatio-temporal and currently available causal ways. This does not prevent us from agreeing that the range of objects of cognition and the range of intentional objects may overlap.

Finally, nothing has been said in this characterization that would rule out propositions and concepts being indeterminate in ways similar to what we said about ontological indeterminateness. Indeed, in the last part this sort of a theory for the objects of cognition will be worked out in our theory of language.

Some philosophers have described what we call the object of thought as its content. This seems misleading. For a thought, as we use this term in this essay, is a mental, psychological entity. Thus its content would have to be so too. But that would mean that properties and propositions can be reduced to psychological entities. This would clash with the realism defended in the first part. Thus barring the success of such a reductionist programme, it is better to keep the terminology of 'object'. As we saw in our survey of semantics, the word 'content' has been appropriated

196

already by logicians for a very different purpose. In some cases thought processes not only have objects but also lead to products. Such are: what we associated with certain linguistic outputs, theories we construct, explanations or proofs we offer, conclusions we reach, works of art, etc. The internal structures of these too may be relevant to the characterization of cognition and the understanding of certain aspects of it.

Having freed ourselves from the constraints of naturalism and pragmatic pictures, and having seen the unique way in which cognition has its objects, let us go back to basic common sense, and restate the basic constituents of its concept of cognition and its key components.

First, the objects. Though in the previous pages the focus was on elements of propositions, and complexes or propositions such as theories, this conception of cognition allows for various aesthetic structures such as those of music and the other art-forms to be appropriate objects too. This account leaves the issue of musical thoughts, aesthetic understanding, etc. open, providing a conceptual place for these, without any specific commitment as to their nature. Earlier it was claimed that having these objects for cognition involves some articulation into parts, and building up complexes. This claim must not be confused with the obviously false one that a thinking or theorizing person must have a grasp of the latest analysis of what a proposition is by a philosopher or logician. Concepts can be analysed into 'parts' on a common-sense level without a commitment to a philosophical theory about these entities and without assuming an atomistic picture. While a proposal about the semantics of lexical items, and thus about a set of concepts, will be made in the last part, the main claims of the 'objectual approach' are independent of that particular analysis.

Second, phenomenal experience. This includes conscious experience of thought, plans, decisions, concepts, and other conscious representations of abstract patterns such as those of music. We shall argue later that many of our thoughts and mental operations are non-conscious. Hence phenomenal experience cannot be utterly reliable. This is so not only because it does not cover all of cognition but also because it it not an infallible guide to what we really think, plan, etc. At the same time, it is essential to our deliberations, planning, predicting, etc. that some of our cognitive life should take place on the conscious level. This allows us to be reflective, introspective creatures. Furthermore, in ways that are left unspecified, phenomenal experiences are causally related to both linguistic responses to what is happening to us and to our attempts to change the environment and ourselves.

Basic common sense assumes that cognition has an agent. As we saw, however, the exact nature of this agency is not specified by common sense. Our proposal is that it should be left this way by philosophy as well. We can say a great deal about what must take place in the mind on the basis of analysis of the objects and of biological and psychological constraints without a detailed ontology and map of the agent. If someone objects that our analysis does not leave room for disembodied and agentless thoughts, our answer is that faced with such a possibility the presuppositions of our current notions break down, and we would not know what to say. As was argued before, our concepts do not cover 'all logical possibilities'.

The fourth ingredient is the combination of processes and stimuli. The existence of processes is claimed by basic common sense. That is to say, we assume that some processes and activities take place as parts of cognition, even though many of these are not conscious, and we cannot specify in detail the nature of these processes. It is also assumed that, as a result of these processes, we often end up taking practical and theoretical stands of various sorts. But beyond this rather bland commitment, common sense leaves the matter alone. This is even more so in the case of stimuli. Basic common sense neither affirms nor denies the ontological spontaneity of thought, and conjectures about environmental and genetic causes are matters for science or peripheral common sense. We can think of ourselves as thinking, planning creatures without taking stands on such matters as the stimuli.

The philosophic proposal is that we build on this conception of basic common sense a concept of cognition in which the four factors and the assumption of their convergence are retained, the factors of phenomenal experience, process, and agency as well as that of the stimuli are left to empirical research to fill in. The philosophic stress should be laid on efforts to reach an adequate analysis of the objects. On the basis of such an analysis we can reach perceptive general characterizations of the human mind and human cognition. A general constraint on empirical work on the various ingredients should be the retention of the link between phenomenal experience and the other factors as well as the unique way in which cognition has its objects. This conception also fits well our earlier claim that thoughts and other more complex parts of cognition are individuated by their objects.

Within this philosophical conception, called 'objectual' since the whole stress is on the objects and their significance for human thought, we can make room for what we said earlier about the human mind as explanation-seeking. For we can think of thoughts as elements in the larger complexes of explanations, and thus representing either that which is problematical of that which is part of what renders the problematical unproblematical. Thought also has an evaluative component, i.e. that which can assess the simpler elements from the point of view of veracity, and the larger complexes as perceptive, adequate, illuminating, or lacking these attributes.

The viability of this conception depends partly on our being able to say something informative about what can be discovered with regard to the objects of cognition that will help us to say something illuminating about the human mind. There have been already some efforts in this direction, without a commitment to the philosophic conception that I propose here. For example, people have attempted to characterize an interesting level of complexity that the grammars of natural languages reach, and correspondingly a level of complexity that the human language processing mechanisms must attain (Chomsky, 1963). Similar questions have been asked about semantics and thus about the level of abstractness and complexity of the objects of cognitive representation. For example, are there structures in the quantificational schemes of natural languages that force humans to use higher-order logics? As another example we can take the fact that humans can process complex reiterated sequences of tenses in discourse, and ask what the complexity of these sequences is. Similar questions arise in connection with reference. It is obvious that we can refer to things present to our senses at the time of reference. But we also use anaphoric reference to refer to items of a wide variety which were introduced into discourse at earlier stages. How abstract can the items be that we pick out in this

199

way? The exploration of such issues gives us a preliminary conception of the richness, range, and variety of human thought. In light of this we can formulate further and more empirical questions about cognitive processing and its external conditions. As mentioned above, one could ask similar questions about art and science. For example, is there something non-trivial and not purely logical that all human scientific explanations have in common? Or in virtue of what can the human mind recognize melodies of varying complexity in widely differing cultural contexts? Can we say something non-trivial about what human melodies across all cultures have in common? Even if we advance no further than answers to such questions, we shall have learned a great deal about the human mind. But it is possible that we can use answers to these questions to set the framework for exploring in more detail the other components, i.e. process, agency, and stimulus. Though this conception places the key conceptual stress on the objects, it leaves open the possibility that in studying the four factors we shall find mutual constraints. For example biology might constrain the possible objects for human cognition, and an adequate presentation of the objects might help formulate the appropriate research programmes for exploring both phenomenal experience and the correlated physiology.

Thus the proposed philosophical conception of cognition serves well as the scientific concept of cognition too. Our exploration of the relation of the various sciences to common sense suggests that unless we can attain an account of cognition that covers all four factors, we shall not have accounts of cognition with the explanatory force of accounts that we do attain such as for physics or biology.

The epistemological corollary of the objectual thesis is that the best way to approach cognition and its many aspects is to specify as well as we can the objects, and then attempt to study the various processes under idealization. Only after all this is accomplished, and we have some idea about what the other parameters are that enter into actual public expression of cognition, should we attempt to formulate theories about what actually takes place, milli-second by milli-second in the mind or brain. The fruitfulness of this approach will have to be shown by detailed suggestions about logic, semantics, grammar, etc., and how these help us to analyse different parts of cognition.

The claim that we should study cognition under appropriate idealizations and abstracting it from other factors that also influence performance should not be confused with the untenable view that we could do psychology even if we consider the objects of cognition without taking into consideration any of the biological and psychological factors that affect the way humans represent these objects. We mentioned that there is most likely to be a two-way dependency between the way we want to characterize the objects of cognition for the purposes of studying human thought and the way we give initial characterizations to the biological and psychological agent and the processes and activities that constitute cognition.

We shall now consider proposals about how to determine how much of cognition is on the observable level. There is an obvious crude distinction between what is observable by our senses, such as coloured surfaces, stars, and sunsets, and unobservable elements such as causal forces and some sub-atomic elements. This distinction needs a host of qualifications. There are many in-between cases such as dispositional qualities like flexibility. Furthermore, the distinction is relative to historical periods in which technology changes what the senses can reach. But for our purposes the distinction will have to do in this rough shape. In terms of it we can distinguish theories that focus on the observable from those that focus on the unobservable. As an example of a question about observables consider: 'Why do leaves turn from green to brown?' Questions about unobservables include: 'What are the fundamental underlying constituents of observable matter?' We shall label theories asking questions primarily about observable entities 'shallow' theories, and theories focusing mainly on the unobservable as 'deep' theories, without meaning thereby to imply anything normative about which is better. The distinction classifies theories in terms of their chosen subject matter, and not in terms of how abstract and refined the conceptual machinery is in terms of which the phenomena are explained. A theory inquiring into observable phenomena might carry a lot of mathematical structure, and a 'deep' theory could have a crude conceptual framework. Deep theories are not necessarily better than shallow ones. For example, given our use of these terms, a theory about human images would count as shallow since it deals with entities that are

201

observable via introspection, and recently we have seen interesting theories emerging to explain some of the properties of these phenomena (Kosslyn, 1980). Also, early astronomical theories that aimed solely at describing and predicting the movements of the celestial bodies were 'shallow' in this sense, but many of these were better than some highly speculative 'deep' theories about the actual nature and constituency of the celestial bodies. These reflections show that if one is to argue for a 'deep' theory of cognition, this requires considerable justification.

As was mentioned earlier, humans have a preference for shallow theories of cognition because, under certain assumptions, this gives them more promise of control over their own destinies. (For examples and discussion, see Bracken, 1978.) But not only can a deep theory account for our moral life; it also gives an additional advantage. The deep theory leaves much less room for certainty about what our fundamental convictions are, and thus leaves more room for tolerance. If I cannot be certain what my deepest convictions really are, how can I be sure what the convictions of others are, and hence how can I have any epistemological basis for a stance of intolerance?

Having got these preliminaries out of the way, let us look at cognitive phenomena in terms of the distinction just drawn. We shall distinguish between three types of elements of cognition. One of these is the class of those phenomena that can be observed behaviourally or introspectively. The second class is made up of thoughts, concepts, etc. that are not observable but can be brought to consciousness. The third class is that of elements that are in principle unobservable. The basis for these contrasts can be seen from everyday examples. With regards to certain propositions it makes sense to contrast 'I really believe that p' with 'I think that I believe that p'. Likewise, we can contrast 'I think that I have the concept C', with 'I really have the concept C'. These cases are analogous to the case of linguistic intuitions, covered in our survey. We saw that 'Jones thinks that he has linguistic intuition Γ' is not the same as 'Jones in fact has linguistic intuition Γ'. Along with many of our fundamental beliefs, we do not wear our linguistic intuitions on our sleeves.

It is easy to think of having beliefs, thoughts, and concepts that are introspectively observable. Most of our singular beliefs about our environment and many of our generalizations fall into this category. Indeed, humans could not function as explaining, decision-making creatures if this were not the case. These activities require that at any given time we should be able to consider consciously a small number of thoughts and beliefs. Our assigning probabilities, utility, etc. to various alternatives depends on this. At the same time, we can see that since consciousness can focus only on a relatively small number of thoughts at any given time, many of our beliefs that are brought to consciousness in such contexts must be stored somehow in our minds without being observable either by agent or outside observer.

Apart from information stored that is used for explanation, prediction, or decision-making, there may be thoughts that are unobservable under normal circumstances but can be brought to consciousness by special techniques. Psychoanalysis relies heavily on this fact. We may suppress some unpleasant thought for a long time because of painful associations, but under certain circumstances we can regain these for conscious inspection.

We deal with these two classes mainly in order to contrast with them the third one, i.e. those that are in principle unobservable. As we consider examples and offer justification for our classification we should keep in mind that what is 'deep' is the mental phenomenon of thought and belief, not their objects. For example, there may be a rule of grammar that operates in our mind in such a way as to make its work in principle unobservable. But the rule itself could be an object of conscious belief. To take another type of example, we can accept consciously the commutative law for addition in arithmetic. But the working of this law in our minds, as we learn and use arithmetic, is in principle unobservable. We cannot say, on being presented with the commutative law: 'Oh yes, this is what I have been using all along.' Introspection gives us no evidence for such a claim. We infer on the basis of indirect evidence that our mind employs this principle in calculations.

The last example brings us to the observation that those mental processes that are parts of operations requiring extreme speed are likely to be in the third group, since if we had to go through all of the stages of language processing required to interpret bits of conversations on the conscious level, we would never to able to complete the task within reasonable time limits. Likewise, if checking our account in monthly statements involved going consciously through all of the required steps, completing the task would probably take us longer than a month, and thus we would not have time to spend money during that month and take care of our daily needs and useless luxuries.

Not only the actual steps of calculations and language processing, but also the representation of the rules and principles whose applications these steps embody are in principle unobservable for the same reason that we gave for the individual steps. This also explains why our linguistic intuitions, e.g. about grammaticality, should be 'deep'; they too play important roles in rapid processing activities.

Still another class that seems to belong to the third kind is the set of our most fundamental beliefs about morality, religion, human nature, and the physical world. These include general beliefs about causality, God, justice, goodness, etc. Let us take, for example, ascribing to someone the belief that God exists. Introspective evidence by the agent would be relevant but not decisive. Behaviour – e.g. crossing himself – would also be relevant but not decisive. A person might claim that he believes or does not believe, but could be easily mistaken about himself in this regard. The most plausible solution is to interpret the belief as in principle unobservable and take behaviour, introspection, answer to questions, etc. as indirect evidence on the basis of which we form empirical hypotheses about the person – who could be ourselves.

An alternative explanation would be that a belief like 'courage is good' is a cluster involving conscious belief, behaviour, justifications, etc. and that there is no need to posit in addition to these factors also a non-conscious belief, or similar mental state. Our answer to this is that the elements just mentioned cannot be so many separate items with no common source. If there is a conflict between them, then our cognitive processes have misfired in some place. In the ideal case all of these elements should point in the same direction. We can explain this by positing the unconscious state of mind as the source of all of the other elements.

There is a good reason why these fundamental beliefs should be 'deep' in our sense. For we hold these over long periods of time, and have them play key underlying roles in our deliberations and explanations. We can thus use the same arguments as before. Having to invoke these concepts on the conscious level in each case in which they in some way affect what we think, or plan, would make reasoning and justification pragmatically unfeasible.

Adopting the objectual theory commits us to claiming that the study of the objects of cognition such as logic, language, art, etc. cannot be separated sharply from the study of the key elements of cognition. Such a conception undercuts any sharp distinction between the sciences and the humanities. This is, however, hardly a drawback of the proposal. Any time we come to understand a poem, painting, or symphony in terms of structure, and can relate that structure to human appreciation and interpretation, we learn something just as important about cognition as any detailed physiological location of a certain type of processing in a specific part of the brain.

Beyond Mere Thought; Understanding and Explanation

The phenomenology of understanding is familiar to us from experiences in classrooms in which mathematics or logic is taught. The instructor wants the class to understand a proof. His task is not like that of someone who simply wants to convey information. Information is to be stored, a proof needs understanding. I might need to *know* that Oxford is west of Cambridge; I need to *understand* a proof in mathematics or geometry. If the instructor is successful, students will have a certain experience which we describe metaphorically as 'suddenly seeing' the proof. This experience is not linked infallibly to genuine understanding, but is a typical sign of it. The instructor cannot really implant the proof in people's minds the way we can implant mere information into the mind of someone who speaks our language. The instructor gives the proof over and over again, in different forms, with different examples, etc. In short, he 'helps the students to recollect', as one might put it within a more classical terminology. The same point can be made in different contexts. A candidate for the post of Minister of Foreign Affairs in France once described what he saw as the key difference between himself and his main rival in the following terms: 'He knows everything but understands nothing; I know nothing, but I understand everything' (relying on the difference between the French *savoir* and *connaître*). This semi-serious remark makes the claim that the rival possesses a lot of information, but lacks the insight to understand the fundamental nature of the entire situation, while the speaker claims not to have a great deal of information but to have insight.

Our first example introduced understanding informally in the context of an *a priori* discipline, and the second one within an empirical context. This shows that the contrast between understanding on the one hand and being well-informed or knowledgeable on the other cuts across the *a priori*–empirical distinction.

There is also linguistic evidence for the status of understanding. We understand proofs, explanations, theories, languages, definitions; and though we can be said to know these things, this has very different implications. To know a definition, theorem, etc. is to know how to recite it. That shows the ability to memorize and not necessarily any understanding. The two notions of knowing and understanding converge only in the case of language. To know a language is to be able to understand it. That is because language understanding is typically manifested by responses involving the appropriate manipulation of linguistic symbols. Particular items such as trees, tables, etc. do not serve as appropriate direct objects of 'understand'. Only persons and certain living beings are exceptions to this, and this is because of analogies between abstract systems and our conceptions of some living beings (Moravcsik, 1979).

As the examples above illustrate, we are dealing here with the construction of 'understand' and direct objects. Our analysis also applies to 'understanding what. . .', but not to constructions involving 'understanding that. . ., why. . ., etc'.

The hermeneutic tradition argued that understanding has a unique nature and non-propositional objects. Their argument is in the context of wanting to show something unique about humanistic understanding. They claim that it is different from scientific understanding, because it involves special processes such as *Einfühlung* and *Übertragung* (Göttner, 1973). We need not agree either with the need to posit these special processes, or with the alleged chasm between the sciences and the humanities, and still profit from pondering about some of this material.

Proofs, theories, and explanations are collections of propositions related in special ways. In a deductive proof the relation is that of validity, for theories it is logical structure, and for explanations we have a variety of links such as deductive structure, analogy, building models for the phenomena to be explained, etc. It cannot be an essential mark of the objects of understanding that their components be propositions or sentences, since musical compositions are also potential objects of understanding, and the components of the structure of a Beethoven quartet, whatever they may be, are not propositions. But in the case of music too, understanding involves fitting abstract elements into patterns of appropriate sorts.

Even in the cases in which the objects are complexes of propositions, merely having knowledge of the elements and their relevant relation such as validity, entailment, etc. is not sufficient for understanding. If I really understand a proof, theory, etc., then I should also see its elegance, insightfulness, depth, or its lack of these attributes. Some theories are logically impeccable, but lack insight or depth. Understanding, then, involves not only getting the elements of the complex right and the relation that ties these in the relevant way, but also the ability to assess the object in terms of the characteristics mentioned, and that in turn involves being able to comprehend the complex and to fit it into patterns, and to see it in certain ways that cannot be exhausted in terms of mere propositional knowledge. We can either say that the depth, explanatory power, etc. are parts of the objects of understanding and thus understanding has an object that is not merely propositional, or that the object is propositional, but the cognitive process of understanding involves more than the knowledge of these. Analytic philosophy has produced some formal analyses of propositional knowledge (see, e.g., Hintikka, 1962). We do not have such analyses for 'understand' or 'explain'. This is hardly surprising, for the notions of understanding and explanation are more elusive and less likely to be analysable solely within the framework of modern symbolic predicate calculus, than propositional knowledge, where the analysis can treat knowing and believing as analogous to logical operators, with sentences or propositions in their ranges. For our purposes the key point is that both understanding and explaining something are more than merely the cognitive process of having knowledge of the sum of the parts and the relation that yields the relevant tie.

Though the examples above dealt with understanding, the same thing can be seen for 'explain'. Again, we are not dealing with all of the constructions such as 'explain that', 'explain why', 'explain how', etc., but only with 'explain what. . .' and 'explain' and a direct object. Here too, the direct objects are proofs, theories, and other complicated abstract systems, including musical compositions. Also, we cannot explain a tree or an iguana, but we can explain a person, or an action. Explanations thus restricted can still take many forms. As we said above, analogies, models, etc. are all appropriate in given contexts.

The results of explanations are a series of statements. But in assessing the explanation it is not enough to assess the truth of the statements. One has to see if the statements add up to something that has explanatory power. Can we see the series of statements as an explanation? For example, I might concede that a certain set of statements offered, p^1, p^2,. . . p^n, entail p^x, but I might at the same time deny that they explain what is described by 'p^x'. Seeing something as an adequate explanation is to be able to fit the parts into an intellectually satisfying complex that renders something previously problematic as unproblematic. Hence our ability to characterize explanations as adequate or inadequate, powerful or weak, insightful or shallow, etc. And, as in the case of understanding, we can either say that the object is not wholly propositional, or that it is, but within a good explanation that series of propositions fits into an intellectually satisfying pattern the nature of which cannot be explicated by further steps of propositional knowledge.

Some of the objects of understanding such as games, systems of logic, parts of mathematics, etc. also include rules. This adds another aspect of understanding, namely grasping that some principle functions as a rule. This cannot be defined solely in terms of knowing that and knowing how. Knowing that something is designed as a rule is not the same as having it actually functioning, as represented in our minds, as a rule. Knowing how to use a principle as a rule presupposes that we treat it as a rule.

So much for the objects of understanding and explanation. The two notions are related both conceptually and empirically. One might be able to understand something such as a proof, and not be able to articulate the understanding in terms of explanations. On the other hand, if one can give insightful explanations of certain phenomena, then one also has understanding of these items. Both understanding and the ability to generate explanations of the right kind seem to rely on having similar mental representations.

Let us look at the cognitive phenomena in a little more detail. Understanding a proof involves propositional knowledge, e.g. of the premisses and conclusion. It also involves knowing how. One must be able to know how to generate the proof, restate it in slightly different terms, etc. But, as we argued above, it also involves something else that is easier to illustrate than to define. This is the ability to see the complex in certain holistic patterns that allow us to understand why some proofs are deeper and more insightful than others, and why some proofs are so clumsy as hardly to deserve this label at all. This leads us back to what we said about humans seeing things as problematic and then being able to reduce the problematic to the unproblematic. Understanding something transforms it for us from the problematic to the unproblematic. This 'resolution' is an intuitive state or process that resists analysis in terms of more fundamental notions.

The same holds for the mental state of someone who has a good explanation for something. Again, in the typical case we shall have propositional knowledge, e.g. knowing that elements of the explanation are true. We shall also have know-how, e.g. knowing how to construct models in terms of which the explanation might be given. But we need also the holistic intuitive grasp that enables us to see why something explains, why something renders a phenomenon no longer problematic, and in virtue of what feature an explanation represents occasionally fundamental intellectual progress.

These remarks about understanding and explaining barely break ground in an exciting philosophic territory. But if we are ever to understand cognition and its various aspects, including such obvious but as yet theoretically recondite facts as finding something interesting, worth exploring, etc. then this terrain will have to be charted and analysed. These comments should serve as the introduction to approaches that will hopefully avoid both the Scylla of trying to reduce everything to propositional logic on the one hand, and the Charybdis of falling back on what to me at least are murky notions of *Einfühlung*, etc.

Apart from showing an important part of cognition, the purpose of these observations has been to sketch in the broadest outlines the part of a conception of cognition that will have to underlie the picture of humans as *homo explanans* that we have hinted at throughout this book.

What is intellectually unproblematic? What are deep and illuminating explanations? Are the criteria relative to history and culture, or are there some that are culture- and history-invariant? At present we are not yet in a position to answer these fascinating questions. Meanwhile, let us return to concepts and thoughts. Within the framework sketched here, these have the following roles:

1. Presenting something as unproblematic because we can locate it within a network of propositions and concepts that is intellectually satisfactory.
2. Presenting something as problematic from the point of view of the questions with which at a given time we approach reality.
3. Being parts of explanatory structures that render a certain range of phenomena, abstract or empirical, unproblematic.

To be sure, thought can lead to belief, and belief is judged as true or false. But within our scheme, gathering and processing true (i.e. correct) information is not all there is to cognition. Thus thought does more than present units of veracity and information. It contributes to the holistic cognitive patterns that we ultimately aim at, and that we call powerful or insightful explanations. In the third part we shall see some consequences of this view for lexical semantics.

Our claim of an objectual theory and its dimension beyond information processing should be separated from other purely psychological claims according to which even objects that can be articulated propositionally may be represented in the human mind in non-propositional ways, such as imagery. (For examples, see Block, 1980.) Let us consider a city. The locations of different streets and buildings can be represented either by a complex series of descriptions or by devices such as a map. It is an empirical question whether humans form a conception of a city and find their way around unaided on the basis of purely imagistic representations or propositional ones.

Having outlined the objects and nature of understanding, we shall turn to the question of how one would find out whether a person is in this mental state with regards to a proper object. Two claims will be advanced. First, that there is no certainty in these matters, and secondly that no combination of knowing that and knowing how is completely sufficient for the ascription of understanding. These combinations give us merely empirical grounds on the basis of which we infer the underlying state. We can see these points by considering the following illustration. Suppose it is claimed that someone understands a proof. Furthermore, we have ascertained the following:

1. The agent knows that p', p'',. . .p^n are the premises of the argument.
2. The agent knows that s', s'',. . .s^n are the steps of the argument.
3. The agent knows that c is the conclusion.
4. The agent knows that rules r', r',. . .r^n can be invoked to generate the proof, and knows which step is justified by which rule and which previous steps.
5. The agent knows how to produce the proof.
6. The agent knows how to apply the proof to different instantiations and interpretations.

Conditions 1–4 involve propositional knowledge while 5 and 6 involve knowing how. One can imagine conditions under which all of 1–6 are fulfilled but the agent still lacks understanding. For example, the propositional knowledge listed above could derive from authority rather than from working through the proof. Meeting 6 could also have other sources than understanding. One might try to expand the list, and add abilities to see the significance of the proof, its consequences, to know explicitly that the argument is valid, etc. but the sceptical doubts will still linger.

We have to deal with the following objection. Even if we grant that meeting these conditions is not sufficient, there may be other reasons for this besides understanding being an underlying mental state, for one might claim that understanding is not a precise notion and admits of degrees. Hence there will be no sharp guidelines for the ascription of this state. And indeed, as we shall see in chapter 6, an adequate conception of lexical semantics should entail that a term like 'understand' does not have an exact meaning. But this is not enough to replace our suggestion of understanding being an underlying state. For precise or not, the point of the psychological posit is to give some unity in the sense of a common source to the variety of phenomena covered by 1–6. It is not a part of this proposal to claim either that the phenomena to be accounted for or the underlying state can be gathered under sharply delineated concepts.

Understanding, then, is an underlying mental state, with a variety of facts closer to the observational surface, to be used as evidence for its ascription. Thus the epistemology of understanding resembles the epistemology of what we called 'deep' or unobservable states of knowing. In such cases of propositional knowledge too, the key element is the underlying state, and the variety of surface phenomena related to that state never provides logically both necessary and sufficient conditions for the ascription of the mental state. The epistemic structure of understanding differs from that of propositional knowledge of the 'deep' variety, since some of the evidence for understanding is propositional knowledge of this sort. Thus in these cases understanding is 'twice removed' from the observational level.

This analysis of understanding is logically distinct from the more general theory of cognition that was presented in this section, but it fits into it well. For what we can say today about understanding, as we saw, centres on the objects, and the direct link between these and cognition, whatever the details may turn out to be. We can see today some of the empirical implications; Osherson (1977), for example, started to work out a characterization of the humanly possible logical connectives, i.e. those that humans can use in normal processing of language and thought, under normal circumstances.

Postlude

In this part of the proposal we have developed the outlines of a theory of cognition. It distinguishes basic common sense from other superficially related notions and shows that there is a continuum between science and common sense. It proposes an ontologically indeterminate stance for many of the key notions of cognition, with the proviso that these notions in terms of which we analyse cognition will not be abandoned merely because this or that ontological reduction might fail. It construes notions like those of belief or thought as neither behaviouristic nor purely functional, but as complexes with certain constraints on agency, objects, felt experience, and process. The proposal opts for a non-naturalistic stand on the ground that naturalism is unduly restrictive, and argues also against a pragmatic picture of thought. It shows that the alternatives are as empirically viable as the options rejected. It culminates in an 'objectual' proposal, i.e. the claim that thoughts are individuated in terms of their objects, and that the basic direct link between the objects and cognition is a necessary part of any adequate account of cognition. It also stresses the extent to which relevant analyses of the objects of cognition can provide the key ingredient for insightful characterizations of the human mind.

We then went on to add a specific proposal according to which within a general 'objectual' approach we should explore understanding and having or giving an explanation as parts of cognition that go beyond mere propositional knowledge and know-how. This topic brought us back to a theme that surfaced earlier in this volume, namely that of humans as *homo explanans* and not primarily as mere information processors.

This proposal fights at a disadvantage when compared with other proposals surveyed in our section on problems. For the other proposals assume a commonly shared vocabulary and set of concepts, and spell out various options in terms of these, i.e. the theory of propositional knowledge and traditional empiricist epistemology. My proposal, however, requires the forging of a new set of concepts. These include: basic and peripheral common sense, ontological indeterminateness with respect to the dualist–materialist choice, the dichotomy between 'deep' and 'shallow' theories, objectuality, and conceptions of understanding and explanation giving that cannot be reduced to a combination of propositional knowledge and knowing how.

Thus the proposal needs to be assessed in two stages. One of these is the viability of the new notions introduced. To reject these on the ground that, as of now, they are not susceptible to analytic descriptions of the same precision as the more traditional notions would be to put the cart before the horse. The issue is rather: can we really have an adequate account of cognition as related to the use and understanding of language without some such notions? The second step is the assessment of the proposal made within this conceptual framework. But this assessment cannot be solely in terms of what facts we unearth about cognition. As we saw, differences between proposals are affected by differences in stands about ontology and theories of language. Thus the adequacy of any account of cognition has to be judged in this wider context. In chapter 6 we shall see how a proposed theory of lexical semantics completes our picture of language and thought.

CHAPTER VI

Language

On the basis of the previous chapters we can rely on a realist ontology and a non-naturalist theory of cognition centred on the conception of humans as explanation seeking creatures. We shall consider how descriptive words and phrases in natural languages have meaning. I shall present a theory that differs both from what was described in our survey of problems as the Frege–Carnap model, and the model associated with Kripke and Putnam. This is a theory of meaning according to which descriptive words and phrases do not have meanings in the sense of necessary and jointly sufficient conditions, nor does their having extensions resemble the way in which proper names in natural languages acquire reference. The theory is called a lexical theory of meaning since its data are pieces of information that one would gather from entries in a lexicon. It differs both from theories of the logical vocabulary and that of syncategorematic words on the on hand, and the rules for compositional semantics, i.e. rules specifying how we build larger semantic units of smaller elements, on the other.

  The proposal is linked to the conception of humans as primarily explanation- and understanding-seeking creatures. It attempts to show how this central fact is reflected in semantic structure. For according to this view, roughly speaking, to know the meaning of a word 'w' is to have a representation of that in virtue of which something counts as a *w*: hence to have a rough explanatory scheme for *w*s. Meanings will turn out to be necessary conditions for application forming explanatory patterns within which we can show why and how some elements fall within the extension of a given word. They need to be supplemented with other socially shared cognitive processes in order to arrive at sharply delineated extensions for descriptive words. Thus within this theory meaning alone does not determine extension. The proposal will show also that the determination of extensions for descriptive words has a normative aspect. This, in turn, has important consequences for how we conceive of philosophic activity.

Homo Explanans and Semantics

According to one conception humans think about reality by sorting elements into groups according to similarities, and then build the more complex structures of thought, such as arguments or explanation, out of the concepts arrived at by the sorting procedures. According to the conception adopted in this book humans are primarily questioning, explanation-seeking, and understanding creatures, and sorting things out according to similarities takes place only within this framework. Human cognition gets its main impetus from finding various parts of experience problematic. This leads us to ask 'why. . . ?' or 'what. . .?' questions. Pursuing some of these leads us to positing underlying natures for some elements of reality and to explaining what seem to be simpler phenomena in terms of relating them to these 'natures'. Thus we explain that certain things act, appear, change, etc. in certain ways because of what their nature is. By forming such accounts we gain understanding, and reduce some of what is problematic to the non-problematic. The underlying natures are complex properties the structure of which will be explained in more detail below. These 'natures' posited need not be explained in terms of strong metaphysical notions such as immutable essences. For the purpose of the theories of cognition and lexical semantics to be proposed we can leave such issues open and simply assume that elements of reality have complex structures in virtue of which they can interact causally or conceptually, with variations both in the interactions and in the complex natures allowed, within certain limits to be specified below.

To explain or understand something, in the sense spelled out by an analysis of the direct construction, or to explain and understand what something is, involves the positing or discover-

216

ing of properties related in certain specific ways so as to allow us to see relatively simple phenomena accounted for by the underlying more complex properties. Let us consider, for example, the report: 'The animals ran from the fire.' This makes sense to us because, on the one hand, animals are the sort of thing that can run and sense danger, and on the other hand, fire is the sort of thing that is destructive. Or, to take an example from a very different domain, let us consider the claim: 'Evolutions bring better changes than revolutions.' This makes sense and is thus open to assessment from the point of view of veracity, because evolutions and revolutions are the kinds of process that can bring about change. This analysis applies also to abstract domains like numbers or shapes. Not all natures have the same complexity. From the point of view of everyday understanding, some entities like colours or shapes have less complex natures then biological species or physical kinds.

We shall now consider the distinction between giving explanations in general, and forming explanatory concepts in particular. There are many different kinds of explanations. Some of these merely correlate the exemplification of certain properties, as in 'Where there is fire, there is smoke.' What we shall call explanatory concepts are those that correspond to what we called 'nature' above. As the example about smoke and fire illustrates, one can give many explanations without invoking explanatory concepts. One can explain where a meeting will take place, when it will take place, explain correlations between seasons and seasonal changes, etc. In contrast, we can explain why two chemical substances interact the way they do by referring to their natures, and on the everyday level why rain and wood interact the way they do, as we learn when inspecting the roof after a heavy cloudburst. When we report mere observations – e.g., that there are horses on the range – our concepts 'flatten out', we do not utilize them to the fullest. But then in other contexts we utilize them in all of their articulations as in 'It took elephants rather than horses to get Hannibal through the Alps.'

So far we have made some general observations about cognition. Let us see now how these relate to lexical semantics. My proposal is that explanatory concepts, in our sense, are potential meanings of descriptive words; or, more precisely, since one would want to distinguish within a realist ontology between given meanings and mind-dependent concepts, the explanatory concepts are correlated to potential meanings. Humans, on this hypothesis, have a set of explanatory concepts. Some of these are global in the sense that everyone has them. Others are local in the same sense that they vary from culture to culture. Various languages embody various subsets of explanatory concepts. The global ones are presumably embodied in meanings of descriptive words that can be found in every natural language while others are embodied in different ways. Natural languages do differ in their vocabularies.

This proposal relies on the suggestion canvassed in earlier sections that the primary function of language is to articulate thought. We can add to this now the suggestion that human thought involves fundamentally finding some parts of experience problematic and then forming explanations that seem to us – in ways difficult to articulate – adequate, and thus gives us understanding. In addition to providing us with ways of representing explanatory schemes, language needs to furnish tools in terms of symbolic representations that enable us to interpret and to interact with particular elements of reality. These interpretations and interactions require that descriptive terms should have ranges of application or extensions. The determination of these is a function of many factors. Human needs, limitations, perspectives, etc. all enter into this process. Thus the task of meanings is not just to provide us with terms that have explanatory meanings, but also with some of the elements that determine what counts as falling under a given word. We shall have more to say about the difference between explaining the natures of things and explaining what counts as falling under a descriptive term, i.e. being part of its extension.

Meanings

A theory of lexical meaning is a theory about the nature of meanings of words such as what are called common nouns, adjectives, and verbs in Indo-European languages. A crucial element in the use of such words and related compound phrases is that they can be applied descriptively to elements of reality and that such applications are subject to assessment from the point of view of veracity. This is what we call the semantics of descriptive words and phrases, and for the sake of abbreviation we shall use 'word' in this sense here. The following is the proposed delineation of what the meaning of a word is:

- The meaning of a word 'w' is that in virtue of which an element of reality counts as a *w*.

For example, the meaning of 'eat' is that in virtue of which something counts as part of the extension of 'eat'. The meaning of 'number' is that in virtue of which something counts as an element of the extension of 'number'. As our proposal on pp. 202-3 showed, the key cognitive processes involved in language interpretation are mostly subconscious. This applies to meaning construction and representation. The task of the theoretician is to present an explicit articulation of the structure of meanings. My proposal is that such articulation yields explanatory schemes of what it is in virtue of which something counts as a part of the extension of a word *w*. Hence the link between this semantics and the previous discussion of humans as primarily explanation-seeking and forming creatures.

Let us reflect on three features of explanations and explanatory schemes, in order to appreciate the advantages of this proposal. First, explanations are explanations for intended audiences. The intended audience may be very specific, such as one's own child, or very general, such as all future generations of mathematicians. We explain the same phenomenon in different ways, depending on the intended audience. For example, we explain what a mother is to a biology student in a different way from that employed in explaining the same phenomenon to a small child. Secondly, explanations can be more or less detailed, more or less illuminating. This does not mean that the more detailed correlates with the more illuminating, or that we should always aim at as detailed explanations as possible. For example, there is a lot of detail we want to include in an explanation of what a plant is for the student of botany, and considerably less for a suburbanite. Thirdly, explanations vary on whether they are intended only for an observer, or for someone who will interact with the explananda. For example, it is one thing to explain what a lawyer (judge, bailiff, etc.) is to an observer of different legal systems, and another to explain the same roles to a laypersom who is being sued and needs legal help.

Though we gave different examples for the different features, it is important to note that the same explanatory pattern can have different forms, depending on the situation warranting different approaches in terms of our three distinguishing marks. Thus we can consider in general the task of explaining what a mother is. The same explanatory pattern can be filled in differently depending on the nature of the audience, the need or lack of need for detail, the demand for a certain degree of illumination, and differences in the pragmatic context, calling or not calling for interaction with what we explain.

These reflections suggest that meanings too can vary along these lines, and that there should be one general characterization of the meaning of a word, within which we can distinguish different 'layers' of meaning, depending on variations along the lines of the three distinguishing factors. There should be a general meaning for 'mother', and within this, different layers having to do with understanding at different levels of maturity, different levels of detail and illumination, and contexts of interaction and observation. Below we shall see how the detailed proposal incorporates this conception of meaning as explanatory and as admitting layers. Such a theory established meaning relations other than just the traditional trichotomy of synonymy, meaning inclusion, and homonomy. Intuitively one wants to say that 'mother' has just one meaning, but has different layers according to the criteria mentioned above.

If the meanings of descriptive words correspond to explanatory concepts in the same sense defined, then a key use of such expressions should be the context: '. . . because it is (a) *w*.' For example, 'It can run, eat, propagate, etc., because it is an animal.' Or, to take an example from a different domain: 'It involved money, required a couple of lawyers, led to bettering our financial status, because it was a sale.' This kind of context tells us a great deal more about the meanings of words than merely identificatory uses such as: 'this is an animal' or 'this is a sale'. We shall see how the lexical theory proposed here can account for the key use better than the currently fashionable alternatives.

Meanings, as interpreted here, are necessary conditions of application of a special kind, namely those that form explanatory patterns. Explanations of what something is also constitute typically only necessary conditions. For example, explaining to a potential player a game like cricket or baseball will typically focus on certain necessary conditions such as some of the rules, skills needed, and accounts of some of the key activities. Within the typical range of interaction assumed for the average player, this is all that is needed. We provide certain salient necessary conditions. For an American exchange student to understand cricket – if this ever happens – it is sufficient to have an idea of what is going on, how the scoring is conducted, what counts as rule violation, and some of the key virtues and vices of a cricket player. He need not possess criteria by which he can distinguish cricket from all other (and future?) actual and possible games. If acumen of this sort becomes necessary in some context, then further conditions have to be provided to approach sufficiency.

So far we have largely discussed meaning, but the last paragraphs here brought the speaker–hearer into the picture. Given the characterization of meaning given, the following is proposed as a delineation of the relevant semantic competence.

- To know the meaning of a word 'w' is to (be able to) explain in virtue of what something counts as in the extension of *w*.
- To understand the meaning of a word 'w' is (under idealized circumstances) to have a representation of the articulation of that in virtue of which something falls within the extension of 'w'.

For example if we know the meaning of 'emergency', then we should be able to articulate or give a rough explanation of what makes something count as an emergency. This amounts to explaining that an emergency, as we use the term, is the sort of state in which there is an impending bad condition requiring immediate response. As we shall see, this kind of an account fits into a general explanatory pattern into which all explications of meanings of descriptive words can be fitted.

There are various factors, differing from person to person, that may prevent an explicit articulation of this sort from taking place. But an articulation of this sort must be represented in the speaker's mind if that speaker is able to formulate and express in language the relevant class of thoughts, i.e. those involving descriptions of emergencies, using the notion as an explanatory factor, questioning some aspect of it, etc.

The second formula links our account of semantics to the notion of understanding that we discussed in the section on cognition. We need to add the idealization condition, because this kind of understanding is non-conscious, and may be very difficult for some people to bring to consciousness. By 'articulate' we mean here giving a rough explanatory scheme within which the various conditions mentioned must fit.

We have linked some remarks about cognition to an account of meaning, and this account to a characterization of the state of mind of the competent language user. None of this should be confused with the epistemological question of how we know when some element of reality encountered falls within the extension of a given word. To make answers to that question parts of lexical competence would be to subscribe to a form of verificationism, according to which to have a grasp of the extension of a term is to know how to verify whether or not a given element is a member of the extension. But empirical verification is often a difficult task, requiring knowledge of the world going way beyond linguistic competence. For example, people can know what counts as a lawyer or judge, but might have great difficulty identifying people of these professions in cultural setting with which they are unfamiliar.

These reflections bring us to a contrast involved in the previous discussion, namely between explaining the nature of a kind, be it that of material objects or events, and explaining what counts as falling within the extension of words correlated to kinds. It is one thing to inquire into the nature of gold, or an activity like walking, and it is another to inquire into what falls under 'gold' and 'walking'; respectively. The former is an investigation of nature, the latter of semantics. To be sure, the two enterprises must be related, since the semantics involves setting up conditions determining when something falls within the extension of a term with which we designate truly or falsely elements of what constitutes a kind. Still, there are important differences. The investigation of gold takes place within science and common sense. The detailed investigation of gold is the task of chemistry. Not everything that chemistry discovered about the nature of gold is or can be part of the semantics of 'gold'. We understand this word, and know how to use it under normal circumstances without a detailed knowledge of chemistry. On the other hand, not all of the factors relevant to the determination of the extension of 'gold' pertain to chemistry or the other sciences. The rough outline of the explanation of gold that the sciences provide is a part of the semantics of 'gold', but some of the factors further narrowing the range so as to arrive at a manageable extension have to do with human interests, interactions, and the role of gold in social and economic life. Thus what gold is used for, how it can have value, and similar other factors are not matters of exploring the substance for the science, but are still parts of what goes into fixing extension. Similar considerations apply to walking. Its nature is explored by physiology and medicine. Some of the basic ingredients, such as being an activity involving locomotion by foot, etc., are also ingredients in the meaning of 'walk'. But walking is a human achievement, and as such is subject to semi-normative assessment. This, in turn, as we shall see, is graded by age and ability. But these matters are not parts of explanations of the nature of walking as a physiological process, but of how this activity is a part of various forms of human flourishing.

Let us return to the use having the pattern: '. . . because it is (a) w'. There are two ways of dealing with this in semantics. According to alternative A, 'w' behaves like a proper name, designating an entity across different possibilities, doing so without having a qualitative meaning that would determine conditions of application. On this view 'w' refers to a kind directly, and when we describe something as a w, we are saying that it is a part of a kind. 'Kinds', as we are using this notion here, can be biological species, activities, or abstract collections. As our culture develops, we associate a number of properties with a given kind. Such associations, according to view A, are not a matter of semantic rules, but shared extra-linguistic knowledge. Thus in the context of '. . . because it is a w', the word has explanatory force because of the associated properties. Knowing at any given time some or most of the associated properties is a part of linguistic competence. The properties can change as our knowledge of the world changes.

According to alternative B, the meaning of 'w' is correlated with an explanatory concept, and thus ingredients of the meaning do provide qualitative conditions for applications, even though it is admitted that these give only necessary, not sufficient conditions. Thus 'w' does not simply refer to a kind, and at the same time, we get a direct account of why it can function in explanatory contexts, even when at the same time a speaker has barely any knowledge of the kind other than what semantic competence furnishes.

Alternative B is part of the lexical theory developed in this section. Let us consider what makes it preferable to alternative A. First, if knowledge of the explanatory properties is a part of linguistic competence, then the burden of proof should fall on those who, agreeing with this, still insist that these are not parts of meaning. Is it really true that if one knows only what is contained in the meaning of a word 'w' of the relevant kind, then one would not know why it can be used in explanatory contexts? Secondly, alternative A assumes that substances, activities, etc. that constitute kinds, as delineated through language, remain fixed through history. This may or may not be good metaphysics, but in any case it seems not to account for the facts of semantics. As human practices, modes of using technology to facilitate observation, institutions, etc. undergo development, this also influences our explanatory patterns, and there is no good reason to assume that the extension of 'gold', or any other substance designating term, has not changed. Thus A posits fixity where B does not, and A does not assign fixed qualitative layers to the meanings of the relevant words where B does.

The following are among the conditions that an adequate theory of lexical meaning should meet:

1. The extensions of terms need not stay fixed; cultural changes will cause certain fluctuations in the range of application without meaning change.
2. Knowledge of some key properties involved in explanatory uses is part of semantic competence.
3. There are layers of meanings for descriptive words, depending on whether the context calls for more or less detailed knowledge of the subject, different audiences, etc.

It seems that alternative B satisfies these conditions better than alternative A.

Meaning, Use, and Application

We proposed that meanings correspond to 'natures' in a rather loose sense of this term. In the sections to follow the conceptual anatomy of these meanings will be analysed. But first we need to deal with two prior questions. If the meanings of words are explanatory schemes, then are there simple basic meanings? How do we move from the grasp of meanings in the sense defined to the extensions of the words?

My account denies that there are basic primitive meanings. The explanatory patterns that lexical meanings provide are interlocking. What is problematic in one context is presented as what is non-problematic in another. A concept will appear simple in one context in relation to another, and complex in other contexts when it is related to others. As in Neurath's analogy to a boat that needs repairs always while out at sea and cannot put into port – the world resembling the *Flying Dutchman*? – everything can be questioned, but not at the same time, else the ship sinks. In our search for understanding we need to keep some things fixed at any given time. Language on this view confronts reality not linguistic atom by linguistic atom, nor completely holistically, but in 'large chunks', shaped by our ongoing activities of investigation and explanation in everyday and scientific activities. (On explanation and investigation, see Bromberger, 1962, 1966.) According to this conception there is no sharp break between everyday and scientific uses of language, provided that we keep in mind that scientific uses include the use of language in research and ongoing investigation, and not only the use invoked when we present large parts of what is claimed to be already known and understood. Investigation and explanation-seeking involve finding things problematic, pointing towards entities whose nature is only partly understood, and thus the forging of concepts that explain only partly and call for further illumination. This aspect of scientific activity resembles much of our everyday activity, both linguistic and otherwise, that is embedded in efforts to cope with changing data, changing intellectual climates, and the steady stream of newly emerging problems. Needless to say, the language we use in conducting research and trying to merge the new with the old can also serve for the use with which we present what is, at least provisionally, taken as known and understood.

If the meaning of 'w' gives us an articulation of that in virtue of which something falls within the extension of 'w', then knowing that meaning should give us the cognitive capacity to employ 'w' in a variety of uses, i.e. those in which the word is fitted into contexts of descriptions, explanations, questioning, etc., in which what is denoted by 'w' is joined to other elements of reality to form the appropriate linguistic complexes. Still, acknowledging this does not get around the fact that meanings as we use this notion do not by themselves determine extensions, since they provide only necessary conditions for application. This notion of meaning 'lets in too much'; not everything that can be explained in ways in which we normally explain baseball or cricket fits into that range which is designated by the respective words, and which needs to be distinguished from all other – including possible – games in order to have the properly delineated extensions. As we shall see in the detailed exposition, there is no simple and single procedure that will delineate extensions in all cases. Fixing extension is partly a matter of knowing what the contrasting linguistic elements are. But it is also a matter of looking at practical, or in some cases observational, contexts for gleaning various disjunctions that provide sufficiency to our conditions, in given contexts. In some cases exigency forces on us precise delineation of extensions, and in these contexts determining the extension is not merely a matter of discovery but also partly a matter of negotiation and decision. The social aspect of these procedures will be discussed later. But this brief sketch should serve in a preliminary way to show the theory of meaning outlined so far can lead to a semantic level at which notions of extension, reference, and truth are applicable.

The World and the Human Agent

So far we have sketched a view about human concepts and about some general conditions of lexical meaning, and arguments were presented against the 'pragmatic' or action-oriented view of human thought. It is consistent with this to argue, as I shall do now, that our concepts, and hence the meanings assigned to descriptive words, are influenced by the fact that humans are necessarily agents and not just observers of reality.

This fact is of independent interest, but it bears also on the thesis articulated in the previous section, namely that what I call meanings are special necessary conditions of application. For, as was illustrated, to explain to a potential agent an activity he will participate in, often requires only necessary not sufficient conditions. This applies also to scientific research. Explanatory concepts we use while research is in progress often yield only necessary conditions. These guide us in our work. Exact delineation of species and kinds can be left till later.

Our being necessarily agents influences the structure and content of the general scheme within which we explain what something is. The exact form of this scheme will be presented in the next section. In this section, in order to support the contention that the agential point of view influences semantics, we shall consider a number of ways in which the view of an agent interacting with reality differs from that of the mere observer. For example, how would one want to explain what heat is if one were to look at the world 'from the outside' so to speak, without being a part of it and without interacting with it? Presumably we would want to know what its most important attributes are, what its constituents are, and how it affects other parts of reality. The same applies to explanations of biological species and other kinds. Once we consider heat or a species like a lion from the point of view of human agents, however, other factors enter into consideration. Heat plays important roles in human survival and in phenomenal experience. Lions constitute in some parts of the world a threat to humans, and they are, unfortunately, also used by humans. From the 'outsider' point of view these may be accidental features of heat and lions, respectively. Nevertheless, given their importance for humans, these features enter semantics. Explaining to a human what counts as heat involves pointing out various ways in which heat affects us. It involves also relating this phenomenon to human experience. Again, explaining what a lion is involves reference to its carnivorous nature, strength, ferocity, etc. It will also refer to the fact that lions are used by humans in various ways (skins, circuses, etc.).

To illustrate the point further, let us consider a game like baseball, and see how its explanation differs from the point of view of a disinterested researcher and that of a participant. The classifier of various sports might define baseball simply in terms of its constitutive rules. Over a period of time, this causes trouble. For one would have to redefine what baseball is with every rule change. Thus even from the disinterested point of view, a more flexible scheme is to be recommended. This flexibility becomes apparent when we consider the rule changes and the meaning of 'baseball'. A rule committee changes some rules almost every spring, and yet no linguist would claim that the meaning of 'baseball' changes every spring. A player knows what baseball is, and hence what 'baseball' means, when he knows the essentials of how to play a game. A fan knows the game, when he has a general idea of what to look for and how to score. As we shall see shortly, this contrast can be seen in connection with many descriptive words of a language like English.

An interesting class of cases is formed by words designating diseases. Our concept of a human disease typically involves descriptions of symptoms, underlying internal causes, and some account of the external conditions causing the disease. When we know enough about these factors, our concept of a disease can function as an explanatory concept. From the point of view of a potential patient, however, these factors vary in importance and detail. The symptoms and the effects on the human of a disease are of great importance to us, even if, from the point of view of merely explaining and characterizing a physiological process, these factors might not be essential. The factors just mentioned will play important roles in determining what falls under the extensions of the relevant words. Let us take 'cancer' as an example. From the human point of view it is crucial that many forms of cancer kill. Thus if we had two very similar internal conditions but only one of these was crippling or fatal, the extension of the word 'cancer' would be delineated in view of the latter condition, not in view of the first. The same point can be seen by reflecting on the meaning of other such words, e.g. 'AIDS'. Here too, having an origin partly in sexual contact and having debilitating effects will influence the determination of the extension of the word, even if it were to be less than crucial for scientific research.

We have made a general claim, and have given some examples supporting it. It is time to make a more detailed view of the various ways in which human interaction with reality can influence word meaning. We shall review five of such ways.

1. *Interactions with other humans.* Such interactions will shape the meanings of terms introducing various human relations, and, one hopes, also words designating our relations to other members of the animal kingdom. Our conception of another human is partly in terms of how our actions and attitudes affect other persons, and in terms of how the actions and attitudes of others affect us. It is one thing for an observer to form a concept of what it is for humans to try not to hurt each other, and it is another for a human to form a concept of another human as a creature he will try not to hurt. Many of our encounters with animals and plants raise the same issues. 'How can we affect each other? What can we share?' are concerns that shape many of our concepts of the sentient world, and thus have an impact on the semantics of words like 'friendship', 'care', or 'sympathy'.

2. *The use of things.* Artefacts and other objects can become instruments in human activities. Many of the words for these are formed not in frameworks of theoretical classification, but in the context of a variety of intelligent practices that lead to the utilization of the environment. Affected words will be, among others, 'hammer', 'wrench', 'telephone'.

3. *Drawing qualitative distinctions.* As agents we find it necessary to distinguish one kind from another, but always in the context of facing only a small part of the world, not the totality of what there is. Thus the qualitative distinctions we draw cover only a small part of all the logically possible states. For example, we want to distinguish the harmful from the useful insect, such as hornets and bees. Similarly, we distinguish ferocious big fish like sharks from harmless big ones like sturgeons. Terms like 'useful' and 'harmless' or 'ferocious' need not have exact extensions in order for our active distinguishing practices to work. The distinctions encoded in ordinary use and meaning go as far as our limited human point of view requires it. Hence the incomplete articulations of the world of insects, colours, shapes, etc.

4. *Observational identifications.* Though this ability has been given a privileged place in the empiricist theories of

229

knowledge and language, it is only one of the many ways of interacting with reality. It is at a premium in distinguishing the secondary qualities of colour, smell, sound, and taste, but it is of little value in learning the meanings of such institutional or occupational words as 'judge', 'legislator', etc. These words have a strong functional layer in their meaning, and this aspect cannot be discovered primarily by observation. Though a certain amount of observation is necessary, we also need conceptual information about how legal systems function in order to understand. In the case of terms introducing purposive activities assumptions about intent, goal, or development are far more important than recognitional capacities. One might have an adequate understanding of the meaning of a verb like 'complete' without being good at recognizing sensibly present members of the extension of this word. The importance of sensory observation was upheld by the verificationist theory of meaning according to which to know the meaning of a word is to know the ways in which the presence of an element of the extension can be verified or disconfirmed. This theory turned out to be unacceptable for the sciences in general. We can see the inadequacies if we reflect briefly on words designating disease. As was pointed out above, in many cases the key element is what underlies the observables, and relations between symptoms and underlying structure may be quite indirect. We can keep the observational ability in proper perspective if we do not confuse knowing what the extension of a term is and knowing how to identify sensible present instances. One can see this confusion by considering that one could know perfectly well what it is to be a banker in Zurich without being able to identify the bankers scurrying around in the street of Zurich.

5. *Constructing, producing, doing.* We learn the meanings of many terms in these contexts. We learn typically what counts as a knot by learning how to tie a knot, not by observing bulges on a string. The same applies to terms introducing some of our attitudes. To learn the meaning of 'approve' involves typically to learn how to form and express approval. It is not a matter of observing instances in our environment. In some contexts we need to master rituals associated in a society with conventional forms of approval. We can see this

230

in the case of explicit performatives like 'promise'. Knowing what it is when someone else makes a promise is linked to having a clear grasp of the first person use. This is not always the case with performatives. In many societies, including our own, a few officially appointed persons, in secular or religious contexts, have to go through a certain ritual involving verbal communication in order for a marriage to be valid. In that case, for most of us it is the recognition of the right performance under the right circumstances that matters most. This example shows that the ways in which semantics interacts with human activities can vary from cultural context to cultural context. What if in our society everyone over forty-five were qualified to say: 'I pronounce you . . .' and have this count as performing the marriage ritual? How would this change the meanings of the words involved?

We have reviewed various interactions that affect semantics. These are human relations, use of objects, distinguishing, observing, and doing or constructing. We can now locate the aspects of meaning structures that are affected by the various interactions. Human interactions will affect the way we see what a relationship is supposed to accomplish and how it is to function. Distinguishing and observing place importance on the qualitative structures of entities falling within certain extensions. Finally, making, producing, and doing affect those aspects of semantics and word meaning that have to do with what something is made of, and what causal antecedents or effects its applying correctly to an item entail. Thus we have within these examples stress on constituency, structure, agency, and function. We shall see how in terms of these one can articulate a general form for meaning structure on the lexical level.

Meaning Structures and the Explanatory Factors

We defined word meaning as that in virtue of which something falls within the extension of a word, and we articulated this as an explanatory scheme for this 'semantic nature'. We shall develop here a general scheme for articulating what it is in virtue of which something falls within an extension.

What can we explain with language? In principle everything for which we have a concept and which we can describe in language. In our review of the influence of the agential point of view on word meanings we uncovered four explanatory factors. In this section we shall see that together these yield the desired scheme.

As we saw in the previous section, one of the key questions we can ask of anything is: 'What constitutes it, what are its parts?' We must get away from too restricted materialistic interpretations of this formula. It applies to everything, from material substances to events and to abstract entities like arguments. Things having basically the same kind of essential constituency fall into the same category. Indeed, on reflection it is obvious that if we are to understand the nature of anything and know how to apply our descriptive vocabulary to it, then we should be able to locate it in one of the fundamental ontological categories. Because of its link with the historically influential Aristotelian doctrine of 'matter', we shall label this the m-factor within a meaning structure. Knowing the m-factor within the meaning of a word enables us to place the members of the extension in the right category. For example, if we understand the meaning of 'number', then we know that the items falling under it are abstract, and if we understand 'walk', then we know that events fall under it. Within my lexical theory the following categories are posited: (a) abstract, (b) material entity, (c) event or state, and certain more complex classes to be explored below. The term 'abstract' might suggest to some the view that what we refer to in that category is abstracted from sense experience. But the lexical theory developed here does not endorse any such epistemological view. Furthermore, reflecting on the abstract–concrete dichotomy helps us to see that belonging to one of the categories posited is a necessary property of any item. Not even in the most bizarre science fiction story can we have an item plausibly changing from abstract to concrete, or from being an event to being a material object. The word 'material' carries all the inexactitude discussed in earlier chapters of this book, but will do for our purposes here. Included in this category are also aspects of the material such as surfaces or lines. (d) certain objects of the senses, such as smells, tastes, or sounds. These are in time, but need not have intrinsic links to material bodies, even though according to current physics

they do. (e) transcategorial constituency. Some items are constituted from items from different categories. Prime cases of these
are words introducing human institutions or parts of our mental
make-up. Institutions typically involve some idea or purpose,
some material realization, and people realizing it. Thus the m-
factor of words like 'university', or 'factory' has to include ideas,
function, certain kinds of human in certain roles, and physical
objects that serve as the place for functioning. Similar considerations apply to artefacts such as prints, poems, and symphonies
which are created both on the abstract and the concrete level.
Certain mental terms are transcategorial because they involve
different aspects of our experience. They are individuated by
their abstract objects, but they have also experiential and
biological components. We can see this in the meanings of words
like 'hope' and 'expect'.

So far we have dealt with descriptive words whose meaning
does not depend on its being linked to other descriptive words.
Intuitively, this is exemplified in English by words in the
categories of noun, verb, and some adjectives. There are also
words whose meaning depends on the words acting as modifiers
of various kinds. For example, adverbs fall into this class.
Nothing can be just 'slowly'; the meaning is such as to function as
modification. For words in this class the m-factor will be the
range of all those kinds of thing to which the word can apply. For
'wise' it is comprised of actions, humans, possibly other sentient
creatures, thoughts and thought products. For 'slowly' the m-
factor includes agents and processes involving speed, while for
'gentle' it includes whatever can count as being gentle such as
humans, thoughts, actions, gestures and thought-products such as
communication. Thus one could say that what counts as falling
under 'gentle' is constituted by these elements.

The m-factor, as we spelled it out, is specified by a list. Its
members are: abstract, event, material, objects of senses,
transcategorial, and modifying elements. We can take any
descriptive word or phrase, and run it through this list, and locate
its m-factor.

Having located the extension of a word within one of our
categories, we want to know how it differs from other things
within the same category. Intuitively speaking, structures differentiate kinds within the same category. Hence the name of

s-factor for this element in the meaning structure. For example, the s-factor of 'number' should tell us how what counts as a number differs from other abstract entities describable in English.

Elements in the same category differ from each other partly in terms of individuation and persistence, and partly in terms of qualitative differences. These are the two ingredients in the s-factor. Some terms like 'iron' or 'water' are called 'mass terms' because they do not carry principles of individuation. We saw in the ontological sections how important principles of individuation and persistence were for those terms that carry these. But elements with the same individuation and persistence principles can differ essentially from each other. Such differences are articulated by further qualitative conditions, separating, for example, the different kinds of insect or shade of colour. The extent to which these qualitative differences separate a class constituting an extension from all else conceivable depends on the circumstances determining use. In some cases, e.g. that of 'number', perhaps the m- and s-factors yield necessary and jointly sufficient conditions, but, as we saw, in many cases this is not so. Knowing the meaning of 'city' will give us, via the s-factor, only marks that tell cities from villages, towns, family tents, etc.; it does not involve being able to tell cities from all other actual or possible forms of human settlement.

In summary, to determine the s-factor of the meaning of a word 'w' involves running the word meaning through the following questions.

1. What if any principle of individuation is tied to it?
2. What if any principle of persistence is tied to it?
3. What are the qualitative conditions that, given ordinary linguistic competence, will separate fully or partially, the items in the extension of the word from other items belonging to the class with the same m-factor, but falling within different extensions?

Some terms such as 'number' or 'mass' have only m- and s-factors in their meaning structures. Other terms have meanings containing also functional aspects and necessary attributes involving causal agency. The fact that so many words and phrases have functional components in their meaning structures supports the claim that we conceptualize the world partly from an agential point of view. Specifying the nature of things involves for us linking them also to what they can do, embody, represent, or effect, and in considering these matters, we keep in mind our salient interactions with the world. This is, then, the f-factor in the meaning analysis, where the 'f' is supposed to remind us of function. It has several aspects, not each of which applies equally to the meanings of all words that contain an f-factor. Something can be defined partly functionally in terms of what it does (e.g., carpenter or locksmith), or in terms of what process or accomplishment it represents (e.g. building a house, or winning a race), and in terms of what effect or upshot it stands for (e.g. a defeat is the functional result of having lost to an opponent, no matter how this was accomplished). Not all words have an f-factor in their meaning structure. As a test one can ask: 'Could this word have any meaning or range of application in a universe in which there can be no purpose, aim, function, or result?' If the answer is negative, then we can go about isolating in the meaning structure the functional element. Our analysis assumes that all terms have m- and s-factors in their meaning, and thus no word can be defined purely functionally. This will become clearer from the examples given in the next section.

Finally, let us consider the factor that ranges over the causal properties that are parts of the meanings of some words. Because of the relation to agency, we shall call this the a-factor. The a-factor is designed to capture the fact that in the explanation of what some things are, their origin or causal potency is an essential ingredient. Terms for artefacts are obvious examples. Artefacts are human productions or in some institutional settings at least ceremonially adopted as such; for example, the ceremonial oak tree where the king sits. Since many biological species are distinguished in terms of their modes of propagation the words denoting these will have in their meaning structures an a-factor. Many action terms require certain kinds of entities as their agents, thus these too have an a-factor in their meaning. For example, 'walk' has an a-factor in its meaning since not all types of locomotion resembling walking count as such, regardless of agent. Words like 'write' or 'cut' have a-factors in their meanings since what counts as falling under them must have certain effects. Cutting severs things, and writing produces sets of symbols. Some words designate processes that are characterized partly in terms of their effects, such as 'purify'; hence the need for an a-factor. The fact that not all meanings of all verbs have an a-factor as a component is not incompatible with the hypothesis that every event has a cause. The fact that the a-factor can be absent shows only that for some events the nature of the agent or effect is not part of the essential attributes.

We concluded the survey of the four meaning factors. We see that the factors found in our survey of the influence of the agent's point of view are not just random items. To articulate the meaning of a descriptive word or phrase is to fill in the relevant information under the four headings, keeping in mind that two of these are optional and might be left blank. The general form of meaning representation is:

R (m,s,f,a)

where the four letters in the parentheses are our four factors, and 'R' stands for the relation that ties constituents, structure, function, and agency together in the appropriate way, that we grasp intuitively when we consider something that has all four of these ingredients. This characterization fills out what we said in the previous sections about what it is to know the meaning of a word. Roughly speaking, it is to be able to articulate in virtue of what something counts as apart of the extension in terms of our four factors. To know meanings is to be able to provide explanatory patterns in terms of our four factors. Examples should make this clear.

Examples

We shall survey a number of examples. This should not only help the reader to develop a better feel for the theory, but also to show the wide range of phenomena that can be accounted for within this framework. The following features of the theory will be covered by the illustrations.

1. The lexical theory can be applied to items from different syntactic categories, such as noun, verb, adjective, and combinations of these.
2. The meaning structures of some lexical items include all four

factors while that of others includes only two or three.

3. The theory accounts for the 'count versus mass' term distinction by showing that some words do while others do not come with principles of individuation, and that the distinction can be found in syntactical categories other than just the category of noun and noun phrase.
4. The fourfold meaning structure applies to words whose extensions arc in any of the ontological categories mentioned: i.e. material, event, abstract, or transcategorial.
5. The application of the theory to transcategorial expressions accounts for certain semantic facts that are of independent interest.
6. In the meaning structures of some expressions a certain factor is 'dominant', i.e. it determines to a large extent the content of the other factors for that expression.
7. We see in the meaning structures of several expressions the influence on semantics of what we called the point of view of the agent.

Let us start with the category of noun, and consider a couple of examples whose extension contains living things. Our first example is 'bird'. In informal intuitive terms one would explain what counts as falling within the extension of 'bird' as a living creature, part of the animal kingdom, with feathers, two legs, two wings, and the ability to fly.

We shall restructure this information within the four factors of our theory. The m-factor is being material. This becomes obvious by just going down the list of categories provided by the theory. One of the layers of the s-factor would provide principles of individuation and persistence. Mere bodily separateness is not enough for individuation. The principle involves that and the unity of agency required by biological functioning. A creature that has one continuous body but has within that several biological organisms functioning, like a committee, violates the individuation condition for 'bird'. Both bodily separateness and the unity of biological functioning is essential to the individuation of what falls under this word. To be sure, the details of the latter are much clearer for the ornithologist than for the layperson. This is true for most biological species. The same applies to the persistence conditions. Bodily continuity is not the preservation

237

of the same parts, but of the continuing biological functioning, as well as continuity in coherent mass. The other part of the s-factor is the qualitative distinguishing factor. This includes having feathers, wings, legs, beak, and these elements in a functionally adequate arrangement. Having feathers distinguishes our extension from that of, e.g. 'flying tiger'. The a-factor does not specify an essential causal effect, but it does specify essential origin. What we count as birds constitute a species. Birds come from birds, in ways specified by the empirical information of the zoologist, not semantics. Not surprisingly, the f-factor is crucial for the layperson. It includes the ability to live an organic existence, to fly, to move on the ground, and to propagate.

This characterization and analysis shows once more what was called above the indeterminateness of certain concepts. One could ask: Why two wings? Why not one, or three? Also can beak, wing, leg, etc. be in any arrangement within the body? Functional conceptions give us an answer but only a rough one. Birds have two wings because that enables them to fly, two legs so they can move efficiently on the ground, etc. Deviations from this structure are not inconceivable, and our semantics leaves it open how one would legislate the semantics if such cases cropped up with sufficient frequency.

There are also exceptions to this characterization. What about penguins that do not fly, and kiwis which have no wings? In these cases we provide developmental stories. Penguins have developed non-functional wings, and kiwis presumably descend from species that did have wings. These supplementary accounts suggest that precision in the meanings for words designating natural kinds is not only not available but even desirable for either layperson or scientist.

Let us take now another example from among the living, but not from the animal kingdom. The meaning of 'tree' bears some similarities to that of 'bird'. As an explanation of what we call 'tree' one could say that it is a living thing, a plant sprouting leaves either continuously or seasonally, with a single self-supporting trunk of wood, and branches and leaves. This example shows once more the difference between specifying the nature of what is called e.g. 'tree', and specifying the nature of the genus from a scientist's point of view. Much more, and in some ways different kinds of things would have to be added for the latter enterprise.

The m-factor is the same as for 'bird', and in this case too we have principles of individuation and persistence. The individuation is in this case also organic functioning unit and bodily separateness, but the latter condition is less crucial than in the case of birds. Trees can grow together and not cause conceptual scandal the way the growing together of two birds would. The qualitative distinguishing part of the s-factor includes trunk, leaves, etc., as mentioned above, but again indeterminateness is manifested. Palm trees and plants somewhere between a tree and shrubbery, like an olive tree, fit the explanation less well than pine trees or elms. In our sense of 'meaning' there is a variation in meaning between the lay use and the scientific uses, but not such as to call for homonymy, or even the positing of different sense. There is also the difference in the relative importance of the s- and the a-factors. For example, there are problems concerning constituency. First, while for the botanist the constituency is clearly an essential feature, it is less clear how crucial this is for the lay use. Years ago, when aluminium sailing boats were introduced and the matter came up for discussion in the New York Yacht Club, a crusty old member is said to have commented: 'If God meant us to sail aluminium boats, he would have created aluminium trees instead of wood.' It is not clear whether this semi-serious remark is trading on semantic anomaly or the extreme stretching of meaning.

The a-factor is the essential origin of trees from trees, while the f-factor contains the conditions of organic existence, or 'life', and the capacity for growth and decay. The matter of growth seems to place constraints on constituency. Alternatively, if we do not dismiss the story about the aluminium tree as a joke, then maybe it cannot be regarded as a *sine qua non* either.

We specified the constituency for trees as wood. Let us look at the meaning of 'wood' now. We count as falling within the extension of this word solid material that constitutes the material for tree below the bark. This will do as an explanation for the ordinary use of the word. Needless to say, it would not do as an explanation for the botanist or chemist. For though they would include the above as holding for the ordinary observable cases, they would want a more elaborate account in terms of the scientifically relevant constituent properties of this substance.

The semantics of the scientist includes that of the layperson, and then some more.

'Wood' is the first word among our examples that is a 'mass'-term and thus carries no principle of individuation. One can ask how much wood there is in a pile, but questions about how *many* woods would have to relate to forests, not to amounts of the substance. Whether terms like 'wood' carry persistence conditions is not above controversy. The affirmative view has been defended by Helen Cartwright (1965), while the negative view says that persistence conditions would have to be tied to phrases like 'piece of wood', 'chunk of wood', etc. Discussing this matter would take us too far from the main task at hand.

The s-factor thus contains only qualitative distinguishing features. These include solidity, but only degrees of hardness (in view of pine trees and other 'soft' wood), and the property of being what trees are made of. Together with our discussion of the previous entry, we see here a rather tight circle between the meanings of 'tree' and 'wood'. They are partially defined in terms of each other. For the scientist investigating the nature of wood, there is a way out of the circle, but for the semantics of ordinary uses there is not.

The meaning of 'wood' does not tell us much about further specification of constituency. Thus it is not surprising that there is no a-factor in the meaning structure. Meaning alone does not place essential conditions on the origin or mode of production of wood. There is, however, an f-factor, namely the property of being usable for the construction of various human artefacts, large or small. This shows the intrusion of what we called the point of view of the agent. From the perspective of a detached observer of nature, being or not being usable for humans in their efforts to shape part of the environment to their purposes is an accidental feature. But for the average human who understands the meaning of 'wood', the relation to members of its extension and our interactions with nature is a crucial element.

The effect of the agential point of view can also be seen when we consider the meanings of such pairs as 'chair' and 'seat'. We count as a chair roughly anything that is made as a separate material object usable for sitting by a human or perhaps two. The m-factor is being material. The s-factor has principles of individuation and persistence in it. The individuation principle centres on being an object that can be used for sitting. It cannot include bodily separateness, since two chairs can be nailed down together, or linked – as they are sometimes in parks – by other means. Persistence is once more not in terms of sameness of material parts, but in such preservation and continuous replacement of material as to maintain the same functioning unit. The a-factor is the property of being made or constructed as an artefact. The qualitative distinguishing part of the s-factor has not been mentioned. That is because this layer of meaning is dominated, in the sense mentioned at the outset, by the f-factor. This is the use for sitting, and at different times in our culture different devices serve such purposes better than others. Shape, having legs, etc., are typical features, but not necessary to any degree of exactness, since functional requirements can change. Still, we need some condition restricting possible occupancy, so as to distinguish 'chair' from 'bench' or 'pew', etc.

In comparing 'chair' with 'seat' we see that the latter covers more, and is defined even more exclusively in terms of function. A seat is something made or used for sitting. Thus a chair is a kind of seat, but so are seats in a bus or in airplanes, etc. The f-factor dominates completely. The m-factor is whatever category everything falls that can be used for sitting. The s-factor carries individuation and persistence only derivatively, i.e. one has to look at the different things used for sitting, see what kinds they fall under, and then see the individuation and persistence conditions of these. The a-factor drops out altogether, since there is no semantic constraint on the origin or causal roles on whatever can be used for sitting. Finally, an item like this shows once more the influence of the agential point of view. The concept and correlated meaning emerges only in the world of humans interacting with and using parts of the environment.

A similar pair is 'house' and 'home'. For 'house' the m-factor is being material, the s-factor includes the principle of individuation of being a living unit for a contextually defined social group, and persistence consists in remaining the same shelter and unit for living, with appropriate occasional replacement of parts. The a-factor is being an artefact, and the f-factor is serving as shelter and living place for a socially relevant group.

Bodily distinctness does not enter into individuation, since there are such structures as row houses. The functional factor plays once more an important role, since in terms of size, shape, material, internal structure, houses vary greatly across cultures and across historical periods. The s-factor includes a qualitative distinguishing part, namely being a solid shelter and living place for a social group, thus separating 'house' from 'tent', 'apartment house', and various other shelters. Needless to say, the distinguishing factor is indeterminate. One could hardly expect conditions that will separate houses from all other possible future constructions serving as living place.

'Home' has a different extension from 'house' since we apply this term to any dwelling place where someone has lived for a reasonable period of time, is familiar with the place, regards it as a place to which one belongs, and can take its comfort for granted. This is again a word in the meaning of which the f-factor dominates, and whose existence is brought about by our conscious interacting with the environment. Houses can serve as homes, but so can many other kinds of dwelling places. The derivatives of 'feeling at home' and 'homesick' can be explained in terms of the f-factor alone. The s-factor is completely dependent on the functional specification; anything will do as it can serve as a home for some living creature.

Undergraduates at a university like Stanford say to their advisers in their first and second years of study that they are going 'home' for vacations. Some time in their second or third, or even fourth, year they switch to saying that they are going 'to their parents' place' for vacation, even if their parents have not moved, and the same house is in focus. One cannot help but wonder what exactly the features are that cause this change of words.

Before we leave the realm of concrete nouns, it is worth noting that our lexical theory provided a more structured framework for meaning within which we were able to reflect on many meaning relations. One could not have done this if one operated merely with the intension–extension dichotomy of the philosopher or the procedure of the lexicographer of introducing an intuitive definition and then just adding various 'senses' in the dictionary entry.

We turn now to nouns with other kinds of extension. Let us consider a noun designating an emotional state such as 'joy'. The m-factor is being an event or state, since the primary location for joy is time rather than place. It is, in principle, a temporal entity, lasting through periods in which certain emotions sway over us. Though not a concrete noun, 'joy' is a 'mass' term, or more felicitously a 'non-count' term, since it carries no principle of individuation. There can be much or little joy in a community, but not 'many joys'. The qualitatively distinguishing part of the s-factor is the property of being an emotional state characterized by spontaneous elation of a positive kind, without utilitarian aspects, and without being the satisfaction of some antecedently given need. Our grandchildren can be a source of joy, but not because they benefited us in some way. The title of the hymn *Joy to the World* could hardly be transformed into *Satisfaction to the World*. Satisfaction is the fulfilment of desires or needs, while there is no such requirement on joy.

'Joy' has no a-factor in its meaning structure since no specific mode of origin or causal efficacy is attached to it solely by semantic structure. The f-factor is the bringing about of peaceful contentment, inner harmony, and release from tension. How this is accomplished is not determined by semantics. Because joy, like many other important states, does not lend itself to mechanistic explanations of the sort employed in the social sciences, it has not been in the focus of psychology or philosophy. Yet it is not only a vital part of human experience, but also a theoretically interesting notion. For example, it illustrates what we said above about being ontologically non-committal between certain alternatives. We know that there is such experience as joy, but we do not know whether it is purely mental in a dualistic sense, or a notion explicable in materialistic terms. It is also clear that we can know a great deal about a state like joy without having to make that commitment.

We shall now turn to nouns with abstractness as their m-factor. The lexical theory is neutral as to various proposals about what abstract constituency is; ultimately primitive properties, Aristotelian 'intelligible matter', etc. As we shall see, the count versus non-count distinction applies to abstract nouns as well. Furthermore, some abstract nouns have persistence conditions contained in their meaning structure while others do not. For example numbers are not temporal entities, hence 'numbers' lack persistence conditions, but symphonies, constitutions, languages, etc., do have temporal origins, hence they are governed by persistence conditions.

Let us start with the example of 'number'. The m-factor is being abstract, and the s-factor includes individuation but not persistence. Individuation depends on which range of numbers we deal with. For the average speaker of English, numbers are primarily positive integers and their fractions. Thus the individuation principle is the successor notion. For the mathematician there is a much larger variety of numbers and individuation becomes more complex. Once more, the lay use is included in the use of the expert but the latter extends also further. The qualitative distinguishing feature in the s-factor is: being the primary units of pure (non-applied) addition, and serving to order quantities into determinate magnitudes. There is no a-factor, since abstract entities like numbers do not have causal powers, and in this case there is no f-factor either. The latter condition need not apply to all abstract nouns. Once more we see that for meaning structures of various sorts not all four factors need be present.

We turn now to the semantically more complicated case of 'freedom'. The m-factor is the category of abstract entities, and in the s-factor we have no individuation principle since 'freedom' is not a count term. There can be much or little freedom, but 'many freedoms' only in the sense of many kinds of freedom. This shows once more why 'mass' is an infelicitous word to indicate the feature under discussion. Ordinarily one does not think of something abstract as freedom as a mass of some sort. The qualitative distinguishing aspect of the s-factor is: that combination of possibility, responsibility, and discipline that enables an individual or collections of individuals to act in a self-determining way. There is no a-factor in this meaning structure, and the f-factor is: bringing about a state of relative self-determination. One can easily convince oneself that we need all three components in freedom. Without possibilities there is no freedom but repression. Without responsibility we have whims not freedom. Without discipline of the appropriate kind, we have chaos or anarchy, not freedom. This, of course, leaves open the questions: How much of each ingredient, and in what combination? Semantics of meaning specification leaves these questions open. They are answered in different ways in different contexts. Furthermore, there can be honest disagreement among people using this word with the same meaning about the extension.

This point about the complex ways in which we move from meaning to determination of extension will be treated in the next section.

This analysis of meaning enables us to see also the semantic link between the abstract noun, and the adjective 'free'. This adjective applies to agents and actions. An agent is free if he has freedom in the sense defined in the appropriate context. Freedom is related to certain spheres of activity: religious, political (etc.) freedom, and freedom to do this or that. An action is free if the agent's being free in the sense defined is one of the key conditions of its coming into being. To be free from some condition C is to act in a self-determining way without having C interfere with the appropriate combination of the three components. We talk about more or less freedom, but this should not be taken to be more increase in the amounts of the three components mentioned. Rather, it refers to degrees of the resulting self-determination that is the source of our activities. This is accomplished in different contexts by different variations on the quantity and kinds of possibilities, responsibilities, and discipline or self-control. Thus we see that 'freedom' has in its meaning structure an inherently normative component. In this respect it is similar to a word like 'health'.

Let us now turn directly to the analysis of an adjective. The adjective 'gentle' can be applied to people, other sentient beings, actions, gestures, etc.; hence these constitute the m-factor. The s-factor does not include a principle of individuation since 'gentle', unlike some other adjectives like 'spherical', is not a count term.

The qualitative distinguishing features have to set 'gentle' apart not only from its opposites like 'rough' and 'violent', but also from the 'neighbouring' terms of 'kind', or 'friendly'. Kindness implies some sympathy while gentleness need not. Being friendly carries with it some willingness of co-operation or help while gentleness need not. To be gentle is to be peaceful and soft in one's dealing with others with a feeling of benevolence. As we consider applications of 'gentle' to entities other than human actions, the s-factor is 'thinning out'. Thus for 'gentle horse', the accompanying feeling of benevolence need not be present, and for 'gentle slope' perhaps only the semi-metaphorical ingredient of not having rough or sudden dips remains. An adjective like this that introduces a certain way of treating things and expressing things does not have a- or f-factors in its meaning constituency.

We shall now turn to verbs introducing states and events, thus having this m-factor. Events, processes, and states involve different time structures, made up of combinations of temporal intervals and instances. States are collections of instances, event periods including intervals of ongoing activity, and processes involve both intervals of activity and instances of completion (Gabbay and Moravcsik, 1980). Let us start with an examination of 'walk', a verb that will figure again in the next section. The s-factor includes individuation and persistence. We individuate walking by agents and the number of ongoing continuous activities, with appropriate gaps allowed as determined by context. This shows that 'walk' is a one-place predicate. Determining the argument structures of verbs has been a problem in both philosophy and linguistics. (For the so-called polyadicity problem see, for example Widerker, 1988.) An agent, Jones, walks quickly or slowly, at a certain place, with or without companions, etc. One can add predicate modifiers almost *ad infinitum*. Our lexical theory proposes that the proper argument structures can be read off from the individuation and persistence conditions. The same walk can be first fast then slow, first with then without a companion, etc. Thus these are purely optional argument places, not entering into individuation and persistence. We need, however, the same agent and appropriate continuity of activity. The result that 'walk' is a one-place predicate agrees with our intuitions. We shall test the hypothesis on other examples as well.

The qualitative distinguishing feature in this meaning structure is: being an activity of movement, placing each foot in front of the other, keeping one foot on the ground at any time. This will contrast walking with different activities and states such as running and standing. But the extent of the contrasting set cannot be specified precisely. For some it is only 'run' and 'stand', for others, as applied to horses, it includes 'canter', 'gallop', 'trot', 'race', etc.

The gaps allowed depend on the nature of the context of walking. 'He walked to the bus stop' does not imply that the agent did not stop to buy a newspaper. It does imply that he did not stop at his friend's house for three hours to play a game of chess.

The a-factor for this verb is being animate and having legs, and the f-factor is accomplishing change in place. All of this does not give us sufficient conditions for the application of 'walk'. How much change in place has to be accomplished? What is the exact nature of the appropriate movement? etc. We shall propose a way to deal with these questions in the next section.

Our proposal about specifying predicate structure in terms of what is necessary for individuation and persistence avoids two problems. One is to wonder what to say about cases in which a predicate argument is not explicitly in the sentence though we know that it is necessary for the event. The other is not to posit innumerable arguments for every verb, thus not being able to draw the appropriate inferences from an event having taken place. Let us consider the sentence 'He ate that day with gusto'. This sentence does not contain an object for eating though we must know that there must have been one, and it contains the modifier 'with gusto', which does not play any role in individuation. Thus on the basis of the lexical theory presented we still posit the object, and ignore the modifier, from the point of view of assigning argument places to the predicate structure.

We shall turn to a verb phrase introducing a state: 'to be ill'. As we saw, events require minimal intervals, contextually defined, and allow gaps in activity. States, on the other hand, are periods of time in which some condition holds at every instant. There are many activities and processes going on while the patient is ill, but the semantics ignores those, encoding only the general condition. The m-factor is the category of event and state, and individuation is by agent and state. Persistence conditions are specified in terms of continued state involving the state of being affected by illness. Some interruptions are allowed by the semantics; hence our talk about 'lingering illness'. Individuation of the state, however, is not in terms of diseases. If a person is ill and he is suffering from more than one disease, we do not say that he is 'ill twice simultaneously'. The qualitatively distinguishing factor must separate being ill not only from being in good health, but also from other disabling conditions such as being unfit for some task, e.g. as a result of weakness, and being disabled, e.g. as a result of amputation. Thus what counts as being ill is to be in bad health as the result of illness or disease.

Again, this gives us only necessary conditions, since one would need to know also how much bad health counts as being ill, and that may depend on context. The a-factor is being animate, and the f-factor is the property of bringing about the resulting lack of healthy bodily functioning.

Before we leave the semantic gold mine of verbs and verb phrases we shall look at a family of verbs to illustrate transcategoriality, and the notion of a 'possible lexical entry'. The family to be viewed is that made up by verbs of expectation. Intuitively, the core meaning shared by the members is: thinking that some event will take place. Such thoughts can differ in certain important ways. The thought may be backed by much or very little evidence, and the expected events may be thought good, bad, or indifferent. This gives us six possibilities. One can think that an event will take place and think of it as good, bad, indifferent, and for each of these three alternatives we have the state of either having or not having reasonable evidence. But we have, in fact, only four words in English covering the possibilities. If we think that what is projected is good, then we have 'anticipate' – in one sense of that verb – for the case where we have reasonable evidence, and 'hope' for the case in which such evidence is lacking. We have 'expect' to cover the case in which the projected event is not interpreted as having necessarily any value marking, and this verb can cover both cases in which we have good evidence as well as those in which we do not. Finally, we have 'fear' for those eventualities that are judged bad, and we can use this verb for all such cases regardless of the state of our evidential basis. Here we have, then, two 'possible lexical entries'; we could have separate words for fearing something on the basis of good evidence or on the basis of very slim grounds. One can only speculate why English covers the four situations it does, and whether we would find across languages the same situations covered, or have in some languages all six conceptual places marked by separate entries.

Expecting requires some object. This is characterized in different ways in different philosophical traditions. For some it could be a possible event, for others a proposition. In any case, since it might not become actual, it should be regarded as an abstract entity. Thus the m-factor for expectation and other activities or states of cognition should be transcategorial, since they are constituted of agent, event, and state, and an abstract entity in terms of which the key individuation criterion is stated. An activity like eating requires agent and object, but in such a case the event can be separated conceptually from the two material entities in a way in which the expectations, fears, hopes, etc. cannot be separated from their object and its mental representation.

Nouns like 'factory' or 'university' are transcategorial in their m-factor. For these human institutions involve human participant, aims, and functions as well as physical objects for housing. For 'university' the m-factor is: the property of having a combination of students, faculty, ideas, and buildings. The individuation condition centres on legal criteria. Two universities could use the same buildings and share one faculty. Persistence too is not a matter of sameness of 'parts' but continuity of a legal entity. In earlier stages of history in which universities might not have had legal recognition, continuation of elected or appointed heads, and overlap of staff and students over time would provide persistence.

In many sentences the noun occurs with full meaning, e.g. 'the best university in Oklahoma is in Norman'. But there are contexts in which we restrict the use to only one or some elements of the m-factor. We can see this in the following sentences.

1. The university was rebuilt in the seventeenth century.
2. The university developed the first proposals for non-Euclidean geometry.
3. The university beat Yale at football.

In the first sentence we are talking about the buildings, in the second about the faculty, and in the third about a selected representative group of students. These are not cases of ambiguity, since, as we saw, there are sentences in which we use 'university' with the full m-factor. Within our lexical theory, there are cases of use with contextually restricted m-factor.

There are cases which seem to be similar to the one just discussed, but can be shown within our theory not to be restricted uses, but matters of straightforward ambiguity. These include the use of words like 'Germans' or 'Israelites'. There are three

249

meanings here, with different explanatory conditions of application; citizenship, ethnic origin, and linguistic community. In some cases, the same word can also cover a religious status. We can see from the examples below, that the respective extensions are not identical.

1. Germans live mostly in Western Europe.
2. Germans love complex grammatical constructions.
3. Germans pay heavy taxes.

In the first we would be referring typically to people of a certain ethnic origin, in the second to a linguistic community, and in the third to a group united by citizenship. Any overlap is accidental. Confusion between these uses is not only semantically wrong, but can lead to ethically deplorable prejudice (e.g. 'the Jews', 'the blacks', etc.).

These examples should give a taste of the range of phenomena this lexical theory can cover. Though what we called compositional semantics in our survey of problems is not a part of this proposal, let us see a few implications that this lexical theory might have for it. (Further exploration of this point was suggested by David Doughty.) For many combinations of noun and adjective into a noun phrase, we can simply add the different meaning components. But we should note that certain features will have priorities in these mergings. The combination of an adjective without individuation and a noun with individuation yields a noun phrase with individuation, as in 'red chair'. This example also shows that when we join an adjective whose meaning does not contain an f-factor to a noun whose meaning does contain such a factor, the resulting noun phrase will have an f-factor.

However, there are complications. We can add certain prefixes to adjectives to produce negatives. Thus 'unintelligent', 'inconsiderate', etc. In some cases the change turns a word with individuation conditions into one without. For example, 'sentient' carries individuation conditions, while 'non-sentient' does not.

Various additions can also turn a verb of one semantic sort into a phrase belonging to another semantic sort. The verb 'walk' is an event verb, but the additions make 'walk from Rome to Naples' into a process verb with point of completion, etc.

Finally the adjective 'exotic' raises problems of its own. It is not like 'fake' or 'alleged' that negate what they modify so that, e.g., a 'fake tiger' is not a tiger. But it singles out certain features of the meaning complex of the word to which it is attached as the domain for rarified features. Thus, e.g., for 'exotic bird' we know that the m-factor or the individuation part of the s-factor will not change. What makes a bird like this rare has to relate to the qualitative distinguishing features, and even among those only some allow such modification, such as plumage. Here we have then one more phenomenon that demands the kind of semantic anatomy that our theory yields.

In summary, this lexical theory provides the right semantic structures to go with our conception of humans as *homo explanans*, and at the same time it serves well also in explaining a variety of empirical facts about lexical meaning.

Going back to some of the criteria of adequacy for lexical meaning mentioned in our survey of problems, we can see this theory meeting these.

It accounts for continuity of use, since the explanatory schemes can stay fixed while scientific uses change. It accounts also for the fact that we have at any given time only incomplete understanding of the various kinds with which we deal. For the explanatory schemes posited can be filled in with more detail, and extensions can be added without changing individuation and persistence. It can account also for the relation between lay use and scientific use of terms, since the explanatory concepts can be shared between the two, while the scheme for the expert will be filled in with more detail as far as the s- and a-factors are concerned.

The theory provides a conceptual framework within which empirical questions about developmental stages in language learners can be framed. For example, do children learn first f-factors with only minimal understanding of the s- and m-factors for words designating certain natural kinds, or roles such as motherhood? How does the recognition that the count–non-count distinction cuts across the material–abstract dichotomy fit into a psychological developmental scheme etc?

Communication within this theory is not guaranteed. Maybe nothing can guarantee this phenomenon, and yet we cannot live without assuming that it takes place often. But the positing of explanatory schemes common among humans accounts for the plausibility of assuming that, more often than not, we end up talking about the same things. In order to see how this takes place, we need to take up the last issue, namely how do we get from meanings as defined here to truth and extension?

From Meaning to Reference

Meanings on the analysis presented do not by themselves determine reference and extension. In what follows I shall try to show that this should not be a surprising conclusion. Reflection on the ordinary intuitive notion of meaning should lead us to the same result. Thus we need to show what factors must be added in order to show how meaning and extension are related. I shall posit a third, intermediary level between meaning and extension for many words, and then show how this helps us to understand how meaning and extension are linked even in the cases in which the positing of the intermediate level is not justified. As an introduction let us consider the following story. Professor Jones, the chairman of a philosophy department, is going on six months' leave to Europe. Before his departure he discusses with his secretary how departmental affairs should be managed in his absence. In the course of this discussion he says: 'Don't phone me except in case of an emergency.' She agrees. I take it that, at this point, both the professor and his secretary understand the meaning of 'emergency'. Nevertheless, further discussion is called for. The situation is not analogous to one in which a wife says to her husband: 'Please get my red dress from the other room.' In that case, understanding what is said, and being able to locate contextually 'the other room' and 'the red dress' is all that is needed for successful communication. But in this case we need to supplement the discussion with having Professor Jones say something like: 'By "emergency" I mean here things like an earthquake, injury to my children, the university going bankrupt, etc.' Even if both Professor Jones and his secretary understand English perfectly, it is informative for Professor Jones to add this. Furthermore, his proposal is subject to critical assessment. One can imagine the secretary simply nodding, or raising questions of clarification, or of a critical nature. In short, there is conceptual room for negotiation, and in such negotiations norms of public and social nature may be involved.

Let us suppose now that Professor Jones returns from abroad, and having cleared away the accumulated administrative work he wants to take off half a day so that he can type his research paper at home. He discusses with his secretary the work to be done in his absence, and in the course of this he says to her: 'Please do not phone me except in case of emergency.' The same situation is repeated. This is the sentence Jones uttered before. Again, both participants understand it. And once more, it is appropriate and informative for Jones to go on with the conversation in some such manner as: 'By "emergency" I mean here things like the students staging a protest, one of my colleagues rushing in hysterically, or a memo from the Dean's office requesting information about enrolment figures within 24 hours.' As in the previous case, there is room for further discussion and negotiation. The nature of the discussion and negotiation is the same as in the other context.

I assume that these stories would be seen by anyone as describing typical occurrences. Here are some philosophical observations concerning the communications. First, the professor is using 'emergency' in both cases with the same meaning: I don't think that a competent speaker would regard the two uses as exhibiting ambiguity. Furthermore, the meaning in these two cases does not determine by itself extension. We have here two occasions of use with the same meaning invoked and with different extensions. Thus we need to figure out how the extensions in the two cases are eventually determined. There is, however, a prior question. Brief reflection should convince us that the two situations in the story could be multiplied indefinitely. In connection with a word like 'emergency' there are many extension determining contexts. There is a father talking to his family as he prepares to go outside and clean the gutters, there is a physician leaving his office to get lunch, a lawyer ducking out early to get in a round of golf, etc. And yet these contexts are not generated arbitrarily. They have something in common that we detect and need to conceptualize.

The different applications in the story generate contradictions. The circumstances under which it is legitimate to phone the professor abroad are also legitimate grounds for phoning him when he is just staying at home half a day, but not the other way around. The students protesting is and is not an emergency. It is not an emergency when the professor is abroad, but it is when he is at home typing. Stories like this can be turned around. If the secretary of a military officer is told that all leaves on base will be cancelled for the next 48 hours, she will phone the officer if he is at home on the base, but not if he is in Washington for two weeks.

These cases show that there is need to talk about three levels of semantics. First, there is the meaning of a word like 'emergency'. Second, on the basis of this meaning and other factors, many extension determining contexts are generated. Thirdly, within each of these contexts we can fix the extension of the word. The last clause needs qualification. One would do better to say: 'It is determined on this level what the extension is or should be.' This suggests that there is a normative element in the extension fixing, and an adequate theory should account for this.

The meaning of 'emergency' is roughly: 'a state of impending or already occurring harmful event, requiring immediate response.' It is easy to show that the conditions embodied in this definition are necessary. An emergency is clearly a state, that is how we individuate emergencies. They are not activities, or material objects or abstract entities like the number 2. It is also true that the event has to be impending or already occurring. If it is still far in the future, then things look grim, but we do not, as yet, have an emergency. That the event need be harmful needs hardly be mentioned. 'Emergency' has negative connotations: the emergency room in a hospital is not so named for nothing. Similar considerations apply to the last condition involving immediate response. When emergencies arise, we want a good person at the helm who is capable of quickly surveying situations.

Having seen that the conditions are necessary, let us consider evidence showing that they are not sufficient. It is obvious that being a state cannot be a sufficient condition for being an emergency: for this only places the elements of the extension in the right category. Nor can being impending lead us to sufficiency, but here matters are more complex. What counts as impending is itself context-dependent, and thus only the 'right' kind of impending will constitute a necessary condition. An event can be impending in a minimal sense and not be enough for evoking a state of emergency. An impending disaster can be 2, or 20, or 200 years away, depending on whether we are talking about floods, earthquakes, or environmental catastrophes. What counts as 'about to happen' depends on the social, economic, or physical contexts and their interpretations. Thus one would have to add: 'sufficiently or appropriately impending' to get the kind of condition that eventually contributes to sufficiency. There are similar problems with something being harmful. An event can be harmful in some sense and still not be the sort of thing that will evoke in a given context a sense of emergency. But there is no way of specifying an intensive quantity of harmfulness 'across the board' that will serve as the right threshold. We have to consider once more whether professors, physicians, or lawyers are in the picture, and whether we are talking about brief periods of forced rest, visits from a mother-in-law, or some other appropriate type of event. Thus merely being harmful in some way is not enough. The same is true of immediacy and being a response. How immediate is the response that is required? For a declaration of war it might be weeks, for a fire fighter it might be minutes, for a surgeon in the operating theatre it might be seconds. Merely being immediate in some sense is not enough. Again, what counts as a response? Shrugging your shoulders? Scratching your head? We need to look at the public roles of the agents involved, the nature of the impending event, etc.

We see, then, that the proposed definition does not provide both necessary and sufficient conditions. One might try to remedy the situation by inserting the words 'sufficiently' and 'appropriately' in the right places, but this move is just a case of playing with words. For it is a roundabout way of saying that in determining extension, we need to look at factors other than what is contained in the definition.

The last point shows also why it is a mistake to try to assimilate the phenomenon considered to the general phenomenon of vagueness or indeterminateness. It may be the case that 'emergency' does not have a determinate meaning and that the boundaries of what it can be applied to are not sharply delineated. But what we have seen above is a semantic feature additional to whatever determinacy or indeterminacy the mean- ing of a word may have. It could be the case that everything we said about 'emergency' is true, but that once we focus on any extension determining context, we find clearly delineated classes as extensions.

The proposal under consideration deals with these facts in the following way. Drawing on what has been argued for in the previous sections, we can characterize meaning as a set of explanatory necessary conditions, given in qualitative terms. On the basis of various parts of the meaning constituents we generate extension determining contexts. Within such contexts extensions for the words are determined. We need, however, to say more about how the contexts and eventually the extensions are determined.

Let us compare what we have unearthed with other semantic phenomena. First, let us consider indexicality, as in cases like 'I', 'you', 'here', etc. Here too there are three semantic layers. There is the meaning, or condition of application, and on the second level the consideration of conditions from the point of view of some person, time, or place, etc. Finally, we have the extensions, reference, demarcated from within such points of view. But the three levels do not correspond to what we have seen in the case of 'emergency'. In the case of indexicals all we need to understand that the same expression can pick out in different contexts different times, places, or persons. But in generating the contexts for 'emergency' a great deal more needs to be considered, having to do with the various meaning constituents and the non-linguistic social contexts within which uses can be embedded. It may be that some of the words to which our three-level analysis applies contain also an element of hidden indexicality. If so, this is an additional semantic fact.

Our phenomenon differs also from what John Stuart Mill said about proper names. To be sure, in both cases it is true that there is no purely qualitative set of conditions determining extension. But in Mill's case this is because on his view names have no 'meanings' at all, while on our view the appropriate words have meanings, but these are not sufficient for determining reference.

Finally, we should also separate what we have seen from other semantic facts, often gathered under the name of 'open-endedness' (Waismann, 1960). We can illustrate this by considering the word 'vehicle'. What counts as being in the extension of 'vehicle'? Technology keeps changing, and new artefacts serving as means of transportation are being produced. Thus there is no way for us now to decide for all times what should count as under the word 'vehicle'. This would be like trying to legislate for all eternity what should count as falling under 'theft', even though we cannot envisage all of the changes that will take place in the evolution of the notion of property and property rights. For example, today we are witnessing the evolution of a new speciality in law, dealing with the theft of ideas in the computer industry. It is absurd to suggest that an all-wise judge should have provided legislation for all such possible cases fifty years ago. In all such cases of open-endedness a key fact is that a part of the denotation range is not yet in existence, and that the natures of future species within that range cannot be envisaged by us. It may be that terms like 'emergency' are affected by this semantic feature too. But in any case open-endedness is not the same as what leads us to the positing of three levels of semantics. What we have seen about emergencies would remain true even if the 'evidence' were to close today, i.e. a powerful spirit would intervene and arrange the future of the world in such a way that no new types of emergency would ever arise again. The intermediate level that we posited is needed to explain the current ordinary cases, not the future and conceptually remote cases.

Let us begin the examination of how denotation is determined in the case I presented. There seem to be three main elements. First, the considerations bearing on the matter are social and not a matter of individual taste. If someone says in the context of Jones going to Europe for six months that emergencies will include the secretary cutting her hand, or a graduate student breaking up with his girlfriend, then we can say that this person is misusing the word 'emergency'. There may be 'grey' areas where taste and individual intention enter, but it would be wrong to ascribe to these factors a key role in reference-fixing. Reactions like: 'He considers *this* an emergency?' or 'She should not call *that* an emergency' or simply 'This is not an emergency' are common, and can be backed by justification.

A second important consideration is that negotiation does have a role in extension determination. In order to appreciate this, let us contrast this kind of extension determination with others. In a science like mathematics we deal with a fixed domain of abstract entities. Some positive integers are even and others are not. We define 'even' as 'divisible by two'. Applying this condition is a simple mechanical task, it neither requires nor leaves room for negotiations, nor do we need an intermediate semantic level between meaning and extension. Let us now consider colour terms. These have empirical applications, and are affected by vagueness. The borders between red, pink, and orange are not sharply fixed. But this does not require the positing of an intermediate level as in the case of 'emergency'. It may be that some discussion and negotiation is needed in order to decide what will count as red in certain contexts, but this is not because of the vagueness of the term.

The negotiation in the story we saw involves a number of factors, such as the chairperson's view of how work can go on, the secretary's view of the same question, institutional expectations, and matters of collegial responsibility. These items are subject to public standards and critical assessment. Viewing this process as a kind of negotiation should not lead us to think of it as much like labour negotiations or the settling of international disputes where often individual will and interest have dominant roles. The maxim of maximizing utility for the affected parties plays much less of a central role in semantics than in political matters. Still, it would be misleading to think of the extension as already there, waiting for us to discover it. In some ways, not arbitrarily, the negotiations contribute to create an extension for a set of circumstances.

The normative factor is the third key element in extension determination. We saw already how easily the question 'What is the extension of "emergency" in this context?' shifts to 'What should be the extension of "emergency" in this context?' The assessment of the outcome is not just in terms of true and false, but also in terms of what the participants should or should not have agreed on. The negotiations terminate not only with what is to be in a particular case, but what is appropriate for a certain type of case. Thus the normative element is constrained, is not arbitrary, carries objectivity, and cannot be explained in purely ethical or prudential terms. To settle what would be best for the professor and the secretary would not be the same as settling what is the best semantics for 'emergency' in English in this type of case. These are, then, the factors entering the process of reference or extension fixing.

This process or activity must have a conceptual link to the meaning ingredients of 'emergency'. It is time to look at this matter in more detail. The ingredients that influence the generation of contexts for extensions correspond to some of the salient ingredients of the 'definition' that was proposed earlier, namely the meanings of 'impending', 'harmful', 'requiring', and 'response'. We can ask about each of these not only 'how much?' but also 'how much is enough or appropriate?' These questions will be answered in different ways, depending on the context. Thus when the answers to these questions are quite different, we have distinct contexts for determining extension. Let us look at individual items.

What is appropriate to be considered as impending cannot be specified in terms of a simple quantitative measure of time. An impending environmental crisis can have a time span of 20–100 years, while an impending crisis in a philosophy department is likely to mean something with the next month or year. An impending crisis in surgery can mean seconds, or at most minutes. The same consideration applies to harm. The 'harm' a person injured receives can constitute an emergency for a hospital, but probably not for the city government. Our key question is not 'How much harm constitutes an emergency?' but 'If you are a father, physician, administrator, social worker, etc., how much harm of what nature will be a part of an emergency?' The question has to be answered from the points of view of these different roles. Going on to the next item we notice that being required is also a role-dependent notion. What is required of a person depends on the social role he plays and the social setting within which he finds himself. The same applies to 'response'. What is a response from the mayor's office might not count as a response from one's mother, and the other way around. Thus as we come to the appropriate items within the meaning structure we can ask 'How much is appropriate?' and in sorting out different answers and linking these to different circumstances, we generate extension determining contexts. Let us look now at different words to which this analysis applies. Our question with regard to each candidate is: 'What constitutes, or what counts as a . . . ?' and if the answer is of the form: 'For agents in such-and-such biological or social roles it is this, but for agents or other elements of reality it is that' then the word falls within the three-level analysis that has been presented here.

Given that the meaning of 'sand' is roughly 'small grain of crushed rock', we need to face the question 'how small?'. In the case of sand this is answered differently depending on the various ways in which we use sand. What counts as sand for purposes of house construction material does not count as sand for purposes of filling up space to build a beach, or filling up the bottom of an aquarium for tropical fish. One might try to get round this by saying that there are different kinds of sand, and we use at times this and at times that. But this is just playing with words once more. Within a context of use something will count as sand that in another context will not. The semantics of 'sand' would be different in a 'possible world' in which the inhabitants have no practical use for sand.

As another example, we can take one that John L. Austin used in informal instruction, for another purpose. The example is hexagonality. Consider the sentence 'France is hexagonal'. This, as Austin pointed out, is true when part of a geography book, but false when part of a geometry text. Hexagonality and other terms designating shapes invite the question: 'How hexagonal, etc., and in what way must the object exhibit this characteristic in order to count in this context as a part of the denotation?' In contexts in which the shape terms are used in various human activities such as navigation by the shapes of rocks jutting out, reading maps by identifying shapes, doing crystallography, etc., the determination of extension will vary with what rationality, practical demands, and communicational possibilities demand.

We see that the three-level analysis applies also to a word like 'picture'. Drawing or painting a picture is an achievement. As such it is graded according to biological and cultural standards. What counts as a picture produced by a five-year old might not count as a picture when produced by an artist. This can be reversed. A painting of a very abstract non-representational sort might not count as a painting when produced during play by a child. In this way, this example differs from the previous one. In the first instance being parts of human interactions with the environment was crucial, in the second it was the element of achievement. Other words exemplify the same phenomenon. The meaning of 'walk' is captured by 'activity of movement placing one foot in front of the other, etc.'. In connection with such movements we can ask: 'How much?' and 'In what manner?' Our answers will depend on factors like age or health. What counts as a walk for an infant taking her first steps is different from what counts as a walk for a healthy adult under normal circumstances. Thus the relevant factors in the meaning of the word help us to generate extension determining contexts. The same holds for the related noun 'walk'. I cannot invite a colleague to go from my office to the neighbourhood coffee house by saying 'let us go for a walk', but I can invite a young child to cover the same distance by saying 'let us go for a walk.'

In concluding this demonstration let us consider words whose meaning resembles that of 'emergency'. To help is to do someone else's work, or to contribute to something happening. For example, we can say that Smith helped Bill in writing that book, or that the economic conditions helped bring about the war. The meaning constituents in the meaning of 'help' invite the questions: How much of someone else's work was done? What kind? Under what conditions? The extent and ways of co-operation involved in helping with a book or article are quite different from the extent and ways in which physicians help each other in operations and treatment. What we said above about negotiations involving social and normative factors apply here too. Surgeons and anaesthetists have to work out what will count as *help* in their interactions, in contrast with *interference*. The meaning of 'interfere' is 'to keep something from happening, or to obstruct the plans and activities of others'. This gives us necessary conditions for application, but we need to look at how much obstruction and what kind will count as interference, and this has to be done by generating extension determining contexts. Such are provided when we assess children's complaints that their parents interfere with their lives, or when we assess the claim that noise interferes with work, or the research of a physician interferes with clinical practice.

The word 'contribute' belongs to the same semantic family. To contribute to something is to add something of significance to a state or project contextually specified, and thus the questions arise: what kind of significance, how much significance, how do we single out a project, etc.? Thus we need again to generate denotation determining contexts.

We see, then, that whenever a word is used to designate achievements that vary within biological and social groups, or interactions involving humans or humans and the environment, there will be factors in the meanings that will lead us to generate contexts for determining extensions.

It is notoriously difficult to convince philosophers of a semantic point by the use of examples. Thus let us introduce the more general consideration of the difference between understanding words and determining extensions.

Understanding the meaning of a word like 'interfere' or 'emergency' involves two things. First, to acquire an explanatory schema of what counts as falling under the relevant terms. This is stated in terms of appropriate necessary conditions. Secondly, to be able to see how the various meaning constituents enable us to generate extension-determining contexts. This much is part of linguistic competence. But I need to know quite a lot about the non-linguistics world to know that some of the extension-determining circumstances involve professors, administrators, naval officers, etc. I am not informed about these institutions by the mere knowledge of words like 'emergency'.

Furthermore, the skills and information required for determining extensions for words in interactions between physicians and nurse, captain and gunnery officer, etc., are quite different from those needed for understanding meanings. People can be good at one of these without being good at the other. Thus mere reflection on the cognitive tasks involved in language understanding and use support the three-level analysis offered here. This three-level analysis applies primarily to the 'Fregean Core'. Further levels need to be introduced to deal with indexicality and other individual-relative specifications.

So far we have dealt with lexical meaning. We need to sketch also how we move within this proposal from lexical meaning to the propositions that sentences express. According to the three-level analysis propositions are generated only after we moved from the first to the second level, i.e. from understanding meanings to contexts within which extensions are assigned to the relevant words. If we have only the sentence 'this notice warns of an emergency', we have from a semantic point of view only incomplete concepts associated with the expressions making up the sentence. When we place the sentence within an extension determining context, we obtain the ingredients needed for associating a proposition, something that is true or false, with the sentence. The material that we added to the meanings in order to get extensions is of a rather loose, disjunctive sort. Furthermore, even after everything is done to have sentence meanings that we can associate with propositions, these need not be conceived of as defined across all 'possible worlds'. As we saw, most of our vocabulary is specified against a background of many general assumptions. Thus for some modal projections the meanings of many words remain undefined. Therefore, the propositions emerging from this analysis are indeterminate in predictable ways. This does not prevent them from doing the jobs one can reasonably expect of propositions introduced by relevant parts of natural languages.

In review we should separate two parts of this proposal. One of these is that in the case of words of certain types we need a semantic level between the standardly recognized levels of meaning and reference. The other is that we need certain sets of procedures involving social, normative, and interactive or negotiative factors in determining within appropriate contexts extensions. The second part of the thesis may hold also in cases in which the first part does not. For example, on closer inspection one might argue that for words like 'red', 'blue', 'factory', etc., the three-level analysis is not needed. But that still leaves us with the claim that even for these words extension determination involves the kind of social intersubjective negotiative process of extension determination as for those expressions to which the three-level analysis applies. Indeed, this coincides with the more general claim that meanings are necessary explanatory conditions that in most cases do not determine reference and extension. This thesis was not meant to be restricted to those expressions to which the three-level analysis applies. Explanations, as we saw, can be adequate without yielding necessary and sufficient conditions. Once we explained adequately a phenomenon or an institution, or some other element of reality, additional factors enter into sharp delineations of extensions, where this is appropriate. For example, 'university' means roughly 'institution of higher learning, producing increase in knowledge and understanding, and learned people'. This explanation fits medieval universities as well as modern ones, institutions in Europe as well as those on the American continent. We need, however, additional information to fix extension. In some historical context there is an official, licensing body, in others there is no such thing. In the American context 'university' contrasts with 'college', or 'state college', and the difference is relevant to the type of degree that can be obtained at these institutions of higher learning. Thus extension determination requires once more a complex process including elements of negotiation. The same thing can be shown about words like 'red' or 'blue', or words introducing artefacts.

On the basis of these considerations we can see how meaning is connected to reference and extension for all descriptive items in natural language. It may be that in some cases the explanatory structure constituting meaning yields necessary and sufficient conditions, as with 'even', or 'positive integer'. We can take these simply as limiting cases, constituting the end of a spectrum of more or less specific explanations. The basic vehicle described in this section shows how we can move from meanings as specified in this proposal to extension and propositions that are not defined for all modal projections. This feature of a natural language is not an imperfection. On the contrary, since a natural language is a diachronic phenomenon, and some legislations need to be enacted as we go along, this characteristic of natural language, steering between the Scylla of too much rigidity and the Charybdis of chaos, enables us to both express thoughts across generations and to communicate with each other in practical contexts. Wittgenstein is said to have maintained that ordinary language is 'all right as it is'. My proposal is one way to bear out this dictum.

Concluding Postscript

In this century philosophic theories of language have had a strong impact on the ways we philosophize. For example, the conviction that we can uncover intensions for words, and thereby provide necessary and sufficient conditions determining extensions across all modal projections, led to assigning to philosophy the task of constructing such definitions, with analytic strength, for words like 'knowledge', 'belief', 'right', 'theory', etc. Disagreeing with this view, Quine and some of the 'naturalist' philosophers deny that there are intensions in this sense, and interpret all of our judgements as having some empirical content. According to this view, there is a continuum between philosophy and science, and the former does not have any special prerogatives for tackling conceptual issues.

This essay defends intensional notions against sceptical attacks. At the same time, the emerging positive view construes our semantic and conceptual investigations as dynamic enterprises. The interpretation of intensions developed here allows for conceptual change and development within stable intensional structures. This view of meaning is placed within a conception of cognition as fundamentally the reshaping, filling out, and continued application of explanatory schemata in a world in which large-scale changes force conceptual decisions between alternatives that one could not have envisaged at earlier stages of history.

In attacking the claim that we can define meanings for most of the standard vocabulary of natural languages across all possible worlds, we should distinguish two claims:

1. What do I say now about the application of a word w if and when I find myself in a fanciful imaginary situation?

2. What can I predict about how I shall in fact apply *w* if and when I find myself in the above mentioned fanciful situation?

The following fragment from everyday conversations lends support to the claim that 1 and 2 are distinct. To questions like: 'What will you do if you ever find yourself in such-and-such a situation?' we occasionally reply: 'Well, I think and I hope that I would do such-and-such, but *I* shan't really know until I find myself actually under those circumstances.' Such a reply shows the difference between one's current intuitions about one's practical or conceptual framework and one's prediction about one's future intuitions about practical or semantic choices when placed within a certain context. I might now say: 'I shall call this thing "*F*" under circumstances "*C*"' only to find that when I am actually involved in the full web of what *C* entails, my linguistic and conceptual behaviour does not conform to my predictions.

This essay takes the stand that human thought is projective, and thus some of our intuitions about conceptual choices in modal projections must be sound, otherwise planning and explaining would not be possible. But this does not exclude the possibility that under certain circumstances informative and well-grounded answers to 1 and 2 are impossible. In fact, the theory contained in this essay suggests some of the contexts in which this will be the case. For if meanings are explanatory schemata, and as such come with certain presuppositions, then our intuitions will give out in contexts in which the presuppositions fail. These include not only the cases in which some background assumptions fail, but also those in which the specifications under our four key semantic factors do not coincide. When these factors as specified for a given lexical item do not coincide, then meaning and corresponding concept are underdetermined. Furthermore, given our 'dynamic picture', the set of circumstances under which the meanings of various items are underdetermined, varies through time.

The main difficulty confronting our efforts to predict semantic response under circumstances in which the background assumptions or the coincidence of the various meaning specifications fail is that we have very little if any evidence about one's behaviour in such contexts. Knowing that one handled a previous conceptual crisis well might give us some evidence that we shall muddle through the next one, but not evidence about *how* we shall decide in that future scene.

Since we posited layers of intensionality, we leave room for ongoing changes in our semantic structures and our philosophic investigations of these. In particular, two types of philosophical activity are suggested by our analysis. Explanations, as we noted, do not function in a vacuum. They emerge in conceptual contexts and these, in turn, keep changing. Thus the reshaping of these explanatory structures is a perennial task. So is filling in the details within different situations. Articulating a schema for explaining various kinds of friendship in a setting within which we can assume a widespread sharing of values, limited horizontal and vertical mobility in our society, and closeness of familial bonds is one thing. Developing a variation of this framework for a context in which there is widespread scepticism concerning values, and the social and familial groups are threatened constantly by dispersal either geographically or in terms of social status, is another. Forging an explanatory schema for types of knowledge in a context in which one person can have an overview of all branches of knowledge is one thing, reworking this schema for a context in which knowledge is fragmented and information processing in its technical aspects has outstripped the human absorbing capacity is another. Similar points can be made about other important notions such as those of a person, a theory, a law, or freedom. Thus much of our philosophizing in traditional areas would proceed, but without the pretension that it should aim at, or think of itself as being able to offer, accounts that can cover all present and future logical possibilities.

The other, equally important philosophical task suggests itself as we reflect on what was shown about the unavoidably normative aspects of semantic processing even on the everyday level. Already in banal contexts, briefly sketched in the last chapter, there is an element of decision involved in what eventually emerges as a use such as that of 'emergency' between professor and administrator during different leaves of absence. Other extension determining contexts call for wider communal interactions to establish or modify usage. For example, we need community-wide interactions to decide at particular times and places what should count as education, religion, or medical practice. This conceptual labour confronting communities can be aided by philosophic reflections. As the lexical theory of this essay shows, there is room, indeed necessity, for rethinking such questions as what should count as freedom, increase in understanding, or health care. The explanatory schemes that we inherit provide the parameters for these activities, but these leave us with such conceptual slack as to force us to face the responsibility of either helping to shape the thoughts of our society on these issues, or by default acquiesce in these questions being settled without the benefit of input from our philosophic heritage. What people will think should count as friendship can be shaped by what we learned from Aristotle, Spinoza, or more recent thinkers; or it can emerge without the introspective and reflective activities in which philosophers excel. Committing ourselves explicitly or implicitly to one or the other of these ways is an unavoidable choice for philosophers.

If we define the domain of ethics in a broad sense so that it includes everything to which normative standards apply across departmental compartmentalizations, then my conception interprets all of philosophy as ethics, since all parts of it will have to deal with analogous normative questions. In arriving at this interpretation we join distinguished company. Though they reach their conclusions on the basis of diverse considerations, philosophers with such different orientations as Plato, Spinoza, and Wittgenstein all agree about this aspect of the nature of philosophy. But such agreement leaves open the possibility of there being many legitimate styles of philosophizing. To some this has meant erecting grand systems covering all aspects of reality. For others it meant wide-ranging conceptual investigations without the architectonic of the great systems.

My describing philosophical tasks as having normative aspects can be misinterpreted. This kind of normativeness is neither that of moral obligation nor that of utility. One can explain it by using an analogy between philosophy and health care, first noted by Plato. Goodness is built into the concept of health definitionally. One cannot explain it by making health obligatory, and though we believe that health is useful to us, this is not the goodness that is built into the concept. Health is what enables a living body to function well, and to fulfill its natural potentialities. Within the stable conceptual framework provided by this account, we need to fill in the details at different times and contexts. relying on our incomplete and fallible understanding.

Philosophical proposals are normative in the same sense. We need to seek out what it is that in a given context is freedom, sharing, knowledge, etc. 'at their best', in a way·similar to that in which physicians wrestle with problems of what a healthy individual is. This interpretation does not reduce philosophy to a torrent of edifying discourses, merely expressing good will and noble sentiment. As in the case of health, so in the case of philosophy the sensible proposals require an interplay between empirical information and conceptual reflection. Some parts of the philosophic enterprise might even require having certain attitudes, just as reflection on health care does. In neither case do the attitudes by themselves determine the nature of the enterprises.

Looking for fruitful ways of circumscribing what can and should count today as understanding, hoping, and interacting with each other and the environment is a more modest enterprise than what was envisaged in the great metaphysical systems of the past, and it yields no final answers. Still, it leaves philosophy with an important perennial task – and an awesome responsibility.

Bibliography

Almog, J. (1986), 'Naming without necessity', *Journal of Philosophy*, vol. 83, pp. 210–42.

Alston, W. (1964), *Philosophy of Language*, Englewood Cliffs, NJ: Prentice-Hall.

Aristotle, *De Interpretatione*, ed, L. Minio-Paluello, 1949 edn, London: Oxford University Press.

Armstrong, D. (1968), *A Materialist Theory of Mind*, London: Routledge & Kegan Paul.

Austin, J.L. (1956), 'A plea for excuses', *Proceedings of the Aristotelian Society*, vol. 57.

Austin, J.L. (1962), *How To Do Things With Words*, J.O. Urmson and Marina Sbisa (eds), Cambridge, Mass.: Harvard University Press.

Barwise, J. and Perry, J. (1983), *Situations and Attitudes*, Cambridge, Mass.: MIT Press.

Bealer, G. (1984), 'Mind and anti-mind: Why thinking has no functional definition', *Midwest Studies in Philosophy*, vol. 9, pp. 283–328.

Benacerraf, P. and Putnam, H. (eds) (1964), *Philosophy of Mathematics: Selected Readings*, Englewood Cliffs, NJ: Prentice-Hall.

Bernays, P. (1964), 'On Platonism in mathematics', in Benacerraf and Putnam (1964), *Philosophy of Mathematics*, pp. 274–86.

Black, M. (1948), 'The semantic definition of truth', *Analysis*, vol. 8.

Black, M. (1952), 'The identity of indiscernibles', *Mind*, vol. 61, pp. 152–64.

Block, N. (1978), 'Troubles with functionalism', in C.W. Savage (ed.), *Minnesota Studies in Philosophy of Science*, vol. 9, Minneapolis: University of Minnesota Press.

Block, N. (1980), 'What is functionalism?', in N. Block (ed.), *Readings in Philosophy of Psychology*, Cambridge, Mass.: Harvard University Press, pp. 171–84.

Block, N. (1981), 'Psychologism and behaviorism', *Philosophical Review*, vol. 90, pp. 5–43.

Bracken, H. (1978), 'Minds and oaths', *Dialogue*, vol. 17, pp. 209–27.

Brand, M. (1977), 'Identity conditions for events', *American Philosophical Quarterly*, vol. 14, pp. 329–37.

270

Bresnan, J. (1978), 'A realistic transformational grammar', in Halle, M., Bresnan, J. and Miller, J. (eds), *Linguistic Theory and Psychological Reality*, Cambridge, Mass.: MIT Press, pp. 1–59.

Bromberger, S. (1962), 'An approach to explanation', in Butler, R. (ed.), *Analytical Philosophy*, 2nd series, Oxford: Basil Blackwell, pp. 72–105.

Bromberger, S. (1966), 'Why-questions', in Colodny, R. (ed.), *Mind and Cosmos: Essays in Contemporary Science and Philosophy*, vol. 3, Pittsburgh: University of Pittsburgh Press.

Bromberger, S. (1988), 'Types and tokens in linguistics', CSLI report, Stanford, Center for the Study of Language and Information.

Burge, T. (1977), 'Belief *de re*', *Journal of Philosophy*, vol. 74, pp. 338–62.

Carnap, R. (1956), *Meaning and Necessity*, Chicago: University of Chicago Press.

Cartwright, H. (1965), 'Heraclitus and the bath water', *Philosophical Review*, vol. 74, pp. 466–85.

Cartwright, N. (1983), *How the Laws of Physics Lie*, Oxford: Oxford University Press.

Cartwright, R. (1962), 'Propositions', in Butler, R. (ed.), *Analytical Philosophy*, Oxford: Basil Blackwell, pp. 81–103.

Cherniak, C. (1986), *Minimal Rationality*, Cambridge, Mass.: MIT Press.

Chisholm, R. (1970), 'Events and propositions', *Nous*, vol. 4, pp. 15–32.

Chisholm, R. (1971), 'States of affairs again', *Nous*, vol. 5, pp. 179–89.

Chomsky, N. (1957), *Syntactic Structures*, The Hague: Mouton.

Chomsky, N. (1959), Review of *Verbal Behavior* (Skinner, 1957), *Language*, vol. 35, pp. 26–58.

Chomsky, N. (1963), 'Formal properties of grammars', in Luce, R.D., Bush, R.R. and Galanther, E. (eds), *Handbook of Mathematical Psychology*, vol. 2, New York: John Wiley, pp. 323–418.

Chomsky, N. (1965), *Aspects of a Theory of Syntax*, Cambridge, Mass.: MIT Press.

Chomsky, N. (1975), *Reflections on Language*, New York: Pantheon.

Chomsky, N. (1977), *Essays in Form and Interpretation*, New York: Elsevier/North-Holland.

Chomsky, N. (1980), *Rules and Representations*, New York: Columbia University Press.

Chomsky, N. and Scheffler, I. (1958), 'What is said to be', *Proceedings of the Aristotelian Society*, vol. 59.

Churchland, P. (1979), *Scientific Realism and the Plasticity of Mind*, Cambridge: Cambridge University Press.

Clark, E. (1973), 'What's in a word? On the child's acquisition of semantics in his first language', in Moore, T.E. (ed.), *Cognitive Development and the Acquisition of Language*, New York: The Research Foundation of the State University of New York, pp. 65–110.

Clark, H. and Clark, E. (1977), *Psychology of Language*, New York: Harcourt, Brace Jovanovich.

271

Davidson, D. (1967), 'Truth and meaning', *Synthese*, vol. 17, pp. 304–33.
Davidson, D. (1969), 'Individuation of events', Rescher, N. (ed.), *Essays in Honor of Hempel*, Dordrecht: Reidel.
Davidson, D. (1970), 'Events as particulars', *Nous*, vol. 4.
Dennett, D. (1978), *Brainstorms*, Boston: Bradford Books.
Donnellan, K. (1974), 'Speaking of nothing', *Philosophical Review*, vol. 83, pp. 3–31.
Dupre, J. (1981), 'Natural kinds and biological taxa', *Philosophical Review*, vol. 90, pp. 66–91.
Etchemendy, J. (1983), 'The doctrine of logic as form', *Linguistics and Philosophy*, vol. 6, pp. 319–34.
Field, H. (1978), 'Mental representation', *Erkenntnis*, vol. 13, pp. 9–61.
Field, H. (1980), *Science Without Numbers*, Princeton, NJ: Princeton University Press.
Fillmore, C. (1968), 'The case for case', in Bach, E. and Harms, R. (eds), *Universals in Linguistic Theory*, New York: Holt, Rinehart and Winston, pp. 1–88.
Fillmore, C. (1971), 'Verbs of judging: an exercise in semantic description', in Fillmore, C. and Langendoen, T. (eds), *Studies in Linguistic Semantics*, New York: Holt, Rinehart and Winston.
Fodor, J. (1975), *The Language of Thought*, New York: Crowell.
Fodor, J. and Pylyshyn, Z. (1988), 'Connectionism and cognitive architecture; a critical analysis', *Cognition*, vol. 28, pp. 3–71.
Follesdal, D. (1965), 'Quantification into causal contexts', reprinted in Linsky, L. (ed.), *Reference and Modality* (1971), Oxford: Clarendon Press, pp. 52–62.
Follesdal, D. (1988), 'Husserl fifty years later – noemata twenty years later', *Proceedings of the XVIIIth World Congress of Philosophy*, Brighton.
Frege, G. (1892, 1956), 'Sense and reference', in *Philosophical Writings*, ed. and trans. Geach, P. and Black, M., New York: Philosophical Library, pp. 56–78.
Frege, G. (1918), 'The thought: a logical inquiry', trans. Quinton, M. *Mind*, vol. 65 (1956), pp. 289–311.
Gabbay, D. and Moravcsik, J. (1973), 'Sameness and individuation', *Journal of Philosophy*, vol. 70, pp. 513–26.
Gabbay, D. and Moravcsik, J. (1980), 'Verbs, events, and the flow of time', in Rohrer, C. (ed.), *Time, Tense, and Quantifiers*, Tübingen: Niemeyer, pp. 59–83.
Gabbay, D. and Moravcsik, J. (1982), 'Negation and denial', in *Studies in Formal Semantics*, ed. G. Guenthner and C. Rohrer, Amsterdam: North-Holland, pp. 251–65.
Geach, P. (1962), *Reference and Generality*, Ithaca, NY: Cornell University Press.
Goodman, N. and Quine, W. (1947), 'Steps toward a constructive nominalism', *Journal of Symbolic Logic*, vol. 12, pp. 105–22.
Goodman, N. (1951), *The Structure of Appearance*, Cambridge, Mass.: Harvard University Press.

Bibliography

Goodman, N. (1955), *Fact, Fiction, Forecast*, Cambridge, Mass.: Harvard University Press.

Goodman, N. (1972), *Problems and Projects*, Indianapolis: Bobbs Merrill, ch. VI.

Göttner, H. (1973), *Logik der Interpretation*, München: Fink.

Göttner, H. and Jacobs, J. (1978), *Der Logische Aufbau von Literaturtheorien*, München: Fink Verlag.

Grice, P. (1957), 'Meaning', *Philosophical Review*, vol. 64, pp. 377–88.

Grice, P. (1962), 'Some remarks about the senses', in *Analytic Philosophy*, Butler, R. (ed.), New York: Barnes & Noble, pp. 133–53.

Griffin, N. (1977), *Relative Identity*, Oxford: Clarendon Press.

Hacking, I. (1975), 'The identity of indiscernibles', *Journal of Philosophy*, vol. 72, pp. 249–55.

Hacking, J. (1988), 'The participant irrealist at large in the laboratory', *The British Journal for the Philosophy of Science*, vol. 39, pp. 277–94.

Halle, M. (1978), 'Knowledge unlearned and untaught: what speakers know about the sounds of their language', in *Linguistic Theory and Psychological Reality*, Halle, M., Bresnan, J. and Miller, G. (eds), Cambridge, Mass.: MIT Press, pp. 294–303.

Harman, G. (1973), *Thought*, Princeton, NJ: Princeton University Press.

Harman, G. (1986), *Change in View*, Cambridge, Mass.: MIT Press.

Harrison, B. (1972), *Meaning and Structure; an essay in the philosophy of language*, New York: Harper and Row.

Hintikka, J. (1962), *Knowledge and Belief*, Ithaca, NY: Cornell University Press.

Horgan, T. (1978), 'The case against events', *Philosophical Review*, vol. 87, pp. 28–47.

Kasher, A. (1975), 'The proper treatment of Montague-grammars in natural logic and linguistics', *Theoretical Linguistics*, vol. 2, pp. 133–45.

Kasher, A. (1976), 'Conversational maxims and rationality', in *Language and Focus: Foundations, Methods and Systems*, Kasher, A. (ed.), Dordrecht: Reidel, pp. 197–216.

Kasher, A. (1977), 'What is a theory of use?', *Journal of Pragmatics*, vol. 1, pp. 105–20.

Kim, J. (1970a), 'Events and their descriptions', in *Essays in Honor of Carl Hempel*, Dordrecht: Reidel, pp. 198–215.

Kim, J. (1970b), 'Events as property exemplifications', in Brand, M. and Walton, D. (eds), *Action Theory*, Dordrecht: Reidel.

Kitcher, P. (1988), 'Marr's computational theory of vision', *Philosophy of Science*, vol. 55, pp. 1–24.

Kosslyn, S. (1980), *Image and Mind*, Cambridge, Mass.: Harvard University Press.

Kreisel, G. (1958), 'Hilbert's Programme', *Dialectica*, vol. 12, pp. 346–72.

Kripke, S. (1971), 'Identity and necessity', in Munitz, M. (ed.), *Identity and Individuation*, New York: New York University Press, pp. 135–64.

Kripke, S. (1972), 'Naming and necessity', in Harman, G. and Davidson, D. (eds), *The Semantics of Natural Language*, Boston: Reidel, pp. 254–355.

Kripke, S. (1975), 'Outlines of a theory of truth', *Journal of Philosophy*, vol. 72, pp. 690–716.

Kripke, S. (1979), 'A puzzle about belief', in Margalit, A. (ed.), *Meaning and Use*, Dordrecht: Reidel, pp. 239–83.

Lesniewsky, S. (1931), 'Über die Grundlagen der Ontologie', *Comptes rendus des séances de la Société des Sciences et des Lettres de Varsovie*, Classe III, pp. 111–32.

Margolis, J. (1984), *Philosophy of Psychology*, Englewood Cliffs, NJ: Prentice-Hall.

Marr, D. (1982), *Vision*, New York: W.H. Freeman.

Michotte, A. (1963), *Perception of Causality*, London: Methuen.

Miller, G. and Johnson-Laird, P. (1976), *Language and Perception*, Cambridge, Mass.: Harvard University Press.

Minsky, M. (1977), 'Frame systems theory', in Johnson-Laird, P. and Wason, P. (eds), *Thinking*, Cambridge: Cambridge University Press, pp. 355–76.

Montague, R. (1974), *Formal Philosophy*, Thomason, R. (ed.), New Haven: Yale University Press.

Moore, G. (1923), 'Are the characteristics of particular things universal or particular?', *Proceedings of the Aristotelian Society*, suppl. vol. 3, pp. 95–128.

Moravcsik, J. (1965), 'Strawson and ontological priority', in Butler, R. (ed.), *Analytical Philosophy*, 2nd series, Oxford: Basil Blackwell, pp. 106–19.

Moravcsik, J. (1969), 'Competence, creativity, and innateness', *The Philosophical Forum*, n.s. vol. 1, pp. 407–37.

Moravcsik, J. (1970), 'Subcategorization and abstract terms', *Foundations of Language*, vol. 6, pp. 473–87.

Moravcsik, J. (1973), 'Reply to comments', in Hintikka, J., Moravcsik, J. and Suppes, P. (eds), *Approaches to Natural Language*, Dordrecht: Reidel, pp. 301–8.

Moravcsik, J. (1975a), *Understanding Language*, The Hague: Mouton.

Moravcsik, J. (1975b), 'Aitia as generative factor in Aristotle's philosophy', *Dialogue*, vol. 14, pp. 622–36.

Moravcsik, J. (1979), 'Understanding', *Dialectica*, vol. 33, pp. 201–16.

Moravcsik, J. (1981a), 'Frege and Chomsky on thought and language', in French, P., Uehling, T. and Wettstein, H. (eds), *Midwest Studies in Philosophy*, vol. 6, pp. 105–23.

Moravcsik, J. (1981b), 'How do words get their meanings?', *Journal of Philosophy*, vol. 78, pp. 5–24.

Moravcsik, J. (1981c), 'Universals and particulars', *Philosophia*, vol. 10, pp. 151–67.

Moravcsik, J. (1982), 'Understanding and the emotions', *Dialectica*, vol. 36, pp. 207–24.

Moravcsik, J. (1983), 'Can there be a science of thought?', *Conceptus*, vol. 17, pp. 239–62.

Bibliography

Moravcsik, J. (1987), 'Conceptions of the self and the study of cognition', in *Logic, Philosophy of Science, and Epistemology*, Vienna: Hölder, Pichler, Tempsky, pp. 294–302.

Osherson, D. (1977), 'Natural connectives: a Chomskyan approach', *Journal of Mathematical Psychology*, vol. 16, pp. 1–29.

Parsons, T. (1980), *Non-existent Objects*, New Haven: Yale University Press.

Peacocke, C. (1983), *Sense and Content*, Oxford: Clarendon Press.

Perry, J. (1970), 'The same *F*', *Philosophical Review*, vol. 79, pp. 181–200.

Pinker, S. and Prince, P. (1988), 'On language and connectionism', *Cognition*, vol. 28, pp. 73–194.

Putnam, H. (1955), 'The meaning of "meaning"' reprinted in *Mind, Language, Reality*, vol. 2 (1975), Cambridge: Cambridge University Press, pp. 215–71.

Putnam, H. (1966), 'The mental life of some machines', reprinted in *Mind, Language, Reality*, vol. 2 (1975), Cambridge: Cambridge University Press.

Putnam, H. (1977), 'Realism and reason', *Proceedings of the American Philosophical Association*, vol. 50, pp. 483–98.

Quine, W. (1953a), 'On what there is', *From a Logical Point of View*, Cambridge, Mass.: Harvard University Press, ch. 1.

Quine, W. (1953b), 'Two dogmas of empiricism', ibid., ch. 2.

Quine, W. (1953c), 'Reference and modality', ibid., ch. 7.

Quine, W. (1960), *Word and Object*, New York: John Wiley.

Quine, W. (1969), *Ontological Relativity and Other Essays*, New York: Columbia University Press.

Ramsey, F. (1931), 'Universals', in *The Foundations of Mathematics*, London: Routledge Kegan & Paul, pp. 112–37.

Rohrer, C. (ed.) (1978), *Papers on Tense, Aspect, and Verb Classification*, Tübingen: Gunter Nass.

Rummelhart, D. and McClelland, J. (eds) (1986), *Parallel Distributed Processing*, vol. I, Cambridge, Mass: MIT Press.

Russell, B. (1905), 'On denoting', reprinted in B. Russell (1956), *Logic and Language*, ed. R. Marsh, London: George Allen & Unwin, pp. 39–56.

Russell, B. (1912), 'On the relations of universals and particulars', *Proceedings of the Aristotelian Society*, n.s., vol. 12, pp. 1–24.

Russell, B. (1918), *The Philosophy of Logical Atomism*, Minneapolis: Dept of Philosophy of the University of Minnesota.

Searle, J. (1969), *Speech Acts*, Cambridge: Cambridge University Press.

Searle, J. (1983), *Intentionality*, New York: Cambridge University Press.

Skinner, B. (1957), *Verbal Behavior*, New York: Appleton-Century-Crofts.

Smart, J. (1963), *Philosophy and Scientific Realism*, London: Routledge & Kegan Paul.

Soames, S. (1984a), 'What is a theory of truth?', *Journal of Philosophy*, vol. 81, pp. 411–29.

Soames, S. (1984b), 'Linguistics and psychology', *Linguistics and Philosophy*, vol. 7, pp. 155–79.

Stalnaker, R. (1984), *Inquiry*, Cambridge, Mass.: MIT Press.

Stich, S. (1983), *From Folk Psychology to Cognitive Science*, Cambridge, Mass: MIT Press.

Stout, G. (1923), 'Are the characteristics of particular things universal or particular?', *Proceedings of the Aristotelian Society*, suppl. vol. 3, pp. 95–128.

Strawson, P. (1950), 'On referring', *Mind*, vol. 59, pp. 320–44.

Strawson, P. (1959), *Individuals*, London: Methuen.

Strawson, P. (1974), *Subject and Predicate in Logic and Grammar*, London: Methuen.

Suppes, P. (1973), 'Congruence of meaning', *Proceedings of the American Philosophical Association*, vol. 46, pp. 21–38.

Suppes, P. and Crangle, C. (1988), 'Context-fixing semantics for the language of action', in Dancy, J., Moravcsik, J. and Taylor, C. (eds), *Human Agency*, Stanford: Stanford University Press, pp. 47–76.

Tarski, A. (1936), 'The concept of truth in formalized languages', reprinted in *Logic, Semantics, and Meta-mathematics*, Oxford: Oxford University Press, pp. 152–278.

Urmson, J. (1952), 'Parenthetical verbs', *Mind*, vol. 61, pp. 480–96.

Van Gulick, R. (1988), 'A functionalist plea for self-consciousness', *Philosophical Review*, vol. 97, pp. 149–81.

Waismann, F. (1960), 'Verifiability', in Flew, A. (ed.), *Logic and Language*, 1st series, Oxford: Basil Blackwell, pp. 117–44.

Wang, H. (1953), 'What is an individual?', *Philosophical Review*, vol. 62, pp. 413–20.

Wang, H. (1986), *Beyond Analytic Philosophy*, Cambridge, Mass.: MIT Press.

Watson, J. (1919), *Psychology from the Standpoint of a Behaviorist*, Philadelphia and London: L.B. Lippencott.

Watson, J. (1925), *Behaviorism*, London: Routledge & Kegan Paul.

Widerker, D. (1988), 'Action Sentences', *Erkenntnis*, vol. 28, pp. 269–91.

Wiggins, D. (1967), *Identity and Spatio-temporal Continuity*, Oxford: Basil Blackwell.

Winograd, T. (1972), *Understanding Natural Language*, New York: Academic Press.

Wittgenstein, L. (1922), *Tractatus Logico-philosophicus*, London: Routledge & Kegan Paul.

Zalta, E. (1983), *Abstract Objects*, Dordrecht: Reidel.

Index

277

Index

according to Stalnaker 48–50; and behaviourism 185; and connectionism 65–6; deep theory of 202, 204, 212; elements of 202; examples of 46; human 76, 215; and idealizations 85, 87; and its objects 195–6; and materialism 52–5; and non-pragmatic conceptions of 77–8; notion of 47–8; objectual theory of 56, 72; on observable level 201–2; ontological status of 51; psychological theories of 58–63; and reality 192; and the senses 182–3; shallow theory of 202; study of 177; summing up of 90–1; unified science of 88–91

cognitive processing 200

cognitive state, and functional characterization 69–70

coincidence, spatio-temporal 40

common sense 89–90; basic 90, 168–71, 198; and functionalism 188; peripheral 90, 171–2; and science 172–9

communication 110, 117

competence/ability, questions of 86

compositional semantics, and R(m, s, f, a) theory 250–1

conceivability 171

concepts 197

conceptualism 16; and constitutive relations 23–4

concert, persistence conditions for 34

connectionism, and cognition 65–6

content 196–7; notion of 14

contextual interpretation, example of 125

contingency, notion of 135

continuity 111; in space, not persistence condition 33–4

counterfactuals 22, 24

Davidson, Donald, on events 36, 37, 38; on natural languages 104; on parsimony 36

De Interpretatione (Aristotle) 92

definition, circularity of 137

Delaney, Neil 7

denotation, three elements of 257–9

dependency proposals 4

Descartes, Rene 55, 70

designating 93

developmental facts 112–13

diachronic phenomena 111

disease, concept of human 228, 230

dualism 51, 55–6, 89; some problems of 178–9

dynamic universe 146

Eleatic monism 21

Eleatics 152

emergency, meaning of 252–6, 259; words related to 261–2

empiricism 8

entities, atomic 145; and identity 166; recurrent and mental 7; various 107

environmental influences 59

epistemology 8

essential-accidental distinction, some examples of 159–61, 165

essentialism 20, 38

Etchemendy, J. 104

ethics, defined 268

event, as mass term 159

event individuation 40–1, 156, 157–8; examples of 42

event universals 36–7, 40–1

events, according to Strawson 31–3; and action theory 35; and causal laws of science 35; and cause and effect 39; described 26–7; and essential-accidental distinction 159–62; existence of 36; fourfold-classification of 156–7; as identical 37–8, 39–40; and material objects 27–9, 44–5; mental and material 42–3; objectless 41; ontological views of 28–9, 30; options for 35–6; as property instantiations 165;

278

3